THE

COALWOOD

WAY

Also by Homer Hickam

TORPEDO JUNCTION
ROCKET BOYS
BACK TO THE MOON

THE
COALWOOD
WAY

HOMER HICKAM

DELACORTE PRESS

Published by
Delacorte Press
Random House, Inc.
1540 Broadway
New York, New York 10036

Library of Congress Cataloging-in-Publication Data
Hickam, Homer H., 1943-
    The Coalwood way / by Homer H. Hickam, Jr.
                    p. cm.
              ISBN 0-385-33516-4
    1. West Virginia—Social life and customs—Memoir. I. Title.
PS3558.I224 C62 2000
813'.54—dc21   00-035884

Book design by Lynn Newmark

Map by David Lindroth, Inc.

Manufactured in the United States of America

Published simultaneously in Canada

October 2000

10   9   8   7   6   5   4   3   2   1

BVG

*To Charlie, Linda D., and Susan Black,
beloved family, who left us much too soon.*

AUTHOR'S NOTE

MEMOIRS ARE TOUGH things to write. How can you remember what somebody said or did forty years ago? I don't have an answer. All I know is that I do. I've changed a few names and disguised some other folks to protect them but, otherwise, this is pretty much the way it happened, I swan.

—Homer H. Hickam, Jr.
Huntsville, Alabama
March 14, 2000

ACKNOWLEDGMENTS

THERE HAVE BEEN many gifts and honors to come my way since the publication of *Rocket Boys: A Memoir* (aka *October Sky*), but none have been so wonderful as the recollections I've received from the citizens of Coalwood, past and present, as well as from folks from all over McDowell County and West (by God) Virginia. There are too many individuals to list so I will simply give my humble thanks and reflect that this book would not have been possible without them. This includes Jim, my steadfast friend and brother. I would also like to thank Frank and Mickey, the greatest agents known to mankind; my editor Tom, who's the very best at what he does; and David, my touchstone. Thanks are also due to Linda, my wife and assistant, who works so hard and does so much, as well as her parents, Walt and Sue, who are among my heroes. Of course, nothing would be possible without the continued, gentle vexations that come my way from one Elsie Gardener Lavender Hickam. As ever, I'm proud to know and love her.

CONTENTS

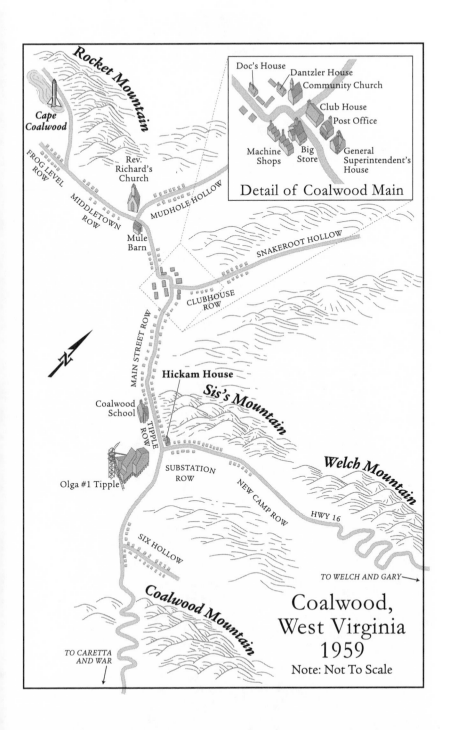

Rocket Mountain

Cape Coalwood

FROG LEVEL ROW

MIDDLETOWN ROW

Rev. Richard's Church

Mule Barn

MUDHOLE HOLLOW

SNAKEROOT HOLLOW

CLUBHOUSE ROW

MAIN STREET ROW

Hickam House

Sis's Mountain

Coalwood School

TIPPLE ROW

Olga #1 Tipple

SUBSTATION ROW

NEW CAMP ROW

Welch Mountain

HWY 16

SIX HOLLOW

TO WELCH AND GARY →

Coalwood Mountain

TO CARETTA AND WAR ↓

Doc's House Dantzler House
Community Church
Club House
Post Office
Machine Shops Big Store General Superintendent's House

Detail of Coalwood Main

Coalwood, West Virginia 1959

Note: Not To Scale

THE
COALWOOD
WAY

Matters of faith are not really accessible to our rational thinking. I find it best not to ask any questions, but to just believe. . . .
—Dr. Wernher von Braun, rocket scientist

The Lord works us . . . even though we don't know it.
—The Reverend Julius "Little" Richard, preacher

There are girls and then there are girls. But that girl there is a woman. Don't ever get them confused.
—Roy Lee Cooke, the Big Creek lovemaster

SONG OF THE CAPE

OF ALL THE lessons I learned when I built my rockets, the most important were not about chemistry, physics, or metallurgy, but of virtues, sins, and other true things that shape us as surely as rivers carve valleys, or rain melts mountains, or currents push apart the sea. I would learn these lessons at a time when Coalwood, the mining town where I had lived my entire life, was just beginning to fade away. Yet, as the fall of 1959 began, and the leaves on the trees in the forests that surrounded us began to explode in spectacular color, Coalwood's men still walked with a trudging grace to and from the vast, deep mine, and its women bustled in and out of the company stores and fought the coal dust that drifted into their homes. In the dark old schools, the children learned and the teachers taught, and, in snowy white churches built on hillside cuts, the preachers preached, and God, who we had no doubt was also a West Virginian, was surely doing His work in heaven, too. At the abandoned slack dump we called Cape Coalwood, rockets still leapt into the air, and boyish voices yet echoed between ancient, worn mountains beneath a pale and watchful sky. Coalwood endured as it always had, but a wheel was turning that would change nearly everything, and no one, not even my father, would be able to stop it. When that brittle parchment autumn turned into our deepest, whitest winter, this and many other lessons would be taught. Though they were hard and sometimes cruel things to learn, they were true, and true things, as the people of Coalwood saw fit to teach me, are always filled with a shining glory.

To me, there was no better time to launch a rocket than in the fall, especially a West Virginia fall. There seemed to be a cool, dry energy in the air that filled us with a renewed sense of hope and optimism. I had always believed that our rockets were lifted as much by our dreams as by burning propellant, and as the lazy summer faded and a northerly wind swept down on us with its lively breath, anything seemed possible. It was also when the school year started and I always felt an excitement stir within me at the thought of learning new and wonderful things. Fall had other marvels, too. At the Cape, we were often treated to V-shaped flotillas of migrating Canadian geese, bound from the far north to places we had only read about or imagined. We always stopped our rocket preparations to gaze longingly at the great creatures as they winged their way high overhead, and to listen to their joyful honking that seemed to be calling us to join them. "If only we could," Sherman said once to my comment. "Even for just a moment, to look down on our mountains and see them the same as angels." Sherman always liked to remind us that we lived in a beautiful place and I guess we did, although sometimes it was easy to forget, especially since we'd never known anywhere else.

Once, a rare snow goose, as purely white as moonbeams, landed on the old slack dump, perhaps fooled by the reflection from the slick surface of the coal tailings. We gathered around the great strutting bird, awed by the sight of her. Then I noticed that her wing tips were as black as the faces of Coalwood miners after a shift. O'Dell said the reason for the black tips was so the geese could see each other inside a white cloud. O'Dell knew a lot about animals so I believed his explanation, but it got me off to thinking. How did the snow geese decide what colors their feathers would be? Did they all get together up north somewhere a million years ago and take a vote? It was a mystery and the snow goose made no comment. She just looked annoyed. When she tired of us gawking at her, she flapped her wings and continued her journey, and I confess I was relieved. I knew the snow goose did not belong in Coalwood. Some people, especially my mother, said neither did I.

Our first rocket of the fall was *Auk XXII-E*. A serious little rocket, it began its journey with a mighty spout of flame and turmoil and its shock wave rattled our wooden blockhouse as it climbed. I ran outside with the other boys, but no matter how much I strained my eyes, I couldn't see it. All I could see were clouds that went, as far as I knew, all the way up to heaven. The seconds ticked by. We had never lost one of our rockets, but I was beginning to wonder if maybe this one was going to be our first. If it had fallen on Rocket Mountain, buried itself into the soft black West Virginia loam up there, maybe we had missed it. "Time, O'Dell," I called nervously.

O'Dell looked at the stopwatch he'd borrowed last year from one of the coal company industrial engineers and forgotten to give back. "I think it's still flying," he said.

"Then where is it?" I demanded. We couldn't lose it. Like every rocket we launched, it held answers we had to know.

"There it is!" Billy yelled as he began sprinting across the slack. I still couldn't see anything but I ran after him anyway. He easily pulled away from me with athletic grace, his muscles like small coiled springs, his shoes sending up little puffs of black grit as he ran. How that boy could run! Nobody could keep up with Billy Rose when he had his sharp eyes locked on a rocket. I, on the other hand, tended to be a pretty slow runner. I think it was because I was so nearsighted. I was always afraid I was going to run into something.

O'Dell trotted up alongside me, putting a hand on my elbow to straighten me out. "Time looks good," he said, and then ran on ahead, his mop of blond hair bouncing as his short legs churned. He held his stopwatch in front of him, his finger poised to click it off the moment our rocket hit the slack.

Roy Lee caught up with me next. He was in his Dugout clothes, a tight pair of draped and pegged black pants, brown loafers, a pink shirt with black piping, and hair thoroughly lacquered down into a swept-back DA. He had a date for the Saturday-night dance at the teen hangout in War and was headed that way right after the launch. "I never can see the blamed things," he griped as he ran by me. Roy Lee's long legs soon had him beside O'Dell, but Billy was still far ahead.

Behind me, I could hear Sherman's uneven gait, his left leg slung in an arc at each step, his built-up shoe scuffing the slack. Polio had given his leg a twist and turned it thin as a sapling. I slowed to let him catch up and run alongside me. "O'Dell said the time looks good," I gasped.

Sherman broke into a grin at my report. "Maybe it's going to be a great rocket," he said.

A "great rocket" was what Quentin, the brains of our outfit, called the rockets that did exactly what we'd designed them to do. I sincerely hoped Sherman was right. *Auk XXII-E* used an untried propellant. With rockets, anytime you changed one thing, a lot of other things changed, too, and it was hard to predict what all they might be. In that, I guess they were a bit like me and the rest of the boys. Even though we were all seniors in high school and thought of ourselves as being grown up, the truth was we had a way to go. I was sixteen, they were seventeen, and every day, it seemed we grew a little, usually in some unpredictable way. Sometimes, I had trouble recalling who I had been the day before, or might be tomorrow. Coach Gainer called it the "teenage boy crazies." When I got too afflicted with it, my mom always jerked a knot in my tail and said, "Straighten up and fly right." And so I did.

Quentin was downrange so that he could measure the altitude of our rocket using trigonometry. To do it, he had to see the rocket at peak altitude and aim at it with a device he had built out of a broomstick, a nail, a wooden ruler, and a plastic protractor. He called his invention a theodolite. But clouds had defeated him today, the rocket disappearing through the heavy layer that hung overhead. We would have to depend on O'Dell's stopwatch.

"Whoa! Stop!" Billy cried as we ran up to him. He had his arms outstretched to hold us back. I could hear the rocket whistling as it came in, and then, a hundred yards ahead, there was a big metallic retort and a plume of slack. The Auk had struck nosefirst. "Come on!" Billy yelled, and we ran on.

"Thirty-one seconds," O'Dell reported as we reached the rocket. I did a quick mental calculation. I had designed *Auk XXII-E* to reach an altitude of 6,000 feet. It had reached, according to the formula we used, less than 4,000 feet. That was a disappointment. The Big Creek Missile Agency (or BCMA, as we liked to call it) had been in business for nearly two years, ever since the sight of the Russian *Sputnik* flying through the starry sky over Coalwood had first inspired us to join the space race. We'd started off slow, our rockets mostly blowing up, but after a while we had gotten the hang of it. We had already sent rockets higher than a mile using our old rocket candy propellant. The new propellant we were using should have easily gotten us past the mile mark. Something had gone seriously wrong with this little rocket, and I itched to find out what it was.

The smoking Auk was too hot to touch, so I gave it a quick eyeball once-over. The casement, which is what we called the body of the rocket, was made from a three-foot-long, one-and-a-quarter-inch-diameter length of seamless steel tubing. Steel tubing of that size and make was incredibly strong, yet it was now slightly bent. That wasn't unexpected, since it was flying at over three hundred miles per hour when it had hit the hard slack. The wooden nose cone that had capped it had been reduced to splinters. One of the four fins welded to the casement had broken off. The machinists in the coal company machine shop would be interested in the damage. They had become dedicated rocket builders, sneaking in the work between jobs sent down by the mine. My father, the mine superintendent, had tried for months to stop them but had finally given up. "Bill," Dad had said to their supervisor, "they're your problem. Just remind your boys who pays their wages." The machinists heard Dad's reminder but it didn't make much of an impression on them. Building rockets, after all, was a lot more fun than working on mine equipment.

I wanted most of all to look inside the nozzle, the working end of the rocket. Our new propellant, which we called "zincoshine," consisted of zinc dust, sulfur, and the purest alcohol John Eye Blevins could produce from his still up Snakeroot Hollow. The nozzle and the propellant were the keys to our success. Unless both worked according to our designs, our rockets might fly but they were not going to be "great."

While we waited for the Auk to cool, Quentin decided it was a good opportunity to give us one of his professorial lectures, although he didn't look anything like a professor. He was wearing a flannel shirt that was ragged at both elbows, and his pants legs were about two inches too short. One of his ankle-high leather brogans was untied, too, the tongue lapping out between the laces like the tongue of a tired old hound dog. "Gentlemen, it is time we adopt a new approach to our work," he said, his index finger held aloft. "To date, we have accomplished prodigious results with our rockets. Yet, I perceive a certain tendency among some of you . . ." At this he sneaked a look at Roy Lee. ". . . to see our work as—dare I say it?—fun! This is not fun, gentlemen. We are about important work here. Therefore, henceforth, I challenge all of us to be absolutely, completely, and utterly *rigorous*!"

The other boys looked at him with slack jaws. He'd lost me, too, but I was not one to let Quentin get away with much. "Define rigorous," I said.

Quentin rolled his eyes as he always did when he was disgusted with my ignorance. "To be rigorous in our work, Sonny, means it is absolutely necessary that we have a thoroughly scientific approach to everything we do. And, of course, it also means that we must do everything quickly, without delay, lest opportunity slip between our fingers."

I didn't see what one thing had to do with the other, but nothing ever happened fast enough to suit Quentin. "I don't know how we can work any faster," I told him, "especially since I'm doing all the drawings and seeing to the machine-shop work. I've got other things to do, you know."

"Such as?" Quentin growled.

I stamped my feet, trying to stay warm in the chill breeze

coming down the hollow. Winter would soon stake out its claim in the mountains of southern West Virginia. "Look, Quentin," I said, "try to understand something. I can't spend all my time building rockets. I'm trying to make all A's this semester. And I've got band practice, too. I'm the head drummer, you know."

Quentin looked down his long nose at me. "Your other activities, Sonny, are of no consequence to this group. You must transcend such matters and bear down on your designs. I assure you that without such rigor, we will impress no judges at the science fair. We must present a careful, well-thought-out, *rigorous* scientific explanation as to why and how our rockets fly. You may be exasperated with me, old son, but it is nevertheless an incontrovertible fact."

I simplified all his big words until I'd ferreted out his meaning. Quentin believed that if our rockets won the county science fair and then we went on to the state science fair and maybe even the nationals, somehow that would result in him getting an opportunity to go to college. I sincerely doubted his concept. Boys could get football scholarships in McDowell County, but I never heard of anybody getting much more than ribbons and medals at a science fair. Still, when Quentin got an idea, it was almost impossible to dislodge it from his brain. The boy had a brilliant mind, but it could get off onto some strange tracks sometimes.

The casement finally cooled enough so Quentin could pick it up. He put his eye on the nozzle, clucked loudly, and then shoved it into my face. "Look! Erosion!"

He was right. The hole down through the center of the rocket nozzle had been burned into an ugly irregular oval. That's why it hadn't performed according to its design.

Quentin handed me the rocket with disdain. "Gentlemen, how do we resolve this? Billy, what say you?"

Billy had been hanging back, not looking at the rocket. He seemed to be studying something on the ridge of Rocket Mountain. I looked in that direction but saw nothing but a grove of pines. He came back to us. "Maybe we just need a tougher steel," he said with only a trace of his usual enthusiasm. Billy was painfully thin, and his shirt, neatly laundered but faded and patched, hung on him like he was a scarecrow. His father had quit the mine some months back over a dispute. I didn't know what the dispute was, but I did know his dad tended to drink more than a little. Billy was the oldest of seven children. I had no idea how his family was getting by.

"If we use a tougher steel, it'll take a lot longer to machine it," O'Dell said in answer to Billy's idea. "Anyway, I don't think we can afford much better." O'Dell was the BCMA's chief scrounger, a natural job for the son of Red Carroll, Coalwood's garbageman. O'Dell also came up with various schemes to make money to buy our materials, some of which actually worked.

Sherman kicked at the slack. "Maybe zincoshine's just too hot," he said. "Rocket candy worked pretty good. Maybe we ought to go back to it."

"Of course it's hot, Sherman!" Quentin cried. "That's why it's so good! And going back to melted potassium nitrate and sugar would hardly be rigorous, would it?" He eyed me. "What do you think, Sonny boy?"

I was actually thinking I was going to knock Quentin's block off if he said "rigor" or "rigorous" one more time. "I don't know," I said instead. It was an honest, if unimpressive, answer. Mr. Van Dyke, Coalwood's general superintendent before the steel company sacked him, used to say, "It's better to confess ignorance than to provide it."

When nobody else had any ideas on what to do, we started to clean up the Cape. As usual, we sang as we worked. We never knew exactly what we were going to sing. It just came to us. Today, we launched into "Get a Job." Eventually, we'd work our way around to singing what I thought of as the song of the Cape: "All I Have to Do Is Dream." We surely loved the Everly Brothers.

Our audience was dispersing. There had been just over a hundred spectators, mostly off-duty miners and their families. Coalwood's union chief, Mr. John Dubonnet, was getting into his car. It was a brand-new maroon Chrysler, pretty fancy for a union man, I thought. Mr. Dubonnet rarely missed one of our rocket launches, unlike my father, who'd never been to even one. Dad had tried to stop the BCMA when we'd first gotten started, saying such activities had no place in Coalwood. Then, because of the harassment he had received from my mother and the teachers at the Coalwood school, Dad had given in and turned over the old slack dump below Frog Level for us to use as our rocket range. Although he'd given in, that still didn't mean he approved of us. He kept his distance, pretending ignorance of what we were doing. There were, however, no secrets in Coalwood. The fence-line gossipers made certain of that.

Some of the miners, still in their helmets, huddled on the other side of the road. There was likewise a cluster of women, sharing the day while watching their children playing on the slack. Our launches doubled as social occasions, too. We Rocket Boys had first become popular in 1958 when Big Creek High School's football team had been idle. My dad, as president of the Big Creek Football Fathers, had sued the state high school athletic commission to let the team play in the 1957 championship game. The result, after the suit got tossed out of court, had been a year's suspension for the team. Desperate for distraction when the next fall rolled around, football fans from around the district had started showing up at Cape Coalwood. Pretty soon, they brought the whole family. Even Big Creek cheerleaders came, dressed in full uniform. By order of the court, we had become the only game in town.

As I came up by the blockhouse, I saw a thin, red-haired young woman in a plain brown coat waving at me. I didn't recognize her. "Come here, come here, come here!" she yelled while gesturing with her hand toward her ample breast. Then, when I didn't come, she walked across the slack to me, her long, slender legs taking big strides. "I saw your rocket!" she said breathlessly, coming up to me. "It was the most wonderful thing I ever seed!" She stuck out her hand. "Shake!" she said. "My name's Dreama Jenkins."

I was a little startled by her forwardness. "Pleased to meet you, ma'am," I said, taking her hand. She had working hands, red and hard.

"You called me ma'am." She giggled, then laid a huge grin on me, showing me her teeth. I guess she was proud of them, but it was her eyes that captured my attention. They were the color of moss. I had never seen eyes so green. Her hair was long and shiny and framed her pretty face, which was punctuated by a small nose with a sprinkle of freckles across it. I put her at maybe nineteen years old, but her youthful beauty was spoiled by heavily rouged cheeks and lips coated with a dark red glossy lipstick. By her look, I knew her for what the fence-line gossipers called a "country woman," a girl washed up in Coalwood from some deep West Virginia hollow, ignorant of manners. Such women, with little knowledge of the Coalwood way of doing things, rarely lasted in our town. If the company didn't chase them out right away, the ladies of our town eventually did.

"You can call me Dreama," she said. "Tell your maw I said hello. I hear she's from Gary, just like me. Tell her I'm from up Number Three. Dreama Carlotta Jenkins, that's my whole name. Farlow Jenkins was my paw before he got killed in the mine."

I looked past her and saw a Coalwood miner named Cuke Snoddy walking toward us. When he got near, the woman grabbed his arm. "Oh, Cuke, honey, tell Sonny here how wonderful his rocket was. Go on, tell him now. What's gotten into you? Speak up!"

Cuke looked at me as if I was something that needed to be scraped off the bottom of his boot. That didn't surprise me. I'd known Cuke all my life, one way or the other, and he was always pretty sour. "Cuke" was short for Cucumber, a vegetable he apparently liked above all others. Before he'd come to Coalwood, he had been in prison for something violent—not the usual moonshining or petty larceny that sometimes caught a man in southern West Virginia, but something mean and loathsome that people wouldn't talk about. He lived in a little house set back up on the mountain, nearly in the woods, just down from the Coalwood school. When I was delivering the *Bluefield Telegraph,* I was forced to go into Cuke's house to collect what he owed me, and my nose was always assaulted by its nasty smell, a mixture of tobacco smoke, rotting food, alcohol (probably pure rock gut), and unwashed clothing.

Cuke seemed to stir something inside himself, his shoulders twisting inside his filthy plaid wool coat as if it took all his might to get the words out. "I don't give a good goddamn about any fool rockets," he said, spitting a stream of tobacco juice near my feet. "Big Creek football team ain't worth nothin', that's what the hell I care about. It's your daddy's fault. Your brother wasn't never all that great, neither."

Cuke's sentiment wasn't anything I hadn't heard before. Even though the Big Creek football team was back in action, it wasn't having a very good season and a lot of people blamed my dad for it, saying he'd caused the suspension that had made the team stale. I didn't think it was stale. It was just missing the big, tough players who had graduated. That included Jim, my older brother. Even though he'd been forced to sit out his senior year, Jim had gotten a college football scholarship down at Virginia Tech. A lot of his fellow players, denied a chance to impress football scouts, hadn't been so lucky. Those boys were now either working in the mines or gone off to the military services. Some people blamed my dad for that, too.

The woman clutched Cuke's arm. "Now, Cuke, that ain't nice," she said. "You apologize, you hear?"

Cuke was somewhere in his forties, I guessed, but his face was already that of an old, old man, with deep furrows in his brow and sunken cheeks. He was missing some teeth up front, too, and those that were still there were chipped and broken. Cuke's dirty hand moved to take hers. It was a surprisingly gentle, almost dainty, gesture. "Dreama, I'd do near anything for you. But apologize to a blamed Hickam? Ain't no way!"

"You better do what I say, you old fool." The woman scowled, removing his hand from hers.

Cuke's eyes went soft, then hard. He grabbed her arm and squeezed. She yelped and backed away. Roy Lee came up just then, his fists ready. "Come on, Cuke," he said. "You want to fight somebody? Try me."

Cuke eyed Roy Lee, sizing him up, but then the other boys arrived. He let the woman go and she took a step away. A tear was running down one of her rouged cheeks. "I can't believe you hurt me," she said in a small voice.

"Aw, honey, you know I didn't mean to," Cuke said, and turned toward her but found himself staring instead into the placid eyes of Tag Farmer, Coalwood's constable.

I was glad to see Tag. He showed up for almost all our launches, and I suppose he had spotted trouble about to happen and come down from the road. He tipped his constable's hat to the woman. "Ma'am? I think ya'll should go get in the car. Cuke will be along. I just need to have a word with him."

"Yes, sir," the woman said nervously. She gave me a smile. "I'm sorry, Sonny. I didn't mean to cause no trouble."

"Go on now," Tag said firmly.

The woman walked to Cuke's car, an ancient Chevrolet, and climbed in. Tag took Cuke aside, his big hand on the miner's shoulder. Tag was at least a foot taller than Cuke. He bent low over him, his lips moving near Cuke's ear. Then, after Tag was through, Cuke slouched off, got in his car with the woman, and aimed up the dirt road that led to Frog Level and then Coalwood Main.

The woman rolled down her window and pushed her head out and yelled "Bye-bye, Sonny! You tell your maw about me, hear?" Then Cuke lifted his hand in a one-fingered salute to one and all and floored it, peeling rubber and sending out a cloud of brown dust behind.

Tag strolled over to the launchpad. "Boys, let me tell you something and you listen up good. A man who hurts his woman is a man who most of all don't like himself." He pushed his cap back on his head and scratched up under it, pondering the boil of dust coming from Cuke's car as he raced toward Frog Level. "That's why he does it. It makes him feel big for a minute or two, but it don't last. He's small and he knows it, but knowing it can drive a man crazy." He looked up the road and frowned, then shook his head. "Trouble there," he said softly. "Trouble there."

WHEN I got home, I found Mom sitting at the kitchen table in front of the mural she was painting of Myrtle Beach, South Carolina. Chipper, her beloved pet squirrel, was on her lap, and a stack of drawings she was working on were on the table. They were the plans, I suspected, for Coalwood's Veterans Day float built annually by the Coalwood Women's Club. Mom was in charge of the float this year. "They're not married," she said when I mentioned Cuke and the woman. A lot of people over the years had remarked how beautiful my mother was, saying she looked a bit like Loretta Young, the famous movie actress. She leaned her head on her hand, her curly black hair spilling down her arm. "I hear she's out of Gary," she added.

"She said she's from up Number Three Hollow," I reported.

Mom frowned. Her face was often furrowed with worry over Dad or me or Jim or Coalwood in general. "There's some sorry people been known to come out of Number Three," she said, sighing. Since Mom had been raised in Gary, I guess she was an expert on the denizens of the town. "I heard she was pretty, though," she continued. "God only knows what that child's doing with Cuke." Chipper stretched, his little front paws grabbing her dress. She smiled down on him and tickled his chin. He grunted in ecstasy. "Sometimes a woman like that just takes any man who'll have her," she added, and then I could tell by the set of her jaw she'd finished all she had to say about Dreama Carlotta Jenkins. "Did you have a good rocket launch?" she asked. "Wish I could have made it but I had too much work to do on the float." She nodded toward the drawings.

"We didn't go as high as I calculated," I reported. "There's erosion in the nozzle. We can't figure out what to do about it."

"Well, I'm sure you will, dear," she said placidly. "I notice you've been spending a lot of time on your homework, too. I'm proud of you, Sonny."

"I'm going to make all A's this semester," I told her, making certain I didn't sound puffed up, a Coalwood sin.

She eyed me. "Don't try to do too much. This is your senior year. You're supposed to have some fun, too."

"Yes, ma'am. But if I'm going to college, I've got to make the grades."

She smiled, more to herself, I thought, than at me. "Tell you what I think would be fun," she said. "Just as soon as I get the Veterans Day float done, I'll be figuring out what to do on the Christmas Pageant. How about helping me? We'd make a good team. You could write the script."

It was a temptation. I'd been writing since the third grade when Mrs. Laird, my teacher, had started mimeographing my short stories and spreading them around the school. "Some day, Sonny Hickam," she had told me, "you will make your living as a writer." Although she had retired and moved to Elkins with the Captain, her husband, I'd heard that she was sorely disappointed I had decided to become a rocket engineer. I hadn't completely stopped writing, though. Just last year, I'd written a school play modeled after Shakespeare's *Julius Caesar.* "Beware yon Quintonius Wilsonius, he has a lean and hungry look," was my favorite line in the piece. Everybody laughed at it, but Quentin said he didn't see what was so blamed funny. In Bartley, where Quentin lived, I guess hunger was too real to be amusing.

As tempted as I was to jump into writing a script for the Christmas pageant, I didn't say anything because I didn't know what to say. And as much as I tried to hide it, she saw the anger at the memory of the last Christmas in my eyes. "Sonny? It's time to put what happened last year out of your mind."

"Yes, ma'am," I said. She was right. She usually was. I waited to see if she had anything else to say, and when she didn't, I went off to my room while she went back to her drawings. I sat at my desk for a while, trying not to think, and then got out the stubby pencil and plastic ruler I used to make my rocket designs. We just had to get our nozzles right. The purpose of a rocket nozzle was to direct and compress the hot gases when the propellant burned, causing those gases to speed up. The faster the speed of the gases, the more thrust we got and the higher our rockets flew. Our present nozzle design used steel-bar stock with a hole drilled through its center. It also had countersunk ends, which meant they sloped inward at the top and outward at the bottom like inverted drains. It was a crude design, but it was the best that could be done without getting into a lot of mathematical calculations, something I wasn't confident I could do even though I had been studying calculus and differential equations to prepare myself.

I started to draw another countersunk nozzle, but my eyes fell on the red book on my desk. Entitled *Principles of Guided Missile Design*, it was the book Miss Riley, our science teacher, had given me last winter. Inside it were all the equations we needed to design a sophisticated rocket nozzle called a De Laval nozzle. A De Laval nozzle, I suspected, was the key to a "great" rocket. All I had to do was find the courage to begin using it. I opened the book, gazed at the myriad of complex equations, and then shut it again. There were just too many thoughts richocheting through my mind for me to concentrate on anything. The worst of it was that Mom had started me thinking about Christmas, something I didn't want to do. In all the years I had grown up in Coalwood, Christmas for me had been a joyful, glorious time. Now, the thought of Christmas made me think of poor dead Poppy, and then of my father's eyes, slowly filling with scorn and disgust for what I had done and couldn't do.

2

POPPY

REVEREND JOSIAH LANIER of the Coalwood Community Church used to preach that we should look upon vexations as gifts from God, trials that would strengthen us and our resolve to do and be better. My mother, never one to admire being vexed by anyone, said she and her resolve were about as strong as they were going to get and if the good Lord and Reverend Lanier didn't mind, they could both rest easy on her case. It seemed to me, however, that she was more tolerant of vexes that came my particular way.

"I'm sorry you've got problems, Sonny," Mom told me once when I was complaining about this or that, "but that's called life." At the time, she was up on a ladder, putting in a palm tree on the mural of a beach scene she had been painting on our kitchen wall over the years. "You can't expect everything to go your way," she declared after considering the proper brushstrokes for coconuts. "Sometimes life just has another plan."

Later that day, having overheard what my mother had told me, my father let me know he had a different idea about life and its plans. He came into my room while I was studying. "If you don't like the way things are going," he said, "find the courage to change it. That's called being a man." Then, when the mine phone, which we called the black phone, started ringing, he went off to yell at one of his foremen, leaving me struck with the thought that my parents were the most interesting people I knew.

During all the years I spent in Coalwood, West Virginia, I was called "Sonny" instead of my real name, which was Homer Hadley Hickam, the same as my dad except I had a Junior attached. My older brother's name was James Venable, but everybody called him Jimmie or Jim. The story of how I, as Elsie and Homer Hickam's second of two sons (and no daughters), got tagged with my dad's name had several different versions. The one I think is true, knowing my mother as I do, was that my father took one look at me after I was born and said, "That's the ugliest baby I've ever seen." After he left, the next person in the room at the Stevens Clinic Hospital in the county seat of Welch was a nurse with a clipboard. "And what is the name of your baby?" she asked officiously. I can well imagine my mother's triumphant smile forming as she opened her mouth to speak.

I think it was some relief to my father when people started calling me by my nickname. Even though he and I shared the same name, most people agreed we weren't much alike. He had an intimidating physical and intellectual presence, while I was more relaxed. According to what I'd heard, my grandmother on my mother's side—my Amamma—once came to Coalwood to visit when I was a baby and snatched me out of the cradle and made me wake up. "Gaw, Elsie, this baby's got to move," she said, "or he ain't ever going to amount to a thing." Then she put me down on the floor and made me crawl around for the rest of the day even though I fell into slumber every time she took her eye off me. Mom said I pretty much slept through babyhood. That may have been thanks to her daily doses of catnip tea to cure my colic, but I like to think I was just resting up for all the excitement to come.

My mother taught me to read before I went to the first grade, and in the books my parents kept stacked in the upstairs hall, I found a new world past Coalwood and its mountains. I fought pirates with Jim Hawkins, flew above a crystal sea with Wendy and the Lost Boys, went down the Mississippi on a raft with Huck and

Jim, and became one of the last of the Mohican tribe. I had an almost insatiable need to act out the adventures I found in the books I read and formed elaborate games with my boyhood friends, especially Benny Brown and Roy Lee. When we were pirates, we tied bandannas around our heads, hammered together wooden swords, and built rafts, terrorizing mostly the crawl-dads in the creek. "Avast there, wench! Serve us some rum!" I yelled at my mother one time from the creek as she came into the backyard to hang up sheets on the clothesline.

"Wench, is it?" she said, laughing. "I think a certain young man's been reading a little too much *Treasure Island*."

"Arghhhh! I'll see ye keelhauled!" was my reply. I was good at staying in character even under the stress of reality.

After I'd seen the Disney television show about Davy Crockett, the miners trooping home after the day shift became Mexican soldiers. I gave the signal and we boys rose up over the walls of our Alamo of sticks and boards and let fly with horrendous gouts of imagined smoke and fire from our broomstick muskets. The miners, having played parts in my sagas more than once, comprehended their roles immediately and staggered and clutched their chests before righting themselves and moving on down the valley. Benny Brown would usually volunteer to play the last Mexican horde and let me pretend to swing my Old Betsy musket broomstick at him, knocking him down a hundred times before finally I'd collapse, moaning with patriotic fervor for Texas, which I took to be someplace down south. Benny's father died of dust silicosis, and according to the rules of Coalwood, he and his mother had to move on. I still missed him.

In 1954, my father became the mine superintendent in Coalwood, and my mother, brother Jim, and I moved down to what was known as the Captain's house. The coal company tipple, where the coal was brought out, sorted, and loaded into coal railcars, was a mere hundred yards from our house. As I watched the miners go up and down the path that led to the tipple grounds, I thought they looked like soldiers in the newsreels, except instead of carrying rifles, they swung cylindrical tin lunch buckets as they marched, their black helmets shining in the sun or sparkling in the rain. My dad was, in many ways, their general, plotting strategy and tactics against an unyielding foe, the mine itself. Coalwood's miners proudly dug the finest bituminous coal in the world, all of it shipped to the steel mills of Ohio and Pennsylvania. Dad said that without Coalwood and the towns like it, there would be no steel, and without steel, there would be no United States as we knew it. He took it as his personal and patriotic responsibility to keep the coal heading north. Every day, even though he didn't have to, he went to the face where the coal was cut from the seam. There he could see the results of his daily plan. There, also, microscopic coal dust produced by the continuous miners filled the air and coated the men. In 1957, Dad was diagnosed with black spots on his lungs, but he still kept to his daily routine of going to the face. When he coughed at home, my mother's eyes would fill with worry. She knew very well lung spots never got smaller, only bigger.

Both of my parents had come to Coalwood from Gary, another McDowell County coal camp. The two towns were separated by twelve miles, two mountains, and the philosophy of Mr. George L. Carter, Coalwood's founder. When Dad graduated from Gary High School, the Great Depression was in full swing and he found himself among many young Gary men, quietly desperate to make a living wage. Coalwood must have seemed like heaven. Gary was a harsh place of union strikes and bloody heads. Coalwood had steady employment, an honest company-store system, free medical and dental care, and fine, big, sturdy houses provided to each miner for only a small monthly rent. Mr. Carter allowed no union in his mine but paid the best wages in the county. He also worked hard to keep his mine safe, installing a complex ventilation system to flush out the explosive methane that seeped from the coal seams. Gary had coke ovens beside its houses, and their noxious fumes covered its hollows. The drifting smoke made children and old people sickly. Coalwood's air, though dusty from the endless coal trains chuffing from the tipple through the center of town, was sweet in comparison. When Dad applied for work, Captain William Laird, Mr. Carter's right-hand man, saw something in the skinny youth and took him under his wing, teaching him how to mine coal, lead men, and to ferociously love Coalwood and Mr. Carter's social philosophy. A lot of people in town called Dad the "little Captain."

Mr. John Dubonnet, a Gary High School classmate of both my father and mother, began work at the Coalwood mine at the same time. Mr. Dubonnet became a fierce advocate of the United Mine Workers of America and joined the long battle to unionize the Coalwood mine. The union won its battle with Mr. Carter in 1949, causing him to sell out to a steel company in Ohio. The Carter Coal Company was renamed the Olga Coal Company, after the wife of a steel official. Five years after the unionization, the Captain retired and Dad took the mine superintendent's job. About the same time, Mr. Dubonnet took over the union local. Two boys from Gary who'd arrived in Coalwood sharing their poverty and desperation now shared only suspicion and distrust.

Coalwood's houses were jammed between steep, humpbacked mountains pushed so close together a boy with a good arm could throw a rock from one hill to the other. The houses were built in rows down the valleys, each row with a distinctive name: New Camp, Substation, Tipple, Six, Main Street, Coalwood Main, Club House, Snakeroot, Middletown, Mudhole, and Frog Level. Coalwood Main included the central company store (known as the Big Store), the company offices, the general superintendent's mansion on an overlooking hill (vacant since Mr. Van Dyke had been fired), the company Club House (which was a hotel for single miners and visitors and was also used for company banquets and dances), the company churches (the preachers were company men), offices for the company doctor and dentist (still provided free to miners and their families), and the federal post office. When visitors drove over Welch Mountain, the first row they encountered was New Camp on the left followed by Substation on the right. Coming in over Coalwood Mountain from Caretta and War brought visitors past Six and then the mine tipple, where the coal was loaded into waiting railcars. Our house, a big four-bedroom, two-story wood-frame house, was at the intersection of Tipple and Substation Rows.

It seemed to me that life in Coalwood was timeless, that forever men and their sons and their sons coming behind them would tramp to the mine to gouge out the coal. But soon after Dad took his position as the mine superintendent, nearly everything about Coalwood began to change. The biggest change was when the steel company sold the houses. If a Coalwood miner wanted to stay in town, he had to buy his house or leave. The selling of the houses came in the spring of 1959 when I was a junior in high school. Within a few months, the sale was accomplished except for two houses, ours and the general superintendent's, both of which remained company property. The churches were also sold off, along with the utilities. For the first time in six decades of existence, Coalwood was no longer a pure company town, and strangers began to appear in our midst.

Before the houses were sold, when a man lost his job at the mine, the company's rules required him to move out of town and take his family with him. If a man was killed, the rules still applied—two weeks to get the funeral done and get out. But with the houses sold, men who had quit or were cut off could hunker down where they were, defying the mortgage company. Within a few months of the sell-off, there were rumors that Coalwood had families up Six Hollow going hungry. This had never happened to us before. Coalwood was surrounded by poverty-stricken towns like Gary and Bartley and Berwind, towns where the mines had closed or were choked by strikes and where families lined up every week for the commodity food handouts from the government. But Coalwood had always been an oasis of prosperity in the county. Every day, I heard people in town worrying over what was to become of us. Dad especially worried about it over the supper table at night. It seemed to me that ever since his father had died, Dad had been suffering one worry after another.

In the fall of 1958, Poppy had developed a rampant colon cancer too far gone to do anything about. Dad had survived the same cancer five years before, but his father was older and weaker.

It was to be the last insult to a man who, in 1941, had both of his legs cut off in the Coalwood mine. What was left of him after his accident slumped on a chair where someone put him. He never had a wheelchair, didn't want one, refused to use it when Dad got one for him. As a small child, I was terrified of the old man I called Poppy. He had moist blue eyes, stringy arms, and a toothless mouth, but it was his legless lap that gave me nightmares.

Mom said Dad blamed himself for Poppy's accident. It was Dad who had convinced Poppy to leave his job in Gary and come and work for the Captain. It was only a few months after moving to Coalwood that Poppy was standing in the gob at the turnout of his section when a loaded coal car jumped the track, took down the row of posts he had just put in, and slid over him. The razor-sharp wheels of the car sliced his legs off at the hip. It was said that Poppy stayed awake during the whole thing, even while he was carried from the mine. Dad was one of the men who bore him out. He had to listen to his father beg over and over for someone to finish him off.

For a full day, according to the Captain's orders, Poppy's legs were left in the gob where he'd been run over. A sign was nailed to a post. It read: A MAN LOST HIS LEGS HERE BECAUSE HE STOOD TOO CLOSE TO THE TRACK. From what I heard, the Captain's sign worked. For a long time, no Coalwood miner stood anywhere near any track, and the spot where Poppy lost his legs was avoided most of all. Poppy's legs were taken out and buried somewhere up on the mountain behind the mine, but the sign remained for some weeks until it disappeared. Mom said Dad had taken it, maybe the only time he'd done something against the Captain's orders, and chopped it up for firewood.

Poppy, whose real name was Benjamin Venable Hickam, was a well-read man. After his accident, he read nearly every book in the county library until the pain of his lost legs forced him onto the paregoric. A woman who lived up near Panther kept him well supplied with Dad paying for it and delivering it as needed. After he got on the paregoric, Mom said Poppy never read another book.

Dad had found his father a little house up Warriormine Hollow and saw to the monthly rent. Every other Sunday, Mom and Dad and Jim and I visited Poppy and my grandmother, whom we kids called Mimmie, as meek and quiet a woman as I ever knew. When we came to visit, she spent most of her time at the cooking stove and then sat silently at the table during dinner not eating, her hands folded on her lap. Her oval face was always placid, but it seemed to me behind her mask there was something awful going on. One time Mom encouraged me to show Mimmie a model airplane I'd built out of balsa wood. She sat down and handled it, her tiny brown eyes running across the rude fuselage and wings until it occurred to me that maybe she had never seen a real airplane. I'd seen precious few of them myself, mostly at Myrtle Beach, South Carolina, when we went there on miner's vacation. After I'd finished my description of my model plane, Mimmie sat for a moment more, as if waiting to see if I had anything more to say. When I didn't, she silently handed it back to me and rose to go back to her cookstove. Mimmie died of a heart attack in 1956. It was an open-casket funeral, the only time I ever saw her smiling.

By December of 1958, Poppy had been taken to Stevens Clinic. Mom said she didn't think he'd ever leave. While Poppy was in the hospital, Dad rarely spoke at the supper table, my only daily interval with him. His haunted eyes were focused somewhere I couldn't see. Each night, he got in the Buick and drove to the hospital, returning after I'd gone to bed.

One night, Mom came to my room and found me at my desk working on my rocket plans. "Listen, Sonny, you need to go with your dad to see Poppy," she said.

"Why?" I asked.

"You need to go," she said again, and since she had said it twice, the argument, such as it was, was over.

The next night, as Dad was gathering up his hat and coat, she pushed me forward. "Sonny wants to go," she said.

"Guess he should," Dad said, and that was that.

Dad said nothing to me while he drove the Buick across Welch Mountain and I sat shrouded in the darkness of the mountain and my own mind. I didn't want to be going to any old stinking hospital, and I guessed he knew that. Stevens Clinic was on the other side of Welch, so we navigated through the town, resplendent with cheerful Christmas lights and bustling shoppers. Miners still wearing their helmets walked the tilted streets, their wives on their arms, and little children skipping behind, breathless and excited. I envied them.

We crept down the hushed hospital halls, which smelled of medicinal alcohol, cotton sheets, and detergent-scrubbed floors. Poppy lay in his bed with tubes leading in and out of him. A sheet only partially covered his torso, leaving his short stumps exposed. They were horribly mangled things with purplish scar tissue on their ends. Dad spoke so softly that it didn't sound like his voice at all. "Hi, Daddy."

Poppy gasped out something between his twisted lips I couldn't understand. Dad dragged up a white metal chair and sat near the bed. I sat down in another metal chair in a corner and watched. It was all I knew to do. The old man's long, skinny hands lay unmoving by his side. Dad began to talk, very low. I understood occasional words and phrases—"cutting machine," "fans," "ventilation curtain," "roof bolts," familiar mining terms. When Poppy gasped and shuddered, Dad stopped talking and reached into his coat pocket and brought out a small paper sack. He tilted the small bottle inside it to Poppy's lips, and in a moment the old man calmed and Dad put the sack away and started talking about mining again. When Poppy fell asleep, Dad rose, nodded to me, and we stole out of the room.

By the time we drove back through Welch, the Christmas bustle had subsided and the cheerful lights were turned out. When we got home, Mom had already gone to bed. She greeted me in the morning. Before I could bring it up, she said, "Yes, you'll go again tonight and every night your father goes."

"Why doesn't Jim go?" I demanded. My brother was one year ahead of me in school. He was a senior at Big Creek and a football star and my father doted on him. It seemed like a reasonable question to me.

"Because I said so," she said, and then she thought better of her answer. "You asked me one time if your daddy loved you. Do you remember that?"

I did and I said so. I'd asked the question on the night my first rocket had blown up her rose garden fence. She'd challenged me that night to build my rockets and show my dad what I could do. Maybe if I did, she said, he'd let me go to college instead of giving me some menial clerical job at the mine. Ever since, I'd built my rockets with a single-minded determination. I was going to college and then I was going to Cape Canaveral and work for Dr. Wernher von Braun, the great rocket scientist.

"I told you then he loved you just fine," Mom said. "He was just too busy to show it. This is your chance to spend some time with him. Do you understand now why I want you to go?"

I thought I did but I wasn't certain. As we moved deeper into the Christmas season, I helped raise the tree and put up the decorations, I wrapped the presents I'd bought for Mom and Dad and Jim, I did all the Christmas things there were to do, but my heart wasn't in it. I only had one thing on my mind, that dreaded moment each night when Dad would stop yelling on the black phone and start gathering up his things and I knew it was time for me to appear in the kitchen, prepared to go to the hospital with him.

It seemed to me that Welch's Christmas lights seemed less festive each time we crawled through the town on the way to the hospital. Dad's nightly sessions with Poppy seemed endless as I sat on the cold metal chair in the corner and sullenly stared at them. Only once during all the nights I was there had Poppy taken any note of me at all. He'd raised a single finger and looked my way and then mumbled something I couldn't understand. "He can be a good boy, Daddy," Dad said, so I guessed Poppy had said something about me. I stayed in my chair. When Poppy fell asleep, Dad gathered up his things and, without a word, we again went across the cold, dark mountain to Coalwood.

All through the Christmas season, Dad and I visited Poppy. Each night, I stayed in the room with them until I couldn't stand it anymore. There was just something about it that dug at me. Dad sat with Poppy, and even though Poppy didn't say anything, it was clear they were enjoying each other's company. For some reason, that irritated me. Dad would occasionally get a wet cloth and wipe Poppy's brow and then smooth his hair. I had never seen him act so tenderly toward anybody. I knew it was a good thing he was doing, but I could hardly stand to watch him do it. I made a habit of coming up with some excuse to get out of that room, just to walk the halls if nothing else. That I needed to go to the bathroom was my most consistent excuse. I also invented a high school chum with a broken leg on another floor. Dad caught me at that one when I forgot my made-up name for my "friend" and made up another one. Dad remembered the first name very clearly. I think he knew exactly what I was doing even though he didn't know why. I didn't, either, for that matter.

"He likes to see that you're here," Dad said after I'd left the room under one excuse or another for about an hour. "Stop running away."

"Yes, sir," I said, but I couldn't help myself. Whatever Mom's plan was, it wasn't working. It seemed to be driving a wedge between Dad and me.

On Christmas Eve, I begged Mom to let me stay home. Nearly everyone in Coalwood attended the annual Coalwood Christmas Pageant on Christmas Eve. The pageant, sponsored by the Coalwood Women's Club, was conducted on the Club House lawn. There was caroling and sermons and good cheer, and the road in front of the Club House was usually clogged with joyful people. I explained to her reasonably that I hadn't had a night of my own during the entire Christmas season. Sherman had organized a hayride before the pageant began, to be pulled by the two ponies Red Carroll kept in the barn behind his house. Couldn't I have at least one night with my friends? Mom shook her head. "You'll go with your father," she said.

"It isn't working, Mom!" I blurted. "I just make Dad mad by going over there!"

"Give it another night," she said.

"What about you?" I challenged her. "When are you going?"

"Poppy is your blood," she said. "He's none of mine. Now quit stalling and get ready."

On Christmas Eve, I returned to the horrible hospital room and sat, silently outraged and completely miserable, with my father and my grandfather. Outside it began to snow and I wished it would snow ten feet high so that everybody would have to stay home and not be able to go on a hayride or anything else. I could see the feathery flakes drift by, illuminated by the lights from the nurses' dormitory. While I fidgeted, Dad talked on to Poppy, mining more coal. I was desperate to escape. When I could stand it no longer, I mumbled, "Going to the bathroom," and made for the door.

Dad looked at me. "You need to stay."

"I *have* to go!" I said, fairly shouting. I bolted from the room.

In the hall, I practically sang I was so happy to be out of that awful place. A nurse glided by and gave me a look. She stopped. "Sonny Hickam," she said.

I looked closely at the plump, golden-curled woman. It took me a moment, and then I knew her. She'd put on some weight and grown up some since I'd last seen her, but I recognized her all the same. "Charlotte Sheets," I said. She was a Coalwood girl, or had been, some years older than me. Her dad was a motorman in the mine, and her mother grew blackberries in the front yard. Charlotte had grown up and moved away, where I hadn't known, but now I did. She'd become a nurse and returned to McDowell County.

She gave me a quick rundown of where she'd been, how she'd worked her way through nursing school. "I may go to Florida if Jesse gets that job," she said vaguely, and I guessed Jesse was her husband. I looked at the name tag she wore and it said "Dawson" so I supposed that was her married name.

She nodded toward the room I had so joyfully exited. "Mr. Hickam is such a wonderful man," she said. "Not the least bit of trouble. Gets right up on that bedpan and about all that comes out is blood. We don't know how he stands it. We give him all the painkillers we're allowed but it can't be enough, all the cancer he's got inside him."

I didn't reply. The Hickams were taking care of their own on that score, I thought, thinking of the bottle of paregoric in the paper sack Dad brought with him in his coat.

"I really admire you, Sonny," Charlotte continued. "I heard you've been over here every night with your daddy to be with his daddy. A lot of teenagers these days, they wouldn't do that. You're a sweet boy. I remember you growing up that way, too. Always a sweet boy."

And with that she headed down the hall, her rubber-soled shoes squeaking on the dark, waxed floors. I watched her go and then skulked back inside Poppy's room.

Dad was holding Poppy's hand and seemed clenched up somehow, as if maybe his stomach hurt. I sat down in my chair and waited. After a few minutes, Dad let Poppy's hand go and said, "I love you, Daddy." Then he turned to me. "Let's go," he said gruffly, and then stood up and put his coat and hat on and went out the door. I was close behind, thankful to be done with Poppy for another night.

Again, we drove through Welch. To my surprise, Dad stopped at the Parking Building and, without comment, led the way up a street and into the Woolworth's department store. It was staying open late for miners on the evening shift. I followed as he went to the ladies' section and bought earrings and a bracelet for Mom and had them wrapped in pretty Christmas paper and ribbons. Then I followed him back to the car and we turned for home. Mom was still awake when we got there. Dad put her present under the Christmas tree. "Daddy crossed the bar tonight," he told her.

A flush of guilt went straight through me. Tears sprang to my eyes. I stood there while Mom took Dad's hand and they went upstairs. "We got some coal mined before he went," Dad told her. "That man loved to mine coal."

I stood alone beside the lit Christmas tree, feeling miserable. My Poppy had died and I had run from him. Chipper was inside the tree, asleep on one of its branches. I could hear him twittering with each breath as he dreamed. Daisy Mae, my little calico cat, was curled up with the presents, the cotton snow under the tree a soft bed. She purred when I reached down and touched her head. The house, in its silence, smelled of pine needles and wax candles and my guilt. I looked at the clock on the mantel. Christmas Day, 1958, had arrived but I could find no joy in it.

The next morning, Mom came in and sat on my bed and handed over a manila envelope. When I opened it, I was astonished to find an autographed photograph of Wernher von Braun. "I thought he'd like to know who's coming to help him with his rockets," she said, smoothing my hair with her hand.

Dr. von Braun had written me a note. It was filled with praise for my rocket work and suggested that I should go to college. It ended with: *If you work hard enough, you will do anything you want.* I hugged her. "Thanks, Mom. This is the best present I ever had."

Downstairs, I found Dad sitting in the living room, reading the newspaper. I showed him the photo. He glanced at it and then went back to his newspaper. "I'm sorry about Poppy," I said.

Dad made no reply, just rattled his paper.

"I did my best," I said.

Dad let the paper down but he didn't look at me. "Your Poppy loved you more than anything in the world, Sonny, and you couldn't even stay in the same room with him."

"I tried, sir. But I didn't know he was about to die."

"Maybe you didn't care," he said.

I picked up my photograph. "Merry Christmas, sir," I said, not even bothering to disguise the bitterness in my voice. Dad said nothing in reply. Ten months later, he still hadn't.

3

IN ALL MY BORN DAYS

IN THE FALL of 1959, just as I began my senior year at Big Creek High School, something very peculiar began to happen to me. I'd be doing something perfectly normal—studying at my desk, or drumming along at band practice, or loading a rocket in the basement, or even just walking to class—and, all of a sudden, for no reason I could figure out, I would feel sad. It wouldn't last long, more of a twinge, then the feeling would pass. For weeks, I puzzled over it. When I mentioned it to Quentin, he said, with some impatience, "Sonny, as a budding scientist, you should understand that every question on this planet, including any nervous manifestation, can be ultimately determined by a certain application of logic."

I took a moment to let his words register and then responded, "You're saying if I just think logically, I should be able to figure out why I feel sad."

"Quite right," he sniffed.

Quentin was a darkly handsome lad with an aquiline nose, piercing blue eyes, and severely straight black hair. His trademark was a battered old leather briefcase he carried around everywhere he went. It was always filled with books, chewed pencils, and the occasional half-eaten apple. Quentin also had a way of talking that sometimes defied translation, all delivered in a pseudo-English accent. I prided myself on being able to consistently figure out Quentinese.

He continued. "If, however, your mind cannot construct the proper scenarios based on the physical and mathematical realities of the material world, then it is hardly worthy of your concern."

I sorted out his words and made a stab at their meaning. "If I can't figure it out based on math and science, it's not worth worrying about, anyway?"

"Of course!" he fairly shouted, slapping his fist into his palm. "Now you're thinking like a true scientist!" A lock of his hair tended to fall across his forehead when he got excited. He shoved it back with the flair of a conductor waving his baton.

"Thank you, Quentin."

"Anytime, my boy."

Although I appreciated Quentin's advice, it was clear I would have to go to someone else for what I needed. I therefore decided to seek out Reverend "Little" Richard, the pastor of the Mudhole Church of Distinct Christianity at the mouth of Mudhole Hollow. I wasn't a member of Little Richard's congregation—it was the church for the colored people in town—but the reverend had become a friend since junior high school when I'd been Coalwood's delivery boy for the *Bluefield Telegraph*. When I had an extra paper, I always swung by the reverend's church and gave him a free copy. In return, he had given me Bible stories off the cuff. I thought the reverend was about the smartest man I'd ever had the privilege to meet. He didn't know much about science and math, but he knew a lot about everything else. I suspected my "nervous manifestation," as Quentin called it, probably fell into the latter category.

It was a rainy fall day when I rode my bicycle down to the mouth of Mudhole Hollow and went inside the tiny steepled church. There I found the reverend, dressed in his black sermon frock, standing by the front pew, staring up at the ceiling. I didn't know what he was looking at until a big drop of water came down and landed with a *plunk* in a coffee can beside his shiny pointed shoes. When he saw me, his grin in my direction lit up the room with a flash of his gold front tooth. "Well, well," he said. "Sonny the rocket boy. Got a newspaper with you?"

I had to confess that I didn't, seeing as how I hadn't delivered the paper for over two years. I'd stopped when I started high school. Little nodded and looked back up at the roof. My gaze followed his. There was a water stain on the ceiling, and as I watched another big drop of water hit square into the coffee can. "I saw your door open," I said, "and I just thought I'd come in and say hello." It wasn't entirely the truth, but I couldn't just come right out and admit I had a problem. West Virginians just didn't do that kind of pitiful thing.

"Have to leave the door open for the light," Little replied, his eyes still on the ceiling as if perhaps he could stare the leak away. Finally, he turned away from it. "This new electricity company is gouging us, Sonny. I can't hardly afford the bills, and this old church is powerful dark. Could use some windows up front, let in God's sun."

Whenever anybody wanted building materials in Coalwood, their first thought was always getting it out of the coal company. My dad held company property to be strictly for the production of coal, but most people thought that was kind of a quaint idea. Dad usually unbent enough to let weekend carpenters who asked have the odd board or keg of nails. I think he had adapted the old teaching to read " 'Tis better to give than to get it stolen."

I fully expected to hear a request from Little for his windows, and I wasn't disappointed. "Some glass and a little framing lumber would sure come in handy, all right," he said. "Some tar paper for the roof, too. Don't suppose they got any up at the mine, do you?"

I didn't know if they did or not but I told Little I'd ask Dad, and that seemed to satisfy him. He beckoned me forward and scrutinized me. I was sure I was wearing my poker face, but he said, "In all my born days, I don't think I ever seen a boy look so troubled. What you got going on, Sonny?"

I told him then about the sad feeling I got that tended to bubble up without warning. Little pondered for a while and then put his hand on my shoulder. I wasn't used to being touched—we didn't do much of that in my family—so I twitched away. He gripped me tighter and looked into my eyes. "You ever hear the story of the potter's wheel?" he asked. "It's in Jeremiah of the old Bible."

I hadn't and confessed it. Methodists didn't get into Jeremiah that much. Little released me and went behind his pulpit and brought out his ancient Bible, cracked with use. He knew every verse in the book by heart, but he chose to read the words he had in mind. That way, I suppose, he wouldn't seem too proud, a prime West Virginia sin even for preachers. "Now, listen to this, Sonny," the Reverend said, and then he read:

Then I went down to the potter's house, and, behold, he wrought a work on his wheel. But the vessel that he made was marred so he made again another, as seemed good to the potter to make. Then the Lord came to me, saying, cannot I do with you as this potter? Behold, as the clay is in the potter's hand, so are ye in mine.

Little clapped the Bible shut and studied my face for understanding. I must have looked blank. "The Lord works us, Sonny," he said patiently, "shapes us to his liking just like a lump of clay, even though He don't let us know it."

I absorbed the message. "Why does God keep it a secret?" I wondered.

Little thumbed the Bible as if thinking about where to open it, but he left it closed. "You and your daddy getting along?" he asked, deftly changing the subject.

I shrugged. "He hasn't tried to stop me from building my rockets lately."

"Schoolwork good?"

"I'm making all A's so far, even in Miss Riley's class. I'm going to try to make all A's this semester. I've never done that before."

He nodded. "A worthy goal. How's your brother Jim?"

"Off to college. He played first string on the freshman football team. Dad's mighty proud of him."

"Your rockets?"

"Pretty good. We've got some problems with our new propellant, but I'll figure it out."

"Your mom?"

"Same old mom."

"You say your prayers every night?"

"Yes, sir. Unless I fall asleep over my homework."

"What do you pray for?"

I thought about it. "I just ask for blessings. God bless Mom and Dad and Jim and the cats and dogs and the Rocket Boys and Miss Riley and all the soldiers, sailors, pilots, and marines."

"Who's that Miss Riley?"

"She teaches physics. She got us a rocket book, but I haven't figured it out yet. She's my favorite teacher and she's real pretty."

"You don't pray for yourself?"

"No, sir, that wouldn't be right, would it?"

Little raised his eyebrows. "A boy that don't ask for a blessing on himself must be pretty proud, figure maybe he don't need no help from heaven or nowhere else. Put yourself in your prayers, son, ask to see if God will tell you what's making you sad. You know it might just be Him trying to tell you something. Won't hurt to ask. Will you do that?"

I said I would and Little looked pleased. "Don't forget to ask your daddy about the glass and lumber and tar paper, too," he said as I left to get back on my bicycle. He waved from the door of his church until I was out of sight.

That night, as I began my prayers, I considered what the Reverend Richard had told me to do. I tried but I just couldn't do it. The truth was I didn't hold with it. I'd been taught in the Coalwood Community Church that prayer was for laying on blessings for others, not for asking God questions. Whatever was bothering me, even if it was God, would just have to come out in its own good time.

IN early October, Dad was scheduled to go up to Ohio to give a presentation to the steel company on the state of the Coalwood and Caretta mines. Ordinarily, this presentation was given by Coalwood's general superintendent, but when it was announced that the houses were going to be sold, Mr. Van Dyke, our general superintendent for years, had gone to Ohio to protest. As a reward for his sincerity and honesty, the steel company summarily sacked him and sent down a Mr. Fuller to make sure the houses got sold. After that was done, Mr. Fuller went home. Then a Mr. Bundini was assigned the position and made an inspection trip to Coalwood that lasted several weeks. But he had gone back to let his daughters finish out the school year in Ohio. The plan was for Mr. Bundini to return, but until he did, Dad was temporarily wearing the hats of both the mine superintendent and the general superintendent. Mom noted that even though Dad was doing two jobs, at least he didn't have to worry about an increase in his salary.

Dad had been toiling over his pitch to the steel company for days and often worried about it over the supper table with Mom. I caught him working on it when I walked up to the tipple and knocked on the open office door in the grimy brick building that served as his headquarters. His head was in his hands and he was pondering an ancient Underwood typewriter and the sheet of paper rolled into it. Dad looked up, caught sight of me, and said "No," as a general statement.

"Telephone wire," I said, confirming his supposition as to the purpose of my visit. Cape Coalwood needed telephone wire for a new communications system. Despite his greeting, I came inside and stood before his desk, taking on my usual pitiful expression when I was on a scrounging maneuver. "And, if you've got any, some glass, lumber, and tar paper for the Mudhole church," I said brazenly.

Dad cocked his head and made what I supposed was a quick mental inventory of every last scrap of mine supplies, its condition, and likely disposition. "There's a spool of old telephone wire up by the back gate. I asked Filbert to carry it off to Matney's junk yard a month ago and he still hasn't gotten to it. It's yours if you want it. As for the Reverend Little Richard, I am aware of his needs and, even though the company no longer owns his church, I will see that the company provides."

"Thanks, Dad." I nodded toward the typewriter. "Is that your speech?"

"If you can call it that." He fingered the sheet of paper and pushed a single key. He did it with such finality I hoped it was a period.

"I like speech class," I said. "Miss Bryson, my teacher, thinks I'm pretty good."

He pondered me. It seemed to me every time Dad gave me a look, it was like the first time he'd ever seen me. "She's not available for consulting work, is she?"

I guessed she wasn't, seeing as how she was the daughter of the county school superintendent, and probably pretty busy.

Dad waved me out of his office. That night at the supper table, he and Mom had another exchange concerning his upcoming trip to Ohio. "I could make a hash of it, Elsie," he said. There was uncommon worry in his voice.

"So what?" was my mom's unsympathetic reply.

"So what I'll not get what the mine needs," Dad replied.

Her sigh filled the kitchen. "Do you think they really care what you say up there in Ohio, Homer? Seems all they want from you is more coal with less men to do it. You can talk until you're blue in the face and that won't change."

Dad crumbled a wedge of corn bread into his glass and poured it full of milk, his standard dessert. "They have their own problems," he said morosely, digging his spoon into the glass. "The steel business is in decline. Damn cheap imported steel is going to send us all into ruin."

Mom shrugged. "Go to Ohio, have your say, and then come home. Nothing will change in this old place if you do it standing on your head." Then she added: "And stop thinking everything you do is so important. Knowledge puffs up but charity edifies."

"What in Sam Hill does that mean?"

"Just something the preacher said in his sermon this past Sunday. Too bad you missed it."

Dad was notorious for missing church. "Thank you for your support, Reverend Lavender," he said, using Mom's maiden name. That made her laugh into her coffee cup, and Dad looked proud that he had made her do it. I went back to my supper of chicken, corn bread, and beans, Mom's specialty, while secretly mulling Little Richard's story of the potter's wheel. I wondered if God had had any kind of hand in shaping my parents. He'd had his hands full, in that case.

The next day, Dad went off to Ohio. Two days later, he returned and reported the results to Mom while he was still holding his suitcases in his hands. "I was just too nervous," he said, his shoulders down. "I'm lucky they didn't laugh me out of the room."

Mom was at the kitchen table working on her plans for the Veterans Day float. She pointed at the kitchen floor and Dad put the suitcases down, but his shoulders still slumped. "For starters, they spelled my name wrong on the agenda," he said miserably. "Hickham, it said. Then the president of the steel company introduced me and proceeded to call me Homer Hickman. For God's sake, Hickman! I've worked in this mine for thirty years, they've owned the mine for ten, and they still don't know my name!"

Dad was wound up, no doubt about it. When he got that way, he would often start coughing, but Mom had her ways of winding him down. "The sun came up this morning, Homer," she said patiently. "I reckon it'll set later on, too."

Dad absorbed Mom's solar activity report and got her point. "There's a present for you in one of the suitcases," he said. "Perfume."

"What kind?"

"It's orange color. You like oranges."

"I like to eat oranges, Homer," Mom said, suppressing a smile. "I don't know about smelling like one."

Dad shrugged and went off to change his clothes to go to the mine, where at least they knew how to spell and pronounce his name and nobody wore perfume. I was surprised when he came back within an hour. I heard him down in the basement hacking, and then a long, strangled silence followed by another horrible wet coughing fit. Finally, it quieted and I heard him come slowly up the basement steps as if he was carrying a ton of rocks on his back. I guess in a way he was. I came down to see what was going on. When he opened the door into the kitchen, his face was pale. "What the good Lord, Homer?" Mom asked, her voice faintly atremble. "Do you want me to call Doc?"

Dad ignored her question. "They didn't even wait until I got home. Message waiting for me at the office. I either get the tonnage up by ten percent or I've got to cut off thirty more men," he said. "That's not news for anybody but family," he added, giving me a dark look.

"You ran all the way home to tell me this?" Mom asked. "With your lungs, Homer, you're lucky you didn't have a stroke."

"Don't you understand, Elsie?" Dad demanded. "There's no way I can increase production by that much. Thirty good men . . . they have to go by seniority. That means young men with families. I've got to do something about this, come up with a different plan."

Mom slowly put down her pencil. "Buddy, let's get out of here while we still can," she said. When she was looking to calm my dad, Mom often called Dad "Buddy." I never knew why. "Let's go to Myrtle Beach. Peabody Real Estate would hire us both in a second. We'll work together, sell property, get rich as kings. Every day, we'll go down to the ocean, breathe in nothing but fresh, clean air. Coalwood's had its day. We've had a good life here, I swan, but it's over."

Dad brushed past me, heading to the black phone. Soon he was on it, talking to a foreman. "Run East Main as hard as you can tonight, Cecil. Do you hear me?" He stopped to cough into a bandanna, then said, in a strangled voice, "We've got to get that tonnage up!"

I trudged back upstairs. That night, when I heard the evening shift being replaced by the hoot-owlers, I got to thinking about Little Richard's potter's wheel again. If God was shaping us, he was doing it powerfully hard.

4

THE STOOP CHILDREN

THE CHANGES THAT had come to Coalwood arrived at our front door on Halloween. I was doing the answering for the trick-or-treaters. Dad, an adviser to the county Salvation Army Post in Welch, had gone to a meeting. Mom was at the kitchen table worrying over her plans for the Veterans Day float along with her first thoughts for the Christmas Pageant.

To keep me supplied for the trick-or-treaters, Mom had made up a batch of candied apples and popcorn balls. All I had to do was drop them into the outstretched paper sacks of whatever ghouls or goblins came knocking. The kids who showed up reminded me of myself, just four or five years back. I had usually gone out on Halloween nights with Roy Lee because he had a knack for causing excitement. Occasionally, we'd trick our treaters just for the fun of it. It was innocent stuff—knocking on doors and running, or soaping windows. When we were in the fourth grade, we got caught soaping windows at Bunky Smith's house on Substation Row. After he reported us to the authorities, which meant our mothers, Roy Lee and I spent the next day washing every one of Bunky's windows. "Boy, we had fun, though," Roy Lee had snickered while we worked under the close supervision of Mrs. Smith. I told Roy Lee to shut up. Mrs. Smith rewarded my snottiness by giving my behind a good swat with a folded newspaper. When I told Mom on her for doing it, Mom just laughed and said, "She should have used a board."

For years, the Coalwood school had held an annual company-sponsored Halloween party where nearly everyone in town showed up. There were always prizes, usually cakes and cookies, given for the best costume. It was part of the family legend that, before I was born, Mom had gone as a hillbilly, complete with red long johns. She'd pranced around the stage singing about Mountaineers being always free (it was our state motto: *Montani Semper Liberi*) while she received a long, careful appraisal from the judges. She'd also gotten some whoops from the men in the crowd until their wives shushed them, principally because no one had instructed Mom that she might need to button the trap door in her men's underwear. She won the judging, of course. Two years ago, our Ohio owners had ordered the company not to support the carnival any longer, and a Coalwood tradition had died.

A few children came to our door early, dressed in a variety of homemade costumes. Witches were popular with the little girls—a black dress, a glued-together cardboard pointy hat, an old broom, and a painted nose wart was their standard costume. The boys were mostly cowboys—plenty of cap pistols and cowboy hats around town—or ghosts in bedsheets or devils in cardboard horns and dyed-red pajamas. The little kids were cute, but they were also sparse. Coalwood was getting older. In the rest of the United States, the so-called baby boom was still in grade school, but in Coalwood ours was just about busted. The school classes younger than mine were all smaller. A lot of the young men back from World War II and Korea hadn't come home to West Virginia to work in the mine. Once they were out, they had stayed out.

It was around 10:00 P.M., a time when Coalwood's trick-or-treaters were usually home safely in bed, that I heard a nearly inaudible tapping on our aluminum storm door. When I opened it, I found on our front stoop a half dozen or so children dressed as ragged urchins. I didn't recognize any of them. "Trick or treat!" they yelled. Their voices were shrill and oddly anxious. Then, when I took a second look, I realized they weren't wearing costumes at all.

I gave them all the candy and apples I had left and then went into the kitchen. I got a big grocery sack and emptied out all the cookies Mom kept in the drawer beside the sink. She looked up from her drawings and lists. "What do you think you're doing?" she asked tiredly.

"More kids than we thought," I mumbled.

"At this hour? Well, I'll bet they're just coming around again. I made plenty of treats. Let me take a look." She went to the front door with me close behind. The huddled kids shrank away from her. "Oh, my," she said. Her hand strayed to her heart. The children backed down a step, their eyes wide. "Don't you move!" she ordered, and they froze in place.

I followed Mom back into the kitchen and watched her open up the refrigerator and begin tossing baloney and ham slices and cheese into a sack. When it was filled up, she got another sack and put a loaf of bread in it and then opened up her pantry and tossed in cans of soup and a jar of peanut butter. She pointed at the sacks. "Quick, before they get away!"

I did as I was told, handing over the groceries. "Thank you!" the children said over and over, and when I looked out at the gate, I saw for the first time that they'd been accompanied by a woman. She had been just out of sight, hidden behind Mom's rose arbor. The woman wore a thin coat and had a kerchief pulled around her head. She looked tiny and frail, what I could see of her. She waited for the children to come through the gate, and then, whispering amongst themselves excitedly, the family disappeared into the night.

"I wonder where they're from?" Mom said. "Couldn't be from Coalwood. They must have come in over the mountain." She went to the telephone and called Mrs. Sharitz next door. "Rosemary? Did some raggedy kids just come to your house? They did? Did you know them? No, I didn't, either." Mom phoned each lady on Tipple Row, but the answer was all the same. No one recognized the children.

When Dad came in late from his Salvation Army meeting, I was in the basement, contemplating my latest approach to fin design. I thought maybe it would be quicker to just cut two rectangles and bend them around the casement and clamp them together. That would give us four rectangular fins for about what it now took to make two of them. Dad came down the basement steps, and I heard Lucifer, our old tomcat, growl. When Lucifer came into the basement to get warm, he always chose the bottom step of the staircase that came down from the kitchen to make his nest. "I'm not going to step on you, you crazy old thing," Dad said. "Sonny boy—what are you doing up so late?" He had a blue suit on, an unusual sartorial event for Dad, but going to a meeting in Welch apparently demanded it. Although he was forty-seven years old, his hair was as black and full as I guess it had ever been. He and my brother Jim shared the same faded blue eyes, but Dad had a sharper face, his nose thin and triangular.

I showed Dad the drawing of my fin design, and he reached inside his coat for some reading glasses to peruse it. After a moment, he handed it back to me. "You need a sharper pencil" was his only comment. He looked at the furnace and said, "Throw a shovelful of coal or two in there before you come up."

"Yes, sir," I said. He turned to go but stopped at the base of the stairs, straddling Lucifer, who gave him an irritated, heavy-lidded look. Dad pondered me and I thought he was about to say something, but then he went on up the steps. I heard him cross through the kitchen and the dining room, and then he stopped. I knew it was to sort through his mail stacked on the dining-room table. I heard Mom's footsteps on the stairs and then their muffled voices. I was quiet, so I could hear what they were saying.

She told him about the children on the stoop. "Buddy, I talked to everybody on Tipple Row and nobody knew who they were. They couldn't be from Coalwood, could they?"

"I don't know, Elsie," he said. "I hope not but—"

She interrupted him. "Buddy, let's get out of here while you've still got breath left in your lungs."

"It's going to be all right, Elsie," Dad said, his voice low. "I have a plan. We're going to go into . . ." But I couldn't hear what else he said.

I heard Mom well enough. "I won't let this place kill you, Homer."

"For better or for worse," he said.

"Your better, my worse," Mom replied, and then I heard her footsteps going up the stairs.

5

THE COALWOOD WOMEN'S CLUB

MR. DEVOTIE DANTZLER was Coalwood's company-store manager. He was from Mississippi, and he had the soft, courtly drawl of an educated man from a more southerly and genteel clime. He wore three-piece suits and carried in a pocket of his vest a fine railroad watch that had a gold chain attached. In the summer, in a time of no air-conditioning, he took off the coat and rolled up his white shirtsleeves in the office in the back of the Big Store, but I never saw him without his vest.

The company store, which Mr. Dantzler ran with a sure and benevolent hand, consisted of the Big Store in Coalwood, the Little Store on Substation Row, the Six Store near the Number Six shaft, and two stores in our sister town of Caretta on the other side of Coalwood Mountain. Not only could hardware of all types be bought in Olga Coal's company stores, but also groceries, tobacco, clothing, patent drugs, candy, and the best milk shake anywhere to be found in West Virginia. When a miner was down on his luck or had overextended his credit, Mr. Dantzler took a personal interest and helped him manage his financial affairs until he was caught up. He was a man everybody respected, but you didn't want to get caught stealing from one of his stores. When that rare event happened, Mr. Dantzler had no pity. He called Tag and Tag called the state police and then you went to jail in Welch where everybody in Coalwood agreed you belonged.

Mr. Dantzler's wife, Mrs. Eleanor Marie Dantzler, was from Kentucky, where she had played the piano in the silent movie houses while going to the University of Kentucky. Mrs. Dantzler brought her love of music to Coalwood along with a big grand piano and, from the first day of her arrival, let everybody know she wanted to teach the children piano and voice. Coalwood's parents, always glad to add to their children's talents and skills, especially when it didn't cost that much, took her up on it, and soon she had a thriving business. Mrs. Dantzler taught at home, her lessons beginning at 4:00 P.M. on a school day and at noon on Saturdays. She charged two dollars an hour and held four recitals a year. As it happened, there was a piano in my house. Dad had given it to Mom on their first wedding anniversary. Since she had never learned to play, I became the designated piano player in the house as soon as I was big enough to sit on the piano bench and reach the keys and the pedals.

For eight years, while I was in the second through the ninth grade, I arrived at the Dantzlers' house each Wednesday afternoon after school, carrying my lesson books with me. Although I never cared much for playing the piano, I loved going to the Dantzler house. It smelled of light perfume and was cool even on the hottest day in August, the drapes and windows kept closed against the heat. There were fine Persian rugs laid perfectly over a polished oak floor, and the carved furniture seemed to me as if it belonged in a European castle. Sometimes, while I was waiting for my lesson to begin, the Dantzlers' youngest daughter, Ginger, whose real name was Zanice Virginia, would come in and sit with me and we'd read comic books together. I always liked Ginger, but she was two years younger than me, a lifetime when I was in grade school, so I didn't see her very much except when I came for my lessons. I always thought she was a pretty girl, though. She had the face of an alert pixie, a dimple in her right cheek, brown curly locks, and big amber eyes that always seemed to be a second away from mischief.

Mrs. Dantzler was the most glorious woman I'd ever met. She had hair the color and sheen of mercury and the figure of Marilyn Monroe. Her deep blue eyes were large and expressive, and her lashes were long and curled at the ends. She laughed a lot and she had fine, straight, very white teeth. I never saw her when she wasn't wearing a dress and high-heeled shoes. She had beautiful, expressive hands, and her fingers were long and her nails always polished a deep ruby. She was how I imagined a queen would look. I often wondered if she wasn't in fact some sort of royalty that had accidentally ended up in Coalwood.

On Sundays, Mrs. Dantzler played the piano at the Coalwood Community Church. She insisted on a good tempo, no long drawn-out hymns for her. Mom used to laugh and say that "once Eleanor Marie got the bit in her mouth, everybody had to ride or get bucked off." Usually, Mrs. Dantzler didn't sing with the choir, but every so often, at special occasions—Christmas, Easter, and maybe a wedding—she would don the maroon robe of the choir and step out for a solo. She was a glorious sight standing alone beside the pulpit, her face raised to heaven. Her voice was huge in our little church, rattling even the rafters, her great, pearly notes hit sure and strong like a hammer square onto a nail. Sometimes when she was singing, the sun would shine through the windows and her hair would glow almost like molten silver and it seemed to me she had turned into an angel. All she needed were the wings. When she finished one of her solos, I always felt breathless.

Although I had no talent for piano, Mrs. Dantzler kept at me until I at least had developed some playing skill. At her recitals, she always had me last on the schedule, since I was the only boy in her class. To make certain I was presentable for the recitals, which were considered important society events in Coalwood, she taught me to sit up straight on the piano bench and how to bow when I was finished, putting one arm across my stomach, the other across my back.

Although I was perfectly agreeable to taking piano, I hated practicing. "A little more time at your piano at home, Sonny, is in order before your next lesson," Mrs. Dantzler would say routinely. "You know, two dollars doesn't grow on trees."

When I started to go to Big Creek High, I decided it was time to quit the piano. I had a lot of homework and rockets to build, and practicing the piano cut into my time. Mom said it was okay by her if I wanted to quit, but I had to tell Mrs. Dantzler to her face. I think she thought that would stop me, but I was determined.

I rehearsed what I would tell Mrs. Dantzler. I had myself quite a verbal concoction. It wasn't that I was quitting, that's what I was going to tell her. I was just going to play the piano more for myself, that's it. I had learned so much, see, and now I needed a little while to just work on all that I knew. I would keep playing, you could bet on that, now and forever. So thanks a lot, Mrs. Dantzler, you've been grand. While riding my bike, I went over my tall tale all the way down to the Dantzler house, but as soon as she opened her door, my little lies flew out of my head like scared bats. I stammered a bit and then just blurted, "I can't take piano anymore!"

Her big blue eyes opened in shock. "Why not, Sonny?"

"Because . . . because . . . I don't want to!"

Mrs. Dantzler looked at me with disappointment and hurt while I shrank under her gaze, and then she silently led me back to her piano and sat beside me as she had done so many hundreds of times before. She turned on the meter and it ticked as I went through my compositions. She corrected me as if it were a normal lesson and that she would get to see the results next week as she had done for all those years. Finally, the excruciating hour was over, and she turned off the meter and got up and went to the window and looked out at the mountains while I gathered my books and manuals. I left two crumpled dollar bills on the piano bench. "I'll keep practicing," I told her back.

"No, you won't," she said quietly.

I fled, knowing she was right.

SHERMAN was the Rocket Boy I could always call on to help me mix up propellant. For some reason, he enjoyed spending time up to his elbows in chemicals. A day early in November 1959 found the two of us in my basement laboratory mixing the goopy gray gunk we called zincoshine. We followed a set routine, never deviating from what we knew to be safe. First a small amount of zinc dust was measured into a wooden mixing bowl, followed by an appropriate amount of sulfur. After that, we poured enough of John Eye's finest into the mix to make a thick slurry. We'd mix the ingredients in the bowl with a wooden spoon or our hands until it had turned a uniform gray, and then scrape it out on a cookie sheet. A rolling pin was used to squeeze out excess alcohol. Each small batch we produced was enough for us to load a few inches of propellant into a casement. We mixed and loaded, giving a minimum of one hour between loads for the zincoshine to "cure" in the casement. It was a slow, tedious process, but Sherman and I loved to do it. We'd listen to rock and roll on the little Japanese radio I owned, or talk about girls, or gossip about the goings and comings of Coalwood people. We were never bored.

At no extra charge, Mr. Clinton Caton, the machinist who usually did our work, had come up with a slightly higher-carbon steel for the nozzle we were going to use on our next rocket. Luckily, just when we needed it, he'd had a few lengths of the special bar stock left over from a company job. Quentin was certain we would lick the erosion problem with the new steel, but there was only one way to find out: launch a rocket using it. Sherman and I were loading what I'd designated *Auk XXII-F*, pretty much a copy of the last rocket we'd fired except for the new steel.

To mix our propellants and load our rockets, I had built a small laboratory in the basement of our house. It was just a piece of plywood across the washing machine, which sat beside twin laundry sinks over which shelves groaned with our chemicals and mixing utensils. I had liberated most of my propellant-mixing hardware from Mom's kitchen. She'd never asked for any of it back. I think she was afraid of being poisoned or blown up.

For safety, Sherman was wearing rubber dishwashing gloves, a heavy woolen overcoat, and a ball cap with a piece of plastic taped to the brim to protect his eyes. I was pretty much dressed the same way, and we were sweating because not more than ten feet away was a coal-fired furnace. As long as we kept the grate shut, it was safe. We also kept the basement door cracked to the outside to make certain the lab was ventilated.

I heard the upstairs door creak open. "Sonny, what are you doing down there?" Mom asked from the kitchen.

"We're loading a rocket, Mom," I said casually.

Her response was just as casual, although there was a hint of resignation in it. "Well, don't blow yourself up," she said for about the millionth time since I had become a Rocket Boy. "You either, Sherman," she added.

"Yes, ma'am," he said. Sherman seemed to slouch under the weight of all his protective gear, but it was really because he always held one foot at an acute angle from the other and kept his weight on his good leg.

"The Women's Club meeting is going to start in about ten minutes," Mom continued from above. "How about not making too much noise while they're here? Also, I'd appreciate it if you gave the place a little air."

"Yes, ma'am," I answered, and screwed the top on the fruit jar of moonshine and then went over and opened the basement door as wide as it would go. Since we'd gotten into zincoshine, Mom had told every nose-wrinkling visitor to the house, "I'm not running a juke joint here. It's just Sonny's . . ." and then the visitor would chime in unison with her, ". . . rocket stuff in the basement," nodding in sympathy.

There were still some people in Coalwood who believed the Rocket Boys were the town's special burden. I guess we had caused more than a little uproar over the years. One of our first rockets had careened into Dad's office at the mine, causing him to order me to never launch another rocket in Coalwood again. Under pressure, he later relaxed his sentence, but we were banished a mile below Frog Level to the slack dump we called Cape Coalwood. There, Dad expected us to stay out of sight and out of mind of

Coalwood citizenry. In no time, however, we managed to send a missile on a ballistic arc from the Cape all the way to a field not more than one hundred feet from the houses on Middletown Row, a distance of three miles. A steel company official sent down to oversee the selling of Coalwood's houses and utilities had observed the near miss and ordered our blockhouse torn down and launch-pad bulldozed. Dad had taken up for us on that one and we'd kept our range. I guess the way he saw it was that if anybody was going to kick the Rocket Boys out of Coalwood, he was going to do it, not some steel company slicker. We'd also been falsely accused by the West Virginia State Police of starting a forest fire over in Davy. Miss Riley had saved us on that one, pointing out on a map that our rockets couldn't quite reach out that far—not yet, anyway. In the last few months, we'd stayed pretty much out of trouble, although nearly every weekend, our rockets shook the ground from one of our spectacular successes or our devastating but always colorful pyrotechnic failures.

The basement was a good echo chamber, and I could hear nearly everything that happened on the floor above. I heard Mom cross the kitchen floor to the back porch. I supposed one of the women of the Women's Club had arrived. Then the basement door opened again. "Somebody here to see you," she said, and then I heard footsteps down the basement steps and then a pause at the last one. I knew whoever it was was carefully stepping over Lucifer. "Lucifer, I swan," Mom said by way of a complaint as she got past him.

I turned to see who was with her. Much to my surprise, it was Mrs. Dantzler and Ginger. The furnace pipes ran along the ceiling and they had to duck them to get to us. Mrs. Dantzler was especially careful of her hairdo. "Hello, Sherman," she said, giving him a quick smile that she lost when her eyes came to rest on me. "So, Sonny, this is what took the place of your piano lessons." Her large blue eyes flitted across the cluttered shelves. "Elsie, how you keep your house on the ground is beyond me. And the smell of it!"

"I know, Eleanor Marie," Mom sighed. "We do the best we can with what we've got to work with."

"Sonny, take off those gloves and raise your hands," Mrs. Dantzler commanded. "There, you see, Elsie? Long fingers, wide palms. Those are the hands of a pianist. If only Sonny had kept at his lessons . . . It's a shame is what it is."

I glanced at Mom and was rewarded with a twinkle in her eye. "Now, boys," she said, "the ladies and I have some last-minute Veterans Day float issues to discuss today. All I ask is you keep it quiet down here. Got it?"

"Yes, ma'am," Sherman and I chorused.

Sherman said, "I hear our float's going to be the best one yet."

"That's true, dear," Mom agreed.

Ginger looked around her mother's shoulder with a bright smile. She had grown up to be a pretty sprite of a girl, and she still had those curly brown locks and deep amber eyes. She had on a plaid skirt and a white blouse that was buttoned up to her neck, but Sherman and I were both aware that she was a budding, comely teenager. We exchanged smiles when she asked, "Can I stay and watch?"

"Sure!" Sherman said eagerly.

Ginger looked at me. "Is it all right with you, too, Sonny?" she asked.

"Just be careful," I said, playing the big rocket scientist role to the hilt. "And watch what you touch."

"I won't touch a thing," she said softly.

The way she spoke, so meek and mild, made me look twice at her. Then, while I was looking, I had the sudden opinion that Ginger Zanice Virginia Dantzler was the prettiest girl I'd ever seen. It just came out of nowhere and slapped me in the face, don't ask me why. It was like all of a sudden the only thing I cared about in the whole basement was her. Coach Gainer had once spent an entire hour in his health class trying to figure out how the brains of teenage boys worked. He'd finally given up. I sympathized. I had one of those brains all to myself and I couldn't figure it out, either.

"Sonny?" Sherman said, smiling kindly. "If you're finished looking at Ginger now, can we get back to work?"

"Sure!" I squeaked, tearing my eyes away from her. Embarrassed, I cleared my throat and made an attempt to lower my voice an octave. "Sure," I rumbled in a deeper register, and began to stir zincoshine at a rapid rate.

It wasn't long before I heard the scuffling of shoes on the back porch and a babble of voices as the women greeted one another. Mom was shepherding them into the living room. I wondered if any of them knew how Mom had been on her hands and knees all morning polishing the beautiful oak planks Captain Laird had laid down. The house, being company property, didn't belong to us, but she treated it like it did and maybe better.

The McDowell County Veterans Day parade was a huge, patriotic affair. Bands from every high school in the county marched in it, and there was a competition for the best float. As far as anybody could remember, Coalwood had never lost the float competition. Winning it was a point of great pride to the town. The company over the years had spared no expense to keep the string going, providing not only money but machinists and carpenters to do a lot of the work. Mom's design called for a live Statue of Liberty to stand on a revolving disk while soldiers from exotic foreign nations, such as France, saluted her. Most other communities had something simple on their floats such as high school cheerleaders sitting on the lap of old King Coal. Coalwood, everybody was confident, would win the prize yet again.

This year, the guest of honor at the parade was going to be none other than Harry S Truman, the former president of the entire United States of America. President Truman and Coalwood knew each other well because when he had been the president, Mr. Truman had seen fit to send the United States Navy in to occupy us, just as if we were a foreign country. It had happened back in 1949 when Mr. Carter had closed the mine to keep the union out, declaring he had no intention of sharing his company with the likes of John L. Lewis and the United Mine Workers of America. When this subject came up at the kitchen table, Dad said Mr. Carter and "ol' John L." actually respected each other but they had a duty to themselves and their own principles. Mom said if they had any principles, they wouldn't have caused so much trouble just to make themselves appear like big shots.

President Truman came in on the side of the UMWA. The next thing Mr. Carter knew, there was a convoy of gray military trucks rolling into his town and saluting sailors pouring into the Club House. The first thing the sailors did was order the Club House cook to boil their navy beans and bake their bread. Then, they started marching up and down the road, telling the miners to get back to work. The navy commander in charge told Mr. Carter it was time to sign a union contract. While the old man dithered, the commander settled into the biggest room in the Club House and hosted lavish sit-down dinners there, inviting all the bigwigs in the county to join him. He acted pretty much like the king of Coalwood, the way I heard it. The engraved silver cutlery, plates, and bowls used at those dinners were the stuff of Coalwood legend. I knew it was true because, over the years, I saw a lot of it in Coalwood homes. Most of them had pretty daughters in 1949.

Although it took a couple of months before Mr. Carter gave in, he finally signed, "at the muzzle of a gun," as he put it. More than a few swabbies liked our mountains and beautiful women so much they quit the sea and came back to Coalwood to be coal miners. Every once in a while, I'd note an anchor tattoo on a man's arm and suspect he'd once come as an occupier and got occupied instead. Through its grand float, Coalwood was going to show President Truman that, despite him and his navy, it was still a going proposition.

While Ginger watched quietly, Sherman and I got back to our mixing. After a while, he appraised the zincoshine in the bowl. "It looks too dark," he said.

Ginger came over and sniffed it. "It stinks," she said, wrinkling up her pert nose.

I ignored her. "It's the same mix we've been using for the last two rockets," I told Sherman.

He frowned over the bowl. "It still looks too dark. Wish we could test it."

"Your wish is my command," I said, showing off in front of

Ginger. I measured out a tablespoon of the zincoshine mix and scraped it off into a cup, then led the way over to the furnace. Dandy, our cocker spaniel, looked up from the rug Mom had laid down for him. Poteet, our other dog, was outside. It was about the time when the day shift and evening shift at the mine traded places, and Poteet saw it as her duty to bark at them as they passed by our fence. Dandy took one look at me and the zincoshine-filled cup I carried and rushed out the door and up the steps, his tail between his legs.

"Why is Dandy running?" Ginger asked.

I shrugged. "Maybe he remembers that time we blew up the hot water heater."

Sherman looked up. "Your mom said . . ."

I had the confidence that only true ignorance can provide. "Aw, they won't hear this little bit go off," I said.

"Is this safe?" Ginger asked in a small voice.

"Of course it's safe," I said, in patronizing tones, and opened up the grate. "I know exactly what I'm doing."

And I did, too. I mean, was it my fault that that blamed old furnace wasn't constructed for rapidly expanding gases? Or that the big vents that carried warm air into the house acted just like the pipes of a giant musical organ? What monstrously poor engineer had designed such a beast and installed it in our basement, anyway? Those were the questions that rapidly suffused my mind when, under the influence of zincoshine, the furnace happily produced a resounding belch that the devil himself would have been proud to make. The old vent pipes perversely turned the awful grunt into a long, thunderous rumble and then, in a further indication of the furnace's peculiarly awful design, sent out an announcement of smells through the house all too similar to purely rotten eggs.

There was a hushed silence for a moment, and then I heard my mom call out my name. *"Sonny!"* It was amazing how loud and fast she could say it sometimes.

Good scientist that I had become, I made a reasoned observation of the event. "I'm dead," I said, and then cringed at the

coming wrath sure to be heading my way. I could hear windows
being opened upstairs.

Ginger started giggling. The upstairs kitchen door opened and
I heard Mom's heels clicking down the steps, the pause at the
bottom for the step over Lucifer (who hadn't moved a muscle),
and then her pretty face appeared, transformed into a wad of
barely controlled temper. She put her hands on her hips. "I think
I'm going to kill you two," she said, "to save God and the authorities the trouble later on." She appraised Ginger. "Are you all right,
dear?"

"Yes, ma'am. I'm having lots of fun!" Her curls bounced as she
nodded her head up and down.

I gave Mom my very best innocent smile and started to tell her
how much fun I was having, too, but she held up her hand. "I
don't want to hear a word out of you, not one. Ginger, why don't
you come up and join the meeting, honey? As for you two, get out
of my basement!"

"Mom . . ."

"Out, out, *out*!"

Sherman went on home while I skulked into the backyard to
play with the dogs. Dandy and Poteet could be endlessly enter-
tained by just throwing a stick and I guess, to be truthful, so could
I. I further amused myself by thinking about my zincoshine.
Sherman had thought my mix was off. I guessed I'd showed him!
That was one hot propellant. If we could just keep it from eating
our nozzles.

I was still pondering zincoshine and throwing sticks for the
dogs when the screen door on the back porch opened and Ginger
came outside, wearing a Big Creek jacket over her blouse. It was a
typical Coalwood fall day, chilly but not too cold. The trees on the
mountains were aflame. "Need some company?" she asked.

"Can you throw a stick?"

"With the best of them." She picked a twig up from under the
apple tree and threw it for Dandy. Dandy lumbered after it. He
liked to dawdle over the stick, sniff it, carry it around the yard a

few times before he brought it to you, his stubby tail wagging. Poteet was faster. She'd get that stick back to you before it had hardly hit the ground if it hit it at all. Poteet had a special knack of catching a stick in the air. She had been known to catch bats on the wing the same way.

"I'd like to come down and watch you launch your rockets sometime," Ginger said, her eyes on Dandy as he went through his meandering, her stick turning soggy in his mouth.

I took Poteet's stick from her offered muzzle and threw it as hard as I could. She went flying. "We usually launch on Saturdays if we have a rocket ready to go," I said, shrugging. "Around ten o'clock. Watch for our notices. Sherman usually posts them at the Big Store and the post office."

"I will," she said. She walked over beside me. "Sonny, will you tell me something?"

"Sure," I said, throwing the stick again. Poteet had brought it back that quick.

"Do you like me?"

It was a startling question. "What do you mean?"

She shrugged. "I think some other kids don't," she said very seriously. "I think a lot of them think that maybe I'm too big for my britches sometimes because I want to grow up and be a professional singer."

"What kind of professional singer?" I asked.

She looked up toward the tipple where a line of miners were coming down the path, heading home. I could just barely hear the dull clunk of their empty lunch buckets. "I don't know," she said, sighing. "Maybe opera, maybe musical theater. Whatever I do, I know I can hardly wait until I start. When I talk about it, a lot of kids kind of roll their eyes."

I remembered when we'd once read comic books together in her parlor. I said, "Ginger, I think you're one of the nicest, prettiest girls in all of Coalwood." I'd laid it on a bit thick, but I thought she needed it.

Ginger still looked uncertain. "I hope you get what you're after,

Sonny," she said. "The first rocket scientist from Coalwood, West Virginia!"

Ginger had a way about her that made me feel comfortable. "And I'll be proud to tell people I grew up with Ginger Dantzler, the famous singer."

Dandy dropped his stick on the ground in front of her black patent-leather shoes. She had tiny feet. I thought they were cute. As a matter of fact, now that I was paying attention, I thought Ginger Dantzler was pretty much cute all over. Ginger picked the stick up and gave it a toss. Dandy waddled after it, his tail wagging furiously. She gave me a shy smile. "I like you, Sonny. You've always been the nicest boy."

I still didn't have a date for the high school Christmas Formal. A thought burst in my brain like a wad of zincoshine. Why not go with Ginger? She was cute, she was nice, and she was easy to talk to. And we were both planning on heading out of Coalwood aboard a dream.

"Ginger . . ." I began, but before I got my question out, I was interrupted by the scuffling and natter of women on the back porch. The Women's Club meeting was over.

"Zanice Virginia?" her mother called.

Ginger gave me an apologetic look. "Guess I better go."

"Are you really coming down to Cape Coalwood?" I asked.

She tilted her head and gave me a sweet smile that made me feel warm down to my toes. "I'll be there, boy. Don't you think I won't!"

6

FLOAT NIGHT

ALTHOUGH THE VETERANS Day float was designed and built by the Coalwood Women's Club, it was a fully sponsored coal-company enterprise from start to finish. Company materials, workers, and facilities were available to build as grand a float as the ladies wanted. Coalwood's float had always won the award for best float in the parade, and nobody wanted that record broken. It was a matter of town, company, and union pride. As Veterans Day of 1959 approached, the machine shop, where the float was being built, reverberated with the rattling sound of hammers, the buzz of saws, and the spewing of welders. The other float builders in the county didn't stand a chance against a united Coalwood.

The night before the parade was called Float Night. This was when the finishing touches were put on the float and all the ladies in the club, their husbands, and their children were expected to participate. Mindful of the marvelous table of desserts the ladies always set out, I fully intended to be there. I figured to do a few odds and ends, stuff my face with cookies, pie, and cake, and get out early. Mom was aware of my plan, having developed a keen intuition regarding general boy-type behavior over the years. "I'll be keeping my eye on the food table," she told me. "I don't want to see your back every time I look over there. You understand me, Sonny boy?"

"Oh, yes, ma'am," I said, giving her the little submissive smile I reserved for such occasions. Her threat didn't worry me. It would be a long night, and the advantage is always to the persistent over the weary.

Roy Lee and O'Dell arrived at the machine shop on Float Night shortly after dark. I'd been there for about an hour and had already made a sally or two on the plates of cookies. As I figured, Mom was distracted with her supervising and such and had left the goodies to fend for themselves. O'Dell got busy right away helping himself to a slice of apple pie. Interested in another kind of sweetness, Roy Lee went off to scout out the girl situation. I loitered in the background, my pockets full of cookies, happy just to watch the activity. There was a swarm of it, the ladies, their husbands, their kids, and a crew of company carpenters and machinists all bent to their tasks around and on top of the float. Other Coalwoodians were carrying in supplies—paper rolls, paint, nails, and glue, all provided out of the company store for free.

The float was being constructed on a stake and platform trailer ordinarily used by the company to haul heavy machinery. The plan was for a pedestal to be built on the platform where a girl dressed like the Statue of Liberty would stand. Around her would be soldiers (Coalwood boy versions, that is), paying proper homage to our Miss Liberty by saluting her. An American soldier carrying a rifle was to be separate from the group, guarding a copy of the Constitution and the Holy Bible. Everything would be decked out with lots of colorful "flowers" made from toilet paper and crepe paper stuffed into chicken wire. It was a grand design, and everybody was confident of its prospects.

Mom, Mrs. Servant, Mrs. Dent Todd, Mrs. Ada Todd, Mrs. Sharitz, Mrs. Lindley, Mrs. McGlothlin, and Mrs. Mahoney, all supervisor's wives, were in charge of the work. They had a command table over by the machine-shop door where they kept Mom's drawings and the master plan. I knew it was only a matter of time before I was spotted and given a job. Another cookie raid and I figured I'd be ready to do a little before sneaking out. I had a good excuse, since I had to get up early. The Big Creek band was going to march in the parade, and the school bus was scheduled to pick up Coalwood band members at 5:00 A.M.

I was just heading back to the dessert table, taking the long way around so as not to be so obvious, when Sherman arrived. The sight of him stopped me in my tracks. All I could do was gawk. Roy Lee, returning from his girl tour, took one look and burst out laughing. Then, while he covered his mouth, Roy Lee began making little chirping sounds, sort of like a chipmunk on a rock. Finally, he turned away, his shoulders shaking. I tried not to but I started to giggle, too. "Go ahead, you creeps," Sherman grumbled. "Laugh all you want."

We couldn't help it. We had never seen the like. Sherman had on a big floppy beret and a bright blue tunic festooned with golden braid from top to bottom. His pants were bright blue, too, and had a golden stripe down both legs. It was supposed to be a French soldier's uniform, but I thought if the French wore clothes like that into battle, it was no wonder the Germans had beat them up in World War II. The beret was especially peculiar. I couldn't imagine that a real soldier would go around wearing such a sister piece of headgear. As we snorted and guffawed, Sherman took off his beret but otherwise regarded us stoically. "So I look like a dope," he said. "My mother was good enough to make me this uniform, and I guess I'll wear it."

The other boys who were playing foreign soldiers arrived after Sherman. Roy Lee was so staggered by the sight of them he had to lean against a lathe to catch his breath. Jackie Likens, Grant Smith, Jimmy Siers, Phil Sharitz, and Billy Lindley were all wearing uniforms of our European allies (such as Belgium) cluttered with shiny buttons, braid, and stripes. Not only that, they were also wearing berets like Sherman's, which could not be mistaken for anything but ladies' hats. Vincent Curto was the only lucky one. He was playing the American soldier and was proudly wearing his father's uniform from World War II. I later learned that Coalwood moms, frustrated by not being able to find pictures of foreign soldiers, had pretty well made up the uniforms by themselves. It kind of summed up the way they thought about our country's place in the world. American soldiers wore uniforms for fighting, and when war came, we would be the ones to take the brunt of battle. Soldiers from the other countries, the ones our boys were being drafted right out of high school to defend, wore uniforms to look good, not for bloody combat.

"Where's the French soldier?" Mrs. Mahoney called from the float platform. She held a sheet of paper, a list of things to do, no doubt. She spied Sherman. "Put on your beret, dear, and come on and line up. We're going to teach you how to salute."

"Put on your beret, dear," Roy Lee said, holding his stomach. "Put on your beret. Oh, my!" He was having trouble catching his breath.

Mrs. Mahoney frowned at Roy Lee and then at me. "Roy Lee, Sonny, come here!" she commanded. We'd been caught. We trudged to the float, our heads down. Out of the corner of my eye, I looked for O'Dell. As far as I could tell, he'd managed to raid the dessert table and make a clean getaway. He was slick, that boy.

Mrs. Mahoney descended from the platform and gave Roy Lee and me our orders. We were to stuff toilet paper and crepe paper in the chicken wire along the side of the float until she told us to stop. I figured that would be about the time the sun burned out. "Don't let any bare spots show," she said. "It's supposed to look like it's covered with flowers. Now, get to work!"

Mrs. Mahoney had been our eighth-grade arithmetic teacher, and her voice was law to us. We got busy. Then it occurred to me that Billy wasn't there, and then I remembered I hadn't told him he was invited. His mother wasn't a member of the Women's Club, but I'd asked Mom about the Rocket Boys coming to Float Night and she had said any and all were welcome. I had meant to tell Billy but it had slipped my mind. I felt bad about it for a few seconds and then shrugged it off. I figured Billy probably wouldn't have come, anyway. His family had moved to Six Hollow a few months ago, a couple of miles from Coalwood Main. Now that I thought about it, about the only time I saw Billy lately was on the school bus, in class, and at the Cape. Even there, he seemed distant. What was going on with Billy? I made a decision to find out and then promptly forgot it.

After an hour or so of boring paper stuffing, Roy Lee crept off to the table for another handful of cookies. I told him to bring me some and then went around to the back of the float to continue stuffing. When I turned the corner, I was surprised to find none other than Cuke Snoddy's woman, Dreama Jenkins. I was surprised because I knew for certain she was not a member of the Coalwood Women's Club. Membership was by invitation only, and it was never extended to any woman whose husband wasn't either management or a union boss. Besides that, she wasn't even married as far as I knew. Since she didn't have a Coalwood husband or father, that meant, no matter how long she lived here, she wasn't even a Coalwood citizen by our traditional definition.

If Dreama was aware that there was anything wrong about her attendance at Float Night, she didn't show it. She had come to work, that was clear. She was really stuffing that paper in the chicken wire. She was wearing an old pair of bib overalls about two sizes too big for her and underneath it a flowery blouse with puffed arms. I also noticed she had a ton of rouge on her right cheek. It looked as if maybe there was a bruise underneath it, but I couldn't tell for sure. When she saw it was me, she flashed her teeth in a big grin. She really did have nice teeth. "Hidy, Sonny!" she said, and the way she said it was most proud. "This is gonna look so purdy," she continued, eagerly going back to pushing the paper into the chicken wire and fluffing it up. The way she'd said "purdy" was like a note sliding up a scale.

I mumbled some halfhearted reply. The truth was I felt embarrassed to be beside her. She just wasn't where she was supposed to be, sort of like a snow goose on a slack dump. All I could figure was that she had sneaked in when Mom and the other ladies weren't looking. When they saw her, I wasn't sure what they'd do.

Ginger sidled up to me just then, poking me with her elbow and bumping me with her hip. "Hey, Rocket Boy," she said cheerfully. Then she noticed Dreama. "Sonny, have you no manners? No, of course you don't." She stuck out her hand. "I don't think we've met. I'm Ginger Dantzler."

The woman shyly took Ginger's hand. "I'm Dreama," she said in a small voice. "Dreama Jenkins."

"Dreama, I love what you're doing," Ginger said, appraising her work.

"They're flowers," she said, ducking her head and blushing even through her heavy makeup.

"Well, your flowers are very artistic and I don't think there's anybody here doing a better job than you." Ginger then took a look at my work. "Hmm. I can't say the same for you, Sonny." She fluffed up my paper stuffings and shook her head and "tsked" a couple of times at me. "It isn't boys' work, I suppose," she said, and then she was off, saying she had to work with "Miss Liberty," meaning, I supposed, the little ninth-grade girl all the beret-boys were supposed to salute during the parade.

Dreama looked after her. "That's the purdiest girl I've ever seen in my entire life," she said, clearly awed, "and she's so nice. I bet she's going to be a movie star or something someday."

I didn't see any movie stars coming out of Coalwood, even Ginger, but I kept it to myself. When I looked around, I saw a lot of ladies glancing our way with dirty looks, and more than a few seemed to be directed at me. Then I thought maybe they were blaming me for bringing Dreama in! Short of raising my hand and denying everything before being accused of it, I was stuck. It was like being a skunk under the house. It didn't matter how innocent and pure smelling that skunk was, unhappiness was headed its way. I was relieved when Mr. Bolt, the machine-shop foreman, called me over to talk to him. Mr. Skunk made his escape.

I had a code name for Mr. Bolt. If Dad was in earshot when I talked to Mr. Bolt on the black phone, I pretended to be talking to one Leon Ferro, a name I had made up because I didn't want Dad to suspect how much I was using his machine shop. I don't think I fooled Dad very much but I kept doing it. It was sort of like being a spy. "The boys have a new idea for your rockets," Mr. Bolt/Ferro said, speaking of his machinists. He leaned in close after a furtive look around. "*Wings!*" he said.

I squinted at him. "Why wings?"

Mr. Bolt was at a band saw, cutting the pedestal that was going to carry Miss Liberty on the float. "So they'll go farther," he said. "See, they'd glide." Mr. Bolt made a swooping movement with his hand.

I considered his proposal for approximately one second. It might have been less. "Horizontal distance isn't what we're after, Mr. Bolt," I told him. "We want our rockets to go as high as they can, not long. If they went long, we'd lose them."

Mr. Bolt took the pedestal loose from the saw clamps. He looked crestfallen. "I'll tell the guys," he said sadly. "It'll knock them for a loop."

Roy Lee came and got me. "Take a look," he said. He pointed to Mrs. Cleo Mallett. She was the wife of Leo Mallett, the second-in-command at the union local, just one notch below Mr. Dubonnet. I thought Mr. Mallett was a nice man, although a bit meek. His wife, on the other hand, was big and brassy and fancied herself the social conscience of the community, sort of a Coalwood version of Eleanor Roosevelt. To her, I guess that meant she had the right to stick her nose into everybody's business. According to what I'd heard, she held sway among a tiny group of union wives who believed they had married beneath themselves. It was that group of women who were watching Dreama and murmuring low to one another. "They're building up to something," Roy Lee said gleefully. Roy Lee never minded a spot of trouble.

Mrs. Mallett looked sort of grandmotherly, dressed as she was in a shapeless dress covered with bright flowers, but I wasn't fooled. She had the perpetual look on her face of somebody that had eaten something sour. She walked up to Dreama and tapped her hard on the shoulder. We were close enough to hear what she said when Dreama whirled around. "You know you're supposed to have an invitation to come here, don't you?"

Dreama tucked her chin and her big green eyes went wide.

"No, ma'am, I didn't. I thought ever'body who lived in Coalwood could come."

"Well, ever'body can't," Mrs. Mallett said acidly. "You'll have to leave."

Roy Lee nudged me. "Here comes your mom."

Sure enough, Mom had left her command table to come up beside Mrs. Mallett. "It's okay, Cleo," Mom said. "The girl didn't know."

Mrs. Mallett, jerking her head back, acted startled by Mom's comment. "Float Night is by invitation only, Elsie," she replied, crossing her rolling-pin arms. "That's the Women's Club rules to keep out . . . people who don't know what they're doing."

Mom inspected Dreama's work. "Well, I'd say she knows exactly what she's doing." To Dreama, she said, "You can stay, honey." To Mrs. Mallett, she said, "It's my decision, Cleo."

Mrs. Mallett's jowls quivered. It looked like she wanted to reply, but something, maybe the tone of Mom's voice, kept her from it. She turned on her heel and went back to her circle. The glares of those women toward Dreama were shifted to Mom. They were like thrown knives. Dreama said, "Thank you, ma'am." If Mom said anything in reply to her, I didn't hear it. She went back to her table piled high with drawings and plans.

Later that night, I saw Dreama walk over to the food table and get herself a cup of punch. At her approach, a cluster of women stalked off and she was left alone, sipping from the cup and turning around, looking out of the tops of her eyes. I thought she looked small and scared and I found myself feeling sorry for her even though she was someplace she wasn't supposed to be. Then I saw my mother leave her table and stride across the machine-shop floor and go directly to the punch bowl and pour herself a drink. Then she nodded to Dreama. It occurred to me just then that it was a nod from one Gary girl to another.

7

VETERANS DAY

SOMETIME BEFORE THE sun came up on Veterans Day morning, I heard the sound of a truck rumbling past my window and looked at the alarm clock on the table by my bed. It was 4:30 A.M. Coalwood's proud float was rolling past. Mom in her Buick and a bunch of other ladies in their cars followed closely behind, creeping over a frost-slickened road. The float was being pulled by a rusty, dented truck. Dad had advised Mom just the day before that he was going to need all Olga's trucks to "haul mine machinery." The old truck pulling the float had been borrowed by Dad from a little independent mine up Warriormine Hollow that only worked weekends. There were more and more such small, nonunion mines being operated around the county, most of them run by union men who worked for big mines during the week. These little mines skirted safety regulations and union dictates alike, but they made a profit, and some people said that when the big operations finally shut down, the independents would be the only mines still going. Dad said they had their place in the scheme of things but he worried about their safety. "A man who makes an hourly wage will gripe about safety and his working conditions all day long," I heard him say once to Uncle Clarence, his brother. "But you tell him he can make a profit for himself on a ton of coal and he'll forget about everything but the money. He'll hold up the roof with one hand and dig with the other."

Uncle Clarence, who worked for Dad as an assistant superintendent at the Caretta mine, said, "About half my men work those mines every weekend. Sometimes on Monday, they're so worn out they all but fall asleep on the job."

The two Hickam brothers then shook their heads at the strange antics and peculiar attitudes of the men they had been raised with and led for years. Somewhere along the line, they had taken a different turn from their union brethren. When I asked Mom about the reasons for it, she said, "Poppy made them that way. Poppy, and all his books."

It was at the supper table that Dad told Mom about the truck. He also said he wasn't going to the parade. "Things to do," he explained.

"You can't mean it," Mom replied, obviously shocked. "I've worked so hard—we've all worked so hard on this float. You have to be there, Homer. You're the acting general superintendent. It's expected!"

"I just can't," he said. "And it's because I am the acting general superintendent that I can't."

"Homer . . ."

"Elsie . . ."

There was never a satisfactory resolution to any discussion between my parents when they began to call themselves by their first names, and this one was no exception.

I didn't know what it was, but there was something in the works at the mine that had sent Dad into a feverish round of activity. Although he always worked long hours, lately he was at the mine until far into the night. Sometimes I would wake, hearing him as he crept up the stairs to go to bed. He was there for only a few hours. I had to get up before sunrise to catch the school bus but he was always up and gone by then.

At 5:00 A.M., the Big Creek school bus picked me and the other Coalwood band members up at the filling station across from my house. We slept through the trip over Welch Mountain, but I was awakened near the top by a rumble of trucks. I wiped the moisture off the window and saw truck after truck going by, all with Olga Coal Company markings on them. In the back of each of them were canvas-shrouded boxes and unidentifiable equipment. I presumed it was Dad's new mining equipment, whatever it was. I went back to sleep and didn't wake up until we were winding through the low brick buildings that lined the streets of our county seat.

Our first stop was the Welch Norfolk and Western railroad station. The Big Creek band had been given the honor to welcome Mr. Truman to McDowell County. Mr. Polascik, our band director, was in a state of near nervous exhaustion even though we were all formed up, ready to blare out "The Stars and Stripes Forever" the moment the former president's train arrived. A man given to worry, Mr. Polascik gave his worst tendency full rein as he raced in between the rows and columns of the nearly one-hundred-strong band. I thought we were looking pretty sharp in our green-and-white uniforms and our big tall shakos. Mr. Polascik was apparently not of the same opinion. His round face was nearly purple with concern, Or perhaps his necktie—a bright green—was pulled too tight. "Not too loud, Sonny, okay?" he reminded me. "Don't drown out the woodwinds."

"Yes, sir," I replied, perhaps a little too archly for his ears because he gave me a particularly beseeching look. I didn't know why he was so worried. I had trained my drummers well. If I put my mind to it, I could keep them so quiet even the flutes could be heard. That was a particularly good idea, since Ginger was one of the flute players. I hadn't asked her to the Christmas Formal yet but I still planned to do it first chance I got. I had decided it wasn't right to just blurt out an invitation to a girl like Ginger. It required careful preparation and thought. One of the lessons I'd learned with my rockets was that planning was the parent of success. I figured that surely applied to girls just as well.

At 7:00 A.M., precisely on schedule, the Powhatan Arrow, loudly chuffing steam, rounded a curve and pulled into the station. It was a sleek black bullet of a locomotive. Behind it came a proud chain of red Pullman passenger cars. The last car was not the standard little caboose that trailed on the end of the coal trains but a big Pullman densely draped in red, white, and blue bunting. It looked like something I'd only seen in the movies. On the back was a tiny platform and a big circular sign of some sort that somebody said was the presidential seal. Harry Truman wasn't president anymore, so I guessed it was an honorary thing and somehow that didn't seem right to me. If my dad had stopped being the superintendent at the mine, he couldn't go around wearing his white helmet anymore, could he?

The Powhatan Arrow rested for a bit while venting some more steam, and then the door to the fancy car opened in the back and a couple of men in brown suits with wide lapels walked out on the platform. An attractive, smartly dressed young woman in a white suit and high heels followed, and then out came none other than Harry S Truman himself, looking a bit grim. He was surely a small man, I thought. After he looked us over, he suddenly erupted in a huge grin, as if somebody had pushed a button in his back. He took off his fedora and waved it in the air. Mr. Polascik, about to burst a gasket, loped all around us, his hands shaking in the air to gain our attention. We tore our eyes away from Mr. Truman, and at Mr. Polascik's nearly hysterical count "One-Two-Three-Four!" we launched into our march. I was so excited I began to batter my snare drum as hard as I could, and so did the other drummers. Everybody in the band played as loudly as ever we could. Mr. Polascik kept jumping up and down and waving and trying to get us to hit some low points as well as highs, but nobody paid him much mind.

When we'd finished with our ear-shattering rendition of "The Stars and Stripes Forever," surely the loudest version President Truman had ever heard, some men climbed up on the car platform with him. I recognized one of them—Chester Matney, a scrap-iron dealer from Welch and a friend of my parents. He'd even attended a couple of our launches at Cape Coalwood.

Mr. Truman, Mr. Matney, the other men, and the one woman came off the train and climbed in automobiles and took off while

we launched into a sprightly "Missouri Waltz." Mr. Polascik gradually came back into my focus. His tie was undone, his coat in dis-
array, his hair atangle. Then I saw Dreama Jenkins. Her pretty red
hair made her hard to miss. She was waving at the band, so excited
it looked like she was going to fly right up into the sky. I heard her
cry out "Go Owls!" just as if she'd graduated from our high
school. I wondered what her fellow Gary High School Coaldiggers
would think of that. There was no sign of Cuke.

As the "Missouri Waltz" wound down, I noticed other high
school bands had arrived. The Excelsior band formed up beside
us. Excelsior was the high school for colored students in Big Creek
district. It was located about a mile away from Big Creek High. I
was proud of the Excelsior band, although I felt a little jealousy
when their drummers started up. How they managed such complex syncopation was beyond me. It was like their wrists were
double-jointed or something.

Bobby Gray, our drum major, held up his baton to keep us in
place until all the other bands marched past. We were pulling up
the rear in the parade this year because we had been selected to go
into the Pocahontas theater to play the National Anthem before
Mr. Truman spoke. I wasn't certain how we'd managed to get that
honor. Maybe it was just our turn.

The Welch High School band, dressed in smart maroon-and-
white uniforms, led the parade. We watched them with not a little
envy. It was the judgment of Big Creek students that Welch students were all rich, their parents all lawyers and doctors and politicians and such. Margie Jones was our head majorette, and she had
all of her girls especially charged up to match the stellar Welch
girls. When we got moving, I'd never seen Margie and the other
majorettes throw their batons so high.

As we marched down the street, it seemed the crowd grew in
size and enthusiasm. There was wild cheering and applause from
all the Big Creek fans as we tramped by. We paraded down Elkhorn Street, then turned into the steep maze of narrow streets that
made up downtown Welch. We passed Belcher and Mooney, the
men's shop that my brother Jim had almost single-handedly kept

in business before he'd gone off to college; Davis Jewelry, where my mom liked to look but never bought; the Chris-Ann store with women's fashions all the way from the capital city of Charleston; and the Flat Iron Drug Store, where you could get a fountain Coke and a banana split just like, I was told, in New York City.

American flags flapped from nearly every window, and men took off their hats and women put their hands on their breasts as our color guard marched by. I was swept up by the whole red, white, and blue spectacle and felt so patriotic that if the entire Russian Army had landed at that moment, they would have had their hands full just with me. Mr. Turner, our high school principal, had once given us a speech when he said he felt sorry for the Russians because they were going to have to compete with the boys and girls coming out of Big Creek and McDowell County. This was at a time when a lot people in America were saying we ought to just give up, that communism was an unstoppable force. Mr. Turner said the only unstoppable force was us, and we believed him.

At the corner of Wyoming and McDowell Streets, there was a line of American Legion men in their navy-blue caps. We stiffened our spines and cut loose with a rendition of "E Pluribus Unum." The batons of our majorettes twinkled high into the air, and then we turned a corner and approached the stand that had been built to hold Mr. Truman, local dignitaries, and the float judges.

Then we stopped. Drum Major Bobby turned around and held his long green baton with a big white ball on the end over his head. That meant we were supposed to march in place. Something was happening up ahead I couldn't see. We marched and marched with just the drums playing, going nowhere. I saw Mr. Polascik run past and then come walking back. When I looked at him for a sign as to what was going on, he just grimly shook his head.

We marched in place for so long that Patty Cordisco, a flutist in the line behind me, said her feet hurt and she was just going to stop pretty soon. I kept my eye on my drummers. I wasn't going to let any of them stop, nosiree. Finally, Bobby blew his whistle and rared back, jabbing his baton in the air for us to follow him.

"Well, thank the good Lord," I heard Patty say as we shuffled forward. Then we opened up with Big Creek's fight song. *On, on, green and white! We are ripe for the fight tonight! Hold that ball and hit that line . . .*

As we surged ahead, I saw what had stopped us, and the sight of it nearly took my breath away. It was the Coalwood float. Broken down, it had been pushed up on the sidewalk to get it out of our way. The old truck's hood was flung open, and the driver, his miner's helmet pitched to the ground, was furiously grabbing at wires in the engine. Sherman was standing disconsolately on the float squinting down at the truck, his beret tucked up under his arm. All the other boys were looking miserable, too, and had also hidden their berets. Devota Bradley, the pretty little junior high school girl who was playing the Statue of Liberty, was crying, big tears carrying streaks of mascara down her rosy cheeks. Her crown was dislodged, hanging by a lock of hair, and her cardboard torch holding crepe-paper flames drooped low in her hand.

As we passed, I got a glimpse of the Coalwood women standing in a knot in front of the sagging truck. My mother was pale, her lips pressed into a tense, flat line. She looked like she was in shock. Cleo Mallett stood apart, her fists digging into her wide hips. There was a look of total disdain on her face. Dreama Jenkins also watched from nearby, her big green eyes filled with tears, her hand covering her mouth. It was like looking at a scene in a movie when the film got hung up, just before it melted from the light. Then my mother's eyes locked on mine and I saw in them something I had never seen there before: despair.

I tore my eyes away, and my drumming sped up unilaterally. I needed to get away from what I had seen. It was just too awful. The other drummers, the entire band, strained to catch up with me. We were almost running before Mr. Polascik's screams at me to slow down finally penetrated my skull. By then, we were past Harry Truman and the judging stand. We stopped at the Pocahontas theater and to the *clickety-clack* of our sticks on the rim of our drums, my drummers and I cadenced the band inside. We marched up into the balcony and stood in the back. That's when it sank in. Coalwood, for the first time ever, was going to lose the Veterans Day float competition, and my mom, and probably my dad, too, was going to get the blame for it.

I kept thinking about what I'd seen in Mom's eyes as the speakers came up on the stage and made their various pronouncements. A Presbyterian preacher gave the invocation. After that, we played the National Anthem while the audience turned and faced the American Legion color guard and sang the words. The old theater's roof could have lifted up and turned around everybody sang so hard. Then we said the Pledge of Allegiance, and Sonny Pruitt, Big Creek's lead trumpet player, played Taps as sweetly as ever anybody had done it. Then the mayor of Welch spoke briefly, followed by a chorus from Welch High School singing a medley of songs including the West Virginia official song, "Those West Virginia Hills." Sam Solins, a Welch businessman and, according to my dad, a "bigwig Democrat," introduced the former president, and the great man himself stood up and walked to the microphone. He looked about a foot shorter than everybody else onstage, but he strutted to the mike like a banty rooster set loose in the hen house. He only spoke for a few minutes, his reedy voice not entirely pleasant to listen to. I tried to pay attention to what he had to say, but my mind kept wandering back to Mom and the dismal scene of the Coalwood float.

The bus took us back to Big Creek High. I made sure the drums were all put away and helped everybody else clean up their instruments. Then I hitched my way home. When I arrived, I noticed that the Buick hadn't been put in the garage. In fact, it seemed parked at an odd angle, as if Mom had started to put it in and lost interest.

I found her peeling potatoes over the kitchen sink. It looked like she was peeling them pretty hard, as much potato going into the sink as peel. I briefly thought of saying something to her about how pretty I thought the float had been, but then thought better of it. Mom was clearly not in a mood for any foolishness out of me. I went to my room and closed the door. Mom called me down for supper later but she didn't eat, retreating instead with Chipper to the Captain's porch, so called because Captain Laird had originally added it to the house to face the mine. Soon after we moved in, Mom had gotten Dad to send down the mine carpenters to enclose it and put in some Florida windows. The sun kept it warm, even in winter. She liked sitting out there but I don't know if she cared much for the view. When I walked past and glanced at her, she was just staring straight ahead. She was waiting for Dad, I figured. I was in my bed when, around midnight, I heard him come home. There wasn't any yelling, but whatever Mom had to say didn't take long. I heard her come upstairs and go into her room. Dad came afterward. His footsteps on the stairs were slow, as if he was climbing a steep mountain.

8

A ROCKET KIND OF DAY

MELANCHOLY SEEMED TO settle over Coalwood like a layer of brooding clouds. Even the air seemed to have weight. People walked around as if they wore lead boots. It wasn't fair! Coalwood had the best float! The Welch and Gary floats had tied for first prize but they didn't belong on the same street as the Coalwood float. The Welch float was a big fat guy dressed up like Henry the VIII with a sash that said—what else—*Old King Coal* with the Welch High School Maroon Wave cheerleaders sitting on his lap. The Gary float, sponsored by the UMWA, had miners lounging around under a banner that said THE SACRED RIGHT TO STRIKE. (When Dad saw a photograph of it in the *Welch Daily News,* he wondered aloud if they had the sacred right to starve, too.) But since the Coalwood float never crossed in front of President Truman and the judges, it was ruled that it was ineligible, no matter how superb the design or accomplished the craftsmanship or splendid the uniforms of the boys.

Mom took full responsibility for the failure but sent the message down the fence line that, to make up for it, she was going to make sure the Women's Club's 1959 Coalwood Christmas Pageant was the best one anyone ever saw. The fence roared back with anger and disdain. It was more than the truck breaking down. My mom had overreached herself, made the whole thing too complicated. If it hadn't been the truck, it would have been some-thing else. What did she think she was, an artist or something? And what was she talking about, this grand Christmas Pageant? Elsie Hickam needed to remember who she was—a girl from Gary (it was also noted sharply that she'd actually been born in the dreary, dilapidated coal camp of Wilco), not some hoity-toity gen-eral superintendent's wife out of Ohio.

Dad came in for his share of criticism as well. Wasn't Homer Hickam, after all, just a common miner raised up by Captain Laird? Why, the man wasn't even an engineer. Those Hickams needed to be pulled down a peg or two where they belonged!

I heard the fence-line buzz on the school bus from Roy Lee, who'd heard it from his mother. "Gossipy idiots," he concluded. "My mom told them to mind their own business." I shrugged. My family had been raked over the coals by the fence before. There was hardly a family in town that hadn't felt its bite, one time or another.

I went to Mom and reported what I'd heard. She was doing the laundry at the time. She poured in the detergent and closed the washing machine hatch. "It's Cleo Mallett who's spreading most of the poison," she said. "She's a ridiculous woman and everybody knows it. Don't concern yourself."

"What did Dad say about the truck breaking down?" I wondered.

She shrugged. "What could he say? He should have gotten us a better truck. That's it."

"But we lost!" I blurted.

She eyed me carefully. "No, Sonny, *we* didn't lose. I lost. It was my responsibility and I didn't come through. I'm sorry about it but I can't change it. Spilled milk. End of story." She started to fold the laundry. "But we're going to do better with the Christmas Pageant, aren't we?"

My reply just popped out of me. "I don't want to work on the Christmas Pageant, Mom."

"Now look, Sonny . . ."

"I just don't care anything about Christmas anymore." This

was like poking a hornet's nest with a stick. I knew what was going to happen, but I still couldn't keep myself from doing it.

"Hold out your hands," she said. I did as I was told, and she started stacking folded towels on them. "Now you listen to me, young man. Christmas is the best time of the year and you will help me on the pageant. Do you understand?"

I understood very well so I properly "yes ma'amed" her but, before I could stop myself, I thought: *I hope the blamed thing gets canceled*. It was a mean, nasty thing to hope for but that was the way I felt. I even knew why. Mom had forced me to be with Dad and Poppy last Christmas, and I was still mad about it. I wanted my revenge, and if it took cutting off my own nose, and my mother's too, to spite my face, then I guess I was just the boy for it. Then I thought: Is this what makes me sad sometimes—this memory of Poppy and Dad on Christmas Eve? I gave it some logical thought, per Quentin's recommendation, but when I was finished, I still wasn't sure. Then I thought of the Reverend Little Richard's recommendation and took a sidelong glance at heaven, although I was careful not to utter a prayer. You don't have to stir a pot if you don't put anything in it. That was my thinking.

THE night after Veterans Day, I went down to the machine shop to help disassemble the float. There weren't nearly as many people there as on Float Night. The women were divided into two groups. Mom and her group were hard at work pulling tissue paper and chicken wire off the float. Cleo Mallett held sway over the other group. They weren't working much more than their mouths as far as I could tell. I wondered if they were talking about Mom. Roy Lee hung around the edge of their knot and then came over to where Sherman and I were to report what he'd heard. "It's about Cuke's woman," he said. "Mrs. Mallett wants to run her out of town."

"Why?" Sherman asked.

"Because they're afraid she's after their husbands."

I scratched my head. "Why would they think she's after their husbands?"

Both Sherman and Roy Lee gave me disbelieving looks. "Innocent as a lamb," Roy Lee said, shaking his head.

"As a newborn kitten," Sherman added.

"As a fresh egg."

"As a—"

"All right," I broke in. "I get the picture."

When I took a break from paper pulling, Mr. Bolt came up to me with what appeared to be an aluminum cylinder. It had a little hinged hatch on its side. "What do you think?" he asked. "My guys built it for you to put on top of one of your rockets. It could carry cargo, see, like maybe a mouse or something."

I took the cylinder and pretended to be considering it. The truth was we boys were into pure altitude, and extra weight, even a mouse, would cut into that. "It's nice," I said diplomatically. "I especially like the hatch."

"I'll tell the guys. It'll make their day," Mr. Bolt said, obviously relieved that I hadn't rejected their work out of hand. "You want they should catch you a little mouse?"

I told Mr. Bolt I could probably catch my own mouse, and then noticed Ginger working atop the float. She was pulling up the tape that had marked the spots where the soldiers stood. After admiring her for a minute, I made a decision. I was going to ask her to the Christmas Formal right then and there. Roy Lee grabbed my arm. "What are you doing?" he asked. There was concern in his voice.

I shrugged. "Nothing."

"You were looking at Ginger Dantzler, weren't you?" he said. It sounded like an accusation.

"Well . . ."

Roy Lee got between me and the float. "Sonny, don't even think about asking her out."

"How did you know I was thinking that?"

Roy Lee gave me a sad smile. "Because I pay attention, that's why. That and because I'm the Big Creek lovemaster."

"The what?"

"The Big Creek love—never mind, I'll explain later." He shifted his stance, looking uncomfortable. "Look, I've got just the girl for you. I've been working on her for the last couple of weeks and I think I've got her softened up. It wasn't easy, you being a little four-eyed creep, but I think I've done it."

"Name the girl," I said suspiciously.

Roy Lee grinned. "Melba June Monroe!"

Melba June Monroe was an absolutely drop-dead gorgeous girl from Bartley. She was a junior at Big Creek, and I had to admit I'd had my eye on her for some time. What boy at Big Creek hadn't? "I still don't understand why I can't take Ginger out," I said.

Roy Lee frowned. "You got to trust me, that's all."

I laughed. "Get out of my way," I said. "I'm going to ask Ginger out right now. As a matter of fact, I'm going to invite her to the Christmas Formal. I don't think she thinks I'm a four-eyed creep."

"Don't," Roy Lee said, barring my way. "You'll be sorry if you do."

I looked over his shoulder and saw that Ginger had come down off the float and was talking to my mother. I couldn't ask Ginger anywhere with my mother standing there.

"Attaboy," Roy Lee said as I stepped back. "I'll have you lined up with Melba June before you know it."

"I don't want to be lined up with Melba June," I said. I felt a sense of loyalty toward Ginger even though she had no idea of my intentions.

Roy Lee rolled his eyes and smacked his lips. "Oh, yes, you do, boy. Yes, you do!"

Mom came over to us a little later, bringing us some punch. "Hi, boys," she said wearily. I think she wanted to get away from the other women and we were the only alternative.

"Mrs. Hickam, I think you are looking especially lovely tonight," Roy Lee said.

Mom blushed. "Why, thank you, Roy Lee. That's a very nice thing to say."

"The truth never hurt the teller of it, ma'am," he replied, so smoothly it was like grease.

After Mom went off, looking pleased for a change, I stared at Roy Lee. "What in blue blazes has gotten into you?"

"You don't think your mother's a beautiful woman?"

"I guess she is. So's your mom. So what?"

Roy Lee pondered me. "Women like compliments, Sonny. Even mothers. I wanted to show you that."

"Okay, you showed me. So?"

He sighed. "I guess I got to say it to you."

"What?" I demanded.

"Sonny, I can't let you go down to Cape Canaveral the way you are."

"What does that mean?"

He started to run his hand through his hair, but I guess he remembered he'd spent too much time lacquering it down to spoil it, so he just patted at the edges. "Listen, you got to know that's a wild bunch of women down there in Florida. All those men and their big rockets sticking up in the air got to keep them all excited. If you go down there as innocent as you are, those women are going to eat you alive. I got to get you trained."

I was nearly speechless but I recovered quickly. "I don't need to be trained," I said. "I'll just follow your lead."

Roy Lee frowned. "I'm not going to Cape Canaveral, Sonny. That's not my dream, it's yours. But I'm going to get you ready, in my own way."

"So you think Ginger . . ."

Roy Lee nodded. "Ginger's even more innocent than you, if that's humanly possible. Besides, you'd never live up to Mrs. Dantzler's standards. Why, I bet she'd have you playing the piano again. You'd never have time to build your rockets. Wernher von Braun would fire you so fast your head would swim."

His logic was wearing me out. "Roy Lee," I said tiredly, "I just want to ask Ginger Dantzler to the Christmas Formal. I don't want to marry her."

Roy Lee wagged his finger at me. "One thing leads to another. Don't even let it get started, son. That's the advice of the Big Creek lovemaster."

"What is this Big Creek lovemaster thing?"

As unlikely as it was, Roy Lee blushed. "We all got our talents," he said, serious as steel.

That night, while lying in my bed, I could hear the wind howling outside, a bitter blast of freezing air pushing in from the north. I was thinking about all that Roy Lee—the Big Creek lovemaster—had said when I heard something outside. I looked out my window toward the tipple and then, for just a moment, caught a movement in the lights of the filling station. The year before, some boys from Bradshaw had robbed the station, so I watched to see if I could see who or what it was. Then I saw a tiny deer fawn come out into the light, going stutter-step across the concrete. A doe, two more fawns, then another doe and a big buck followed, their heads swiveling nervously. The lights from a car coming down from the mine startled them and they ran off, their white tails flipping. They disappeared into the gloom of the back alley. They were all skinny as rails.

THE following Saturday, the BCMA gathered at the Cape. Although the sky was cloudy, and the temperature was hovering at around the freezing mark, there were only light breezes. It was a rocket kind of day. We ran up the BCMA flag on our blockhouse and got going with *Auk XXII-F*. I'd come up with the name *Auk* for all our rockets when we'd first started building them. The Great Auk was an extinct bird that couldn't fly, but I figured it would've if it could've. That put it in the same boat as us Rocket Boys when we started.

I looked across the slack and saw that our audience included, naturally enough, Mr. Bolt and our machinists. Ginger was there, too. Her mother and father were with her, just stepping out of their big Buick.

I walked over to say hello. "Good morning, Sonny," Mrs. Dantzler replied coolly. She wore a mink stole over her dress. I'd never seen anybody so done up at Cape Coalwood. "Will your rocket fly?"

"Yes, ma'am, it will," I said. The only thing I wasn't sure of was how high. I briefly explained the test objectives of the day while Ginger beamed at me.

"I hope you'll still have some fingers left to play the piano after you're done down here," Mrs. Dantzler said.

Even though I didn't plan on playing the piano anytime soon, I fervently hoped the same.

Mr. Dantzler took his railroad watch out of his vest pocket and contemplated it. "Will you launch soon?" he asked in his languid Mississippi drawl.

"Yes, sir, another ten minutes at most."

"Where will it go?"

"Downrange," I said, nodding in the direction of the Big Branch River, "if all goes as planned."

"Make it fly, Rocket Boy," Ginger said with a wink. That got me going again. I decided that after the launch I was going to ask her to the Christmas Formal, Big Creek lovemaster or no Big Creek lovemaster.

"I don't see your father here today," Mr. Dantzler observed, looking around the crowd.

"No, sir. He never comes."

Mr. Dantzler's eyebrows went up. "Is that a fact?"

I shrugged and headed back to the blockhouse. Before I got there, I was stopped in my tracks when I suddenly felt a passing sadness. I thought and then I thought again, but I couldn't figure out why. I shook it off and found Sherman working on the firing box inside the blockhouse. My undefined blues were replaced by impatience. I thought Sherman was going too slow, being entirely too meticulous. It wasn't that difficult, just some wires to be hooked up. "Hurry it up, will you, Sherman?" I demanded.

Startled, he frowned at me. "Who made you king?"

"We're already late," I muttered.

Sherman put down his screwdriver. "Sonny, I'm working as fast as I can. Now, unless you want to get in here and do it yourself, go away."

Sherman had taken my measure. Roy Lee and Billy were at the pad, checking the launch rod. Billy was whistling. He always seemed to have a good time at the Cape. I walked over and, without a word, knelt to inspect the wires leading into the rocket. There was a heating element inside, a piece of nichrome wire I'd borrowed from my mother's new turkey roaster. As far as I could tell, it had been inserted properly. I stood up and slapped the black slack dust off my knees. Roy Lee and Billy were looking at me. "You don't trust us?" Billy asked.

"I'm just inspecting," I said. "That's the way they do it at Cape Canaveral."

"How do you know how they do it?" Billy snapped, his mood turned as sour as mine.

I was puzzled. I wasn't used to Billy griping. In fact, I couldn't remember Billy Rose ever being anything but agreeable. "What's stuck in your craw?" I asked.

Billy gave me a sharp look. "What's stuck in yours?" The color had risen in his face.

We stared at each other. I couldn't figure out if I was picking a fight with Billy or he was picking one with me. We were both in an odd mood, that much was certain. I blinked first. "Sorry," I grumbled. "Forget it." I stalked away and fumed by the blockhouse until Sherman announced the ignition system was ready. Then I got O'Dell's report that the theodolites were set up. Roy Lee and Billy slouched back from the pad and hunkered down in the blockhouse. I gave a short countdown and pushed the launch button. At least that was something I could do right. *Auk XXII-F* jumped off the pad in a burst of fire and smoke and whistled aloft, a dot against the sky. I'd packed in some high-sulfur propellant at the top of the casement, and, as designed, the rocket began to smoke heavily, allowing us to track it easier. Billy called out that the Auk was wobbling a bit, but the new clamped-on fin design I'd come up with was apparently doing its job. The rocket landed downrange on the slack, and we ran off to begin the inspection process. O'Dell called out the time, and after a mental calculation

I determined the rocket had not performed up to snuff. After it cooled, Quentin put his eye up to the nozzle end. "Erosion," he groaned.

He was right. The higher-carbon steel hadn't helped a bit. We all stood around looking at it. I couldn't think of a thing to do to solve the problem.

Finally, Roy Lee said, "Why don't we line the nozzle with some kind of clay or something?"

Quentin stared at him. "You mean, of course, a ceramic of some kind," Quentin said. "A very good idea, Roy Lee, a very good idea, indeed, prodigious and rigorous."

Roy Lee jammed his hands in his pockets and kicked at the slack. "Well, I just thought . . ."

Quentin looked at him suspiciously. "You came up with this on your own?"

Roy Lee shrugged. "Well, sure . . ."

"Will wonders never cease?" Quentin asked the group at large.

All the other boys nodded their heads, and O'Dell socked Roy Lee in the shoulder, the ultimate compliment. "Oh, hell, guys," Roy Lee said.

"Not bad for the Big Creek lovemaster," I said, giving him a smile. I agreed it was a really good idea, although I had no clue how to do it.

"I shall put on my thinking cap," Quentin said. "It will require rigorous thought."

By the time I got back uprange, Ginger and her parents were in their Buick, just pulling out. Roy Lee caught me looking longingly her way. "Melba June Monroe," he said.

I saw Billy coming up the slack, carrying Quentin's theodolite and his telephone wire around his shoulder. Quentin was crouched by the rocket, his chin in his hands. I supposed his "rigorous thought" had begun. Either that or he was using it as an excuse to get Billy to carry his stuff. I crossed the slack to intercept Billy. "Hey, if I said something wrong, I apologize."

"You didn't say anything wrong," he said. He kept adjusting the wire on his shoulder and wouldn't look at me.

"All I meant—"

Billy walked past me. "Sonny, just leave it alone, okay? Just leave it alone!"

AT the supper table that night, Dad chewed his corn bread and kept looking at Mom out of the corner of his eye. I knew he had something to say and I think she knew it, too, but she wasn't about to make it easy for him by asking him what it was. Finally, he cleared his throat, then took another drink of milk. "Well, Elsie, I got a call from Ohio today," he said.

She sipped her coffee. "Do tell."

He shifted uneasily in his chair and cleared his throat again. "Yes, well. You see, they're on an economy wave this year as you already know and . . ." His mouth stayed open but his lips were moving as if he was having trouble wrapping them around what he had to say. Mom looked at him, her eyebrows raised. "I've been ordered to stop underwriting all nonmining activities."

Mom waited. When he didn't say anything more, she asked "Such as . . . ?"

He took a deep breath. "The Christmas Pageant, for starters."

Mom slowly put her cup down. It landed in her saucer with a soft clinking sound. "What?"

Dad's lips went flat. "I'm sorry."

Mom sat back in her chair. "Homer, this isn't right. You know how everybody looks forward to the pageant."

Dad said, "I fought this decision, Elsie, but they said if I wanted money for the Christmas Pageant, all I had to do was cut off a couple more miners. They knew I wouldn't do that."

Both my parents fell silent while I reflected on how I'd hoped that the Christmas Pageant would get canceled. I'd gotten my wish and it shamed me.

Later that night, while I was studying, Mom opened the door unannounced and came in and sat on my bed. She had Chipper on her shoulder. The little rodent jumped off and swung on the window curtains, stirring the interest of Daisy Mae. She moved underneath and got ready to pounce just in case he lost his grip. He spotted her and moved to the precise spot that was just out of her reach, no matter how hard she jumped. One of her ears went down, a sign of frustration. Chipper giggled. Frustration of all living things save my mother was his ultimate game.

I turned from my books to see what Mom wanted. She seemed to be weighing what she had come to say. That made me pretty nervous. I started going through all the things she could have possibly caught me on. I was pretty sure she still hadn't tried out the turkey roaster Dad had bought her for her birthday. On the sly, I'd pretty much stripped out its guts for our rocket-ignition system. I figured there'd be a problem over that around Thanksgiving time, but I'd worry about that then. And then there was that garden spade she'd bought down at the Big Store to use on her rose bushes. I'd taken it down to the Cape a month or so ago to use to dig out our rockets when they buried themselves in soft ground. I figured I had until spring before she missed it. Then there was . . . "Sonny, let's talk," she said, interrupting my criminal litany. "I know we don't do much of that in this house, but I need to talk to somebody and I guess you're it."

It was about the last thing I expected. "Ma'am?"

"Just listen to me, okay?"

I nodded. What else could I do?

"Do you remember how we lived before your dad took the Captain's job?"

I did, pretty much. It had only been about five years ago. "Was it any different than now?" I asked. Answering one of Mom's questions with a question was sometimes the safest thing for me to do. Sometimes I could get her way off track that way. But not this time.

"Maybe not for you," she said. "But do you remember the women who used to come to the house? Louise, Virgie, Rodie, Naomi, Charlotte? A bunch of women. They were all my friends. How many of them come to see me now?"

I gave it some thought. "Sometimes Mrs. Keneda comes," I said.

"Naomi's the only one," she agreed. "But not the rest. And you know why? It's because of who your father is. Either the other women are mad at him because of something he's done at the mine, or they're afraid somebody's going to accuse them of playing favorites for their husbands. Since your dad took the Captain's job, I've lost almost all of my old friends, Sonny, and that's the truth of it."

I noticed that her eyes had taken on nearly the same expression they had when I'd looked into them at the broken-down float. But it was more than despair. I could see that now. There was loss there, too. I had been with my mother, Mrs. Elsie Gardener Lavender Hickam, nearly every day for going on seventeen years. I'd seen her under almost every situation there was. I'd seen her happy and I'd seen her sad. I'd seen her mad, too, and grieving. I knew her every look and every move. She could crook a finger and I knew what it meant. "I don't blame your dad," she went on. "It was right for him to climb as high as he could go. And," she sighed, "I guess if I worked at it, I could be really good friends with Mrs. Dantzler, or Doc's wife, or maybe some of the Coalwood teachers. But they're all college-educated women. Who am I to push myself off on them?" She shook her head. "You want to get down to it, I guess I'm like a kitten that's been thrown out of the litter. I can't go ahead and I can't go back."

She fell silent, her eyes on the floor. My heart was thumping in my chest. My mom had never, ever told me anything so personal about herself, and I was pretty uncomfortable with it. I didn't know what to say to her, so I didn't try. I just sat there while the seconds passed. Finally, she took a deep breath, and then her face settled into a mask of determination. "I'm going to talk to the club ladies about the Christmas Pageant. Even if the company won't help, we can figure something out. I may not have many friends left in this town, but I'm just not going to let it be said that Elsie Hickam lost the Veterans Day parade and then gave up on the Christmas Pageant, too."

There was something about my character that, every so often, made me as spiteful as a blue jay spying a cat. This was one of those times. I guess it had to do with the resentment I couldn't shake over how Mom had forced me to be with Dad and Poppy the previous Christmas. Whatever it was, her proposal instantly got my feathers ruffled and I wanted no part of it. Rather than confess how I really felt, I just frowned and drummed my fingers on my books, showing her I was trying to study. She saw what I was doing and rose to leave. "I just needed somebody to listen," she said. "Sorry to bother you."

I wanted to say it was no bother, but I couldn't manage even that. Sometimes, the pique that I was capable of surprised even me. Mom plucked Chipper off the curtain and started to leave. She stopped before closing the door. "Don't worry. I don't expect you to help me. I know you've got more important things to do." Then she eased the door shut. I would have felt better if she'd have slammed it. How had Coach Gainer put it in one of his famous boys' health lectures? "A woman's mildness," he'd said, "will provoke a man's guilt far better than ever her wrath." It apparently worked just the same for mothers and sons, too.

Daisy Mae came over and jumped up on my lap, asking to be consoled because Chipper had escaped her again. I scratched her head, but I don't think it consoled her much. I didn't feel very consoled, either. I felt mean and nasty because that's exactly what I was. Selfish, too. What was with me, anyway? Mom had tried to do a good thing by sending me with Dad to see Poppy. It hadn't worked out, but that wasn't her fault. So why was I punishing her? Maybe just because I could? Was this a part of growing up, wanting to hurt the people who loved me the most? If so, I wanted no part of it.

I stared at my bedroom door. I wanted to chase after Mom, tell her of course I'd help her with her Christmas Pageant if that's what she wanted. But I didn't. It just wasn't in me to do. Daisy Mae nuzzled my chin and then curled up on my lap, tucking her nose between her paws. I envied her ability to find tranquillity after disappointment. I doubted, at that moment, I'd ever be able to do the same.

9

THE COALWOOD SKY

THE FOLLOWING MONDAY, Quentin asked me to sit down with him in the auditorium before classes. He looked loaded for bear, and I was the bear. When I sat down beside him, he cracked his knuckles, something he often did when he was preparing to lecture me about something. He leaned forward in his chair and I leaned in, too. "Sonny, I must say I am disappointed in you," he said.

I started to say "Join the crowd," but I didn't. I just listened. "Have you honestly given a moment's thought to Roy Lee's idea of the ceramic-lined nozzle? No? I thought not. Really, my boy, it seems to me you're dragging your feet these days. And when are we going to do the calculations according to Miss Riley's book? All it takes is a little calculus."

"Quentin," I said fiercely, "I had a lot of homework to do over the weekend. Remember, I'm trying to make all A's this semester. Don't ask me why, but I just want to do it because I never have. I know that doesn't mean much to you. You've always made A's in all your classes, not counting phys ed."

"Studying is your excuse?" He sniffed. "I cannot accept such a proposition." He smacked his fist into his palm. "Dammit, Sonny. You must work harder. There's not a day to waste." When I just sat there and looked at him, he shook his head and sighed deeply. Then he performed a little archeological dig into his briefcase and excavated a torn piece of notebook paper. "While it's clear to me that you are losing your ardor for our entire enterprise, perhaps this will get your attention. I hitched to the county library after our rocket launch on Saturday and researched the various methodologies for applying ceramics to metal surfaces. I believe I have identified just the thing we need. It's called water putty but don't let the name fool you. It comes in powder form and all you have to do is add water to it and—*voilà!*—you get a supple, moldable ceramic." He crossed his ankle over his knee to prop up his paper. I noticed one of his socks was blue. The other one was plaid. "My research further shows that it is a very easy material to apply, hardens rapidly, and sticks quite well to metal surfaces. Of course, when and if you ever get around to it, you'll have to make your calculations such that the ceramic layer will not cause inefficiency within the gas flow. Water putty, Sonny. Find some and let's get going! Here, I've even written it down for you. Water putty!"

I took Quentin's grimy scrap of notebook paper with the tips of my fingers. I didn't have any water putty or the slightest idea how to make such calculations and told him so. "Let's wait until after semester exams," I suggested. "Then I'll get right on it. The water putty, the calculations from the book, everything."

Quentin looked aghast. "Sonny, we can't wait!" He looked at his wrist (although there wasn't a watch on it) and then shook his head in despair. "The county science fair is in April, practically tomorrow in cosmic terms! A ceramic lining in our nozzles will be just the thing to distinguish our work. Water putty, my boy! Find some and then get going with your calculations. I can see it in Basil's paper now. *Big Creek boys solve nozzle erosion problem! Wernher von Braun asks for their help!* Our missile program will be by far the most rigorous in the nation!"

Quentin was referring to Basil Oglethorpe, a writer for the *McDowell County Banner,* a grocery store newspaper. Basil had begun to regularly feature us in his column in 1958. "Rocket Boys Vault into the Heavens" was one of his tamer headlines.

"Quentin," I replied, sighing, "if you're so hot to get all this done, why don't *you* get rigorous and do it yourself?"

"And how do you expect me to do that?" he asked, his frost-blue eyes narrowing. "I could do the calculations, certainly, but you're the one who needs the mathematical practice, not me. And as for the required machine-shop work and the acquisition of water putty, clearly that is for you, the Coalwood superintendent's son, to accomplish." He spread his hands. "A poor Bartley boy, the son of a poor, itinerant miner, could hardly be expected to do more than I do already."

At his mention of being poor, I noticed the white shirt he was wearing had a frayed collar. A closer look showed a patch on one of its sleeves. The mismatched socks I had earlier noted were easily observed because the faded khaki pants he wore with his heavy brown brogans were about an inch too short. Except for Roy Lee, the Big Creek lovemaster, none of the Rocket Boys cared much about the clothes we wore, but Quentin had gotten it down to a science. Still, in Quentin's defense, the fact was his dad had been cut off from the Bartley mine for months and there were a lot of mouths at his house to feed. And I was, indeed, the superintendent's son, from whom all riches flowed. He had me dead to rights. "All right, Quentin," I said. "I'll see what I can do."

A grin cracked his thin face. "Prodigious, Sonny! You see what a little pep talk can do?" Now that he'd gotten what he wanted, he turned friendly. "Say, how about that problem of yours—your mental manifestation? The inordinate sadness? Ever get a handle on that?"

"I might have part of it," I said, and then I told him about Poppy and Dad last Christmas. He listened with his head cocked, his eyes quizzical. That was one thing about Quentin. When he listened, he really listened.

He made a fist and rested his chin on it in the classical thinker's pose. "Let us break it down," he said at length. "Because you thought about your problem logically as I suggested, you have perhaps figured out a portion of what is upsetting you. Good! We're making progress! Now perhaps, you may want to consider that your manifestation is so complex that your particular mind simply cannot deal with it."

I sorted through his words. "You think I'm going nuts?"

Quentin shrugged. "I suppose that is a possibility. But what I really believe we have here, Sonny, is a complex mental situation. That is why it is nearly impossible for you to discern it." He leveled his gaze on me. "I have noticed something about you that I am loath to admit but I will tell it to you now. You have a keen mind. When there is a problem with our rockets, I usually come up with the most complex solution possible to resolve it. You, on the other hand, nearly always come up with the simplest solution. Your new fin design is an example. I would have never in a million years come up with the idea to take two rectangles of metal and bend them so as to make four fins. My advanced brainpower can't handle such simplicity!" He shook his head tragically. "But your thought processes are defeated when the problem actually does require a complex algorithm. That is why you can't figure out what is bothering you with standard thinking. The answer is complex! I think, therefore, you must break it down into its simplest forms."

He'd lost me, and I guess my look told him that. "Here's the way to think about this," he said patiently. "Consider that there is no simple answer, or single cause. Review your past and propose to yourself all the issues that might be affecting your psyche. Write them all down. Then every time something else happens that bothers you, write that down, too. Get yourself a nice little list going. After a while, you'll reach a critical mass with all your complaints and be able to make some intellectual and logical sense to them. I'm certain, in your simple way, you will then find the solution to your occasional bouts of depression. If that doesn't work, I'll check out a psychology book and put you into analysis."

That sounded like a potential cure worse than the disease. "I'll make a list," I promised. "I'll make a bunch of lists."

He slapped his hands on his knees. "Good! I'm glad we had this little talk. Say, there's something else I've been thinking about. Do you like orange juice? Yes? Well, what if you were going to hike in the woods and didn't want to carry juice or fresh oranges around? Got you stumped? Well, what if before you went in the woods you took a bunch of oranges and put them in the sun and let them dry out? And then you ground them up into a fine powder? Then, anytime you wanted orange juice, no matter where you were, all you'd have to do is add water to the powder! *Voilà!* Orange juice! What do you think?"

What I thought was it sounded pretty revolting and started to say so, but the bell to classes rang before I got the chance. Quentin, never one to be late, picked up his briefcase and made his way out of the auditorium. I sat there, letting all the students file by. Quentin had given me a lot to think about, and I wanted to get started on it. Then I saw Billy coming up the aisle. I caught his eye, but he looked away and kept going. I thought to chase after him, maybe find out what was bothering him, but then I got to thinking about what Quentin had told me. A list. I needed to make a list. Of course, if it was supposed to include all the things on that list that were bothering me, I'd have to put Quentin on it, too. That thought made me laugh. I loved it when I made myself laugh. It made me feel clever. Of course, Reverend Lanier used to say when a man thinks himself clever, he's but a temptation to God's sense of humor.

IT was not in the nature of the people of Coalwood to look up at the sky. For most of the years while I was growing up, a drifting cloud of coal dust and grit from the mine hung in the air, obscuring what sky there was squeezed between our mountains. But when the railroad tracks were taken out in the spring of 1959, and the tipple operations moved across the mountain to Caretta, the dust cleared. For the first time I could clearly see the velvety blackness of space. I found the stars bright as fireflies and the moon like a giant glowing wheel, and I was fascinated. It was almost as if I could reach out and touch them. About that time, I started to go up on the roof of the Club House to look through a telescope Jake Mosby had provided us boys. Jake was one of the junior engineers and had become a special friend of the Rocket Boys. Not only did he attend almost every one of our launches, but he had also provided us an old trigonometry book so we could figure out how high our rockets flew. Sherman was with me the first night Jake set up his telescope for us. When Jake fell asleep, a jar of John Eye's best whiskey spilling out of his hand, Sherman and I continued to marvel at the wonders of the stars and planets. When I got home past midnight, my mother confronted me in the upstairs hall. "What now, Sonny boy?" she asked in the tired but resigned voice she often used in dealing with my escapades as a Rocket Boy.

"Mom, you've got to come see," I told her, and then described Jake's telescope and the stars he had shown me along with Jupiter's bands and Saturn's rings.

My dad came out of his bedroom, blinking from the hall light. "Was Jake drunk?"

"He was asleep when I left." I answered. It was a nimble response, I thought.

"Drunk," Dad concluded, knowing nimbleness when he heard it.

"We're going there," I said, entirely too loud for the hour. "All of us. Into space!" At that moment, I was as certain of that as anything in my whole life. I could already imagine what I'd look like in a space suit walking around on the moon.

Mom was eyeing my dad as he stood there in his pajamas and she in her robe. "Let me know when you're ready to go," she said. "I'll be the first one on the rocket." Then, as if on cue, my parents turned their backs on each other and went into their rooms, leaving me standing alone in the dark hall wondering what had just happened.

Jake had left us the past summer, finishing his stint as a junior engineer under Dad's hard tutelage. Jake's father owned a fairly large percentage of the steel company that owned us, and I guessed he was back there, learning how to squeeze dimes or something. He'd at least left us his telescope to wander our eyes around the heavens. But still I missed him. Jake was a man of the world, the only one I knew, but mostly he was my friend. Every time I went past the Club House, I looked for his bright cherry-red Corvette, but it was never there. I asked Mom if she'd heard anything of

Jake, if there was any chance he'd come back. "Jake Mosby?" She laughed merrily. "Oh, yes, that boy will be back."

"How do you know?" I wondered.

"Because he loves that mine as much as your dad."

I was thunderstruck by such an idea. Jake was always in trouble when he was in Coalwood. If it wasn't his incessant womanizing, especially with the company secretaries, it was his drunken, outrageous conduct at company parties. His mining engineering could use some improvement, too. Dad had said so out loud.

Mom watched my face as I sorted through all of Jake's misdeeds. "I know what you're thinking, but I know what I'm talking about," she said. "Jake Mosby and Homer Hickam are two peas in a pod. Where Homer leaves off, Jake picks up. He won't stay gone from his hero for very long."

I just couldn't fathom it. "Dad his hero?" I exclaimed. "I always thought Jake hated Dad."

"Trust me," Mom said. "We'll see our boy Jake in these parts all too soon."

It was time that I looked at the stars. For the first time in weeks, the clouds had blown away, so I figured I had better take advantage of it. Dad had gone off to the mine after a phone call, Mom was down Tipple Row to see Naomi Keneda and her new baby granddaughter. I grabbed my bike and headed off for the Club House. I parked beside the big double doors on the vast front porch and started to go inside, only to be met by two men, just coming out. They were wearing long leather coats that almost reached the ground. I had never seen the like. Then I heard them speaking and I couldn't understand a word they were saying. I stared at them. They were both young men, and at first I thought maybe they were a couple of the junior engineers trying out their college Latin or whatever it was they studied, but even their haircuts were odd, severely cut around the ears and swept straight back. The taller of the two had hair the color of wet straw, the other a deep coal black. They took note of me. *"Guten Tag,"* the straw-haired man said to me.

"Good day to you," the other said, and gave me a curt nod.

I just stared. What kind of foreigners were they? Then I thought—wait a minute—they sounded just like Wernher von Braun on television! They were Germans! I had never actually seen a real live German before and a question just leapt right out of my mouth. "Do you know Wernher von Braun?"

The two young men looked at each other and then shook their heads. "*Nein. Herr Doktor* von Braun is in another line of work, eh?" They both laughed and then each stuck out their hands to me to shake. "Gerhard," the straw-haired man said.

"Dieter," said the one with the black hair.

"Sonny Hickam," I said.

"The son of Homer Hickam?" Dieter asked. His English seemed much better than Gerhard's.

"Yes, sir."

"*Ach,* your father is a man who sees."

I didn't understand. "Sees?"

"Sees," Dieter said mysteriously.

I guessed Dad saw, but what he was seeing these days I had no idea. Gerhard held up two envelopes and mimed mailing them.

"Oh, the post office." I pointed it out, just across the street, lit only by a streetlight. "But it's closed." They nodded, although a bit uncertainly. I led the two over to the post office and showed them the slot to put their letters in, but then I noticed they didn't have any stamps on them. I pointed that out and we walked back to the Club House. "You sure you don't know Wernher von Braun?" I asked.

"*Nein, nein,*" Dieter answered, acting a little put out. He looked around. "What is there to do?" He waved his hand at the street. Downtown Coalwood was as quiet as a graveyard.

"I'm going up to look at the stars," I said, and when they gave me an uncomprehending look, I walked to the edge of the porch and pointed at the first twinkling pinpoint of light in the black sky. "Stars," I said again. Dieter and Gerhard came over and looked up, too, but it was clear they didn't understand what I was talking about. "Come on," I said. "I'll show you."

I led them up to the third floor, stopping to get Jake's telescope out of the broom closet where it was stored. I motioned to them to follow me, and we climbed up the rude wooden ladder. We emerged in the total darkness, but I knew the roof as well as my own room and led them over to the telescope base, covered by a canvas. I took the canvas off and attached the telescope to the base. I proudly patted the assembly. "We use this to look at the stars and planets," I said.

I showed them how to manipulate the telescope, and they looked with interest at each planet I pointed out, beginning with reliable Venus, our dazzling, cloud-shrouded, and closest planetary neighbor. "Nobody knows what's under those clouds," I explained as they each took turns at the eyepiece, Dieter translating what I was saying to Gerhard. "Could be the whole place is covered by an ocean or maybe a big jungle." Then I showed them Saturn. "See the rings? Go ahead," I told them as they swiveled the telescope from planet to planet, and star to star. "Look all you want."

While Dieter and Gerhard took turns looking and chattering in German about their various discoveries in the sky, I sat down on the edge of the roof. Sometimes when my eyes got tired of squinting through the telescope, I would gaze down on Coalwood, looking at it with almost the same wonder and curiosity as the sky. After living there my entire life, I suppose I should have learned all that there was to know about the place. Yet I suspected there were many things about my town of which I knew little, including the contest my parents had waged for as long as I could remember as to what my future should be, and my brother's, and their own. The stars were complex and deeply mysterious. Coalwood and its people, it often seemed to me, were vastly more so.

Past the church, I saw the Dantzler house, a big, white two-story box nestled in a stand of pine. What was Ginger doing at that exact moment? Studying, I supposed, or playing the piano or practicing singing the scales. The Dantzlers were about as cultured and fine a family as I guess had ever graced Coalwood. Maybe I was too crude to ever aspire to their level. "Grace, Sonny Hickam," Mrs. Dantzler had told me one time when I'd stumbled over a lesson and sat there beside her, my head hanging in mortification because I had been so clumsy. "Head up," she'd said brightly. "Curve your fingers. Now play. You can do it. Let's go." She put her hand under my chin and physically raised it, then took my hands, curved my fingers, and placed them on the keys. "Play," she commanded, and I had. "Good," she said, and because she'd said it, I knew it was.

I wondered what was life going to be like without Mrs. Dantzler and all the other townspeople I had known my whole life. By next fall, I would be gone from Coalwood, probably to college. Mom had promised I could go if I showed my dad I was capable of something more than just dreaming. I'd already shown him with my rockets and I was going to show him soon with my grades. Still, even though it was what I wanted to do, I felt frightened at the prospect of leaving. And then I thought—wait a minute—is this what makes me sad? Did I need to put "Leaving Coalwood" on my list? My thoughts were interrupted as Dieter and Gerhard joined me on the edge of the roof. Dieter lit a cigarette while Gerhard sat down beside me and kicked his feet over the ledge. "It is a very nice place, Coalwood," Dieter said.

"Um," I grunted noncommittally.

"You are here your whole life?"

"Yes, sir." I looked over at him. "Why did you say you're here?"

Dieter flicked his ashes over the edge while Gerhard hummed a tuneless song. "I didn't say."

I nodded. It was a West Virginia custom to be curious but to never go past a rebuke. I was just passing the time, anyway. I didn't much care why the two Germans were in Coalwood, since they didn't even know Wernher von Braun. I looked out over the Club House lawn. The machine shop across the valley was dark and quiet. I could even hear the gurgling of the little creek that ran behind it.

"We help your dad," Dieter said, flicking his cigarette over the roof. I watched it fall, a tiny meteor that bounced on the lawn, sparks flying.

I looked in his direction. "How do you help him?"

Dieter was quiet for a moment and then got up. Gerhard did as well. They made their way to the hatch in the roof. "We help him at 11 East," Dieter said, and then they went below.

At the mention of 11 East, the autumn air seemed to get suddenly chillier. I thought Dieter surely must have told me wrong. 11 East? How could that be possible? Ever since I was old enough to know what it meant, 11 East conjured up disaster, death, and doom all rolled up into one deep, dark place.

11 EAST

OVER THE NEXT few days, the two Germans became the main topic of fence-line gossip. Some people even made up excuses to go to the Club House just to look at them. Dieter and Gerhard kept pretty much to themselves. It didn't take long, however, before people heard what they had come for, at least to an extent. The Germans had come under a special contract to do some unspecified work at the section named 11 East, which my father had decided to reopen. There was grumbling all over town. Homer Hickam had surely lost his mind on this one. 11 East was a known killer.

I knew the story of the section as well as anybody, having heard it from my parents at the supper table. The Captain had first opened 11 East in 1941. There was supposed to be a huge seam of pure bituminous coal there, seven to nine feet thick, easy to work—prime "high coal" as such was called. The Captain, after a careful engineering analysis, had assigned the new section its number—every section had one—and pointed a crew in that direction. It didn't take long before 11 East turned into the Captain's and Coalwood's nightmare. There were rockfalls, runaway cars, gas flare-ups, flooding, and some men were hurt and a few were killed. A lot of Coalwood miners from the very start said the place was jinxed, but others said the problem was the roof, a jumble of massive slabs of razor-edged rock. "Just get through this bad roof, boys," the Captain was purported to say, "and we'll all be rich as Croesus."

"Okay, Cap'n, but I guess we'll have to spend our money in the hereafter," one miner was supposed to have retorted, although I couldn't imagine anybody ever truly talking back to the Captain. He stood nearly six and a half feet tall, a huge, slump-shouldered, big-footed man who often walked around with a pistol tucked in his belt. Dad said the pistol was never loaded, but Mom said one time the Captain used it to shoot a cigar right out of the mouth of a man who lit it up in the presence of a lady. I'd have paid real money to have seen the Captain make that shot.

Dad had been a day-shift construction foreman at the time when 11 East was opened, but the Captain reassigned him to take the lead foreman's job on the evening shift of the new section. Day after day, the Coalwood men on all three shifts assaulted 11 East like an army at war, trying every way possible to get through the bad rock. Then, to compound their problems, they discovered that the coal seam sloped downward and became narrower. Before it was over, men had to crawl on their hands and knees to get to the face, but the Captain kept urging them on, believing the high coal was always just a few more yards away. Only the Japanese attack on Pearl Harbor stopped the combat at 11 East. With the demand for coal from the War Department, the Captain had to quit and go after the easier coal. Before the Captain closed the section down, so I'd heard, some 11 East miners had volunteered for the army, figuring they'd be safer storming beaches than working under that deadly roof.

In later years, "11 East" became a phrase used in Coalwood for a close-run thing that was a bit too close. Some mothers even warned their unruly kids that, if they didn't behave, they were going to be "sent down to 11 East." Then, in the early 1950's, a few miners going back into the gob near the old section to eat their lunches claimed they had witnessed miners wearing striped, full-bib coveralls and corrugated helmets, the kind that had been worn before the war. The old-timers had said nothing, just kept walking back into the abandoned tunnel that had been the entry to 11 East. After that report, most people believed the old section was haunted. Every mine had such stories, but this one had the ring of truth to it. I couldn't imagine why Dad would want to go back in there.

There was one other awful thing that had happened on 11 East, too, now that I thought about it. That was where Poppy got his legs cut off.

ONE afternoon after school, I rode my bike down to the Big Store to get a bottle of soda pop. Mr. Dubonnet was talking to some of his union men over by the cigar counter when I walked into the drugstore section. He came over and leaned on the counter beside me. "How about I buy you a pop?" he said, shoving his hand in his pants pocket after change.

"No, thanks, sir," I said, showing him I had my own fifteen cents.

Mr. Dubonnet ignored my show of money and called Junior over and ordered me a Royal Crown. He took off his hat and laid it on the counter and ordered himself a Dr Pepper and a bag of peanuts, which he proceeded to pour into the bottle. Then he leaned backward with his elbows on the counter and perused the passing scene through the store windows. A couple of his men started to come up to him, but with an almost imperceptible shake of his head he sent them away. "How's your mother?" he asked after a while. "I guess the Veterans Day float took some wind out of her sails."

"You don't know my mother if you think that," I said. Of course, he did know her. He'd gone through Gary High School with her—and Dad.

Mr. Dubonnet drank his pop and peanuts and then rubbed his chin. He had something on his mind, no doubt about it. "Sonny, if there's ever . . ." He hesitated. ". . . ever anything I can do for you and . . . your mother . . ." He looked around. I guess it was to see if anybody was listening. ". . . you'll let me know?"

I didn't know what to say so I didn't say anything.

"So . . ." Mr. Dubonnet pursed his lips. "So, your dad's opening up 11 East."

Now I thought I knew why he was talking to me. "I don't know anything about 11 East, sir!" I fairly shouted.

Mr. Dubonnet's face clouded and he looked around again. Shoppers moved past, women intent on groceries with kids in tow. "No, I expect you wouldn't," he said after a bit. "Sonny, I've always thought your father was a good man. He isn't a fair man, he's too hard-shelled in what he believes to be fair, but he's still a good man. I want you to know that I know that. Do you understand?"

"Yes, sir, I guess."

"Opening 11 East is going to cause trouble. Best you get ready for it."

I was astonished a Coalwood adult could be so frank to an adolescent not in his family. "Sir?"

He shrugged. "Union trouble, surely, at my level. The men assigned to the section have already come to me. They're afraid of it and I'll make their case for them. These Germans come to work here, even if they are under contract, are breaking union rules. You have to be a member of the UMWA to work in this mine and I'll shortly be reminding your dad of that. It's not only me, Sonny. People in this town are going to get after your dad on this one. After your family, too, I expect."

I thought then I knew what he was getting at. There had been boys, sons of union men, who over the years had cornered me at school and tried to beat me up because of what Dad had done at the mine. They had been wasting their time. Every boy in Coalwood could stomp me to a pulp and I'd never tell my dad about it, one way or the other.

"Just so you know," Mr. Dubonnet said grimly. "Your dad's out to prove something on this one, that's what I figure. Maybe he's just trying to show that the Captain was right after all these years. I don't know, but just be careful is all I'm saying." Then he put on his canvas snap-brim fedora, nearly identical to the kind Dad wore, laid his finger on its brim, and walked out of the store, leaving me with my pop to finish and another mystery to unravel.

As the days counted down to Thanksgiving, Dad continued to stay at the mine until far into the night, going back to work before I got up. One morning, on the way to my rocket laboratory, I found him asleep on the basement stairs. Lucifer had climbed up beside him, his big black tomcat head on Dad's leg. I woke Dad and he looked at his watch, got up, grabbed his white helmet, and headed back up to the mine. Lucifer and I watched him go.

As much as I wanted to, being fundamentally curious, I never asked Dad about 11 East. The mine was a subject I couldn't talk to him about in any form. On a spring Sunday in 1958, he had taken me inside the mine while Mom was at church. On the man-trip ride to the face, he had explained to me what the mine meant to him, and how proud he was to be a miner and a leader of miners. At the face, he'd explained the mechanical choreography of the work there, how the continuous miners ate at the seam like great carnivorous dinosaurs, how the crablike loading machines moved in behind to scoop up the coal and scuttle back to the waiting trams. On the way out, he'd put the question to me: Did I want to become a mining engineer? Because if I did, he said, he'd see that I went to college. Jim was going to play football, maybe be a coach. He wasn't coming back to Coalwood. But Coalwood needed its sons, he explained, and he needed at least one of his to get that "piece of paper" denied him, and then perhaps take his place to keep the good work of coal mining alive so that steel could stay alive and the country, too. I had never seen my dad so earnest, so hopeful, so ready to hear what I had to say. Everything he thought that was right and holy about what he did for a living, and his hopes for Coalwood, he had placed like a sacrifice before me.

On the lift back to the surface, I told my father that Coalwood wasn't in my future, that I wanted to work for Dr. von Braun. It had been one of the hardest things I had ever done. Because of that, and because I had been a coward when Poppy died, Dad's present opinion of me was something of a mystery. I had my suspicions, though. I was now, and probably forever, Sonny, the unforgiven son.

A DISASTER OF SQUIRRELS

I VISITED JUNIOR, the Big Store drugstore clerk, to see about Quentin's water putty. "Water putty," he mused, repeating the words a couple of times. "Water putty, water putty."

"Water putty," I said. "If you don't have any . . ." I almost hoped he didn't. I could tell Quentin and get back to my studies.

Junior brightened. "Be right back," he said.

Five minutes later, Junior reappeared, a small paper sack in his hand. He plunked it down on the counter. "Water putty," he pronounced. "It's a powder. Just add water, comes out rock hard."

I was astonished. Was there nothing the company store didn't stock?

"I guess we're in business, eh?" Junior grinned, his eyes bright behind his wire-rimmed spectacles.

I guessed we were, indeed. As I went out the door, Junior called out, "Hey, Rocket Boy. Don't blow yourself up!"

The purchase of the water putty inspired me to take another big step. I was ready to open Miss Riley's book and begin the calculations required for a more sophisticated nozzle. Quentin hitched over to Coalwood to supervise. It took all night but, after some false starts, I managed to work the equations in the book. Quentin looked it over and nodded. "It'll do," he said. "It'll do."

The next thing I had to accomplish was an engineering drawing

for the machine shop to follow. The new design called for complex angles to be precisely drawn. While I was working, my tongue
protruding out of the corner of my mouth, I heard Dad come up
the steps. I hadn't seen him home for days. He glanced in my room
and saw me bent over my desk. "Rockets, huh?" he said, coming in
to look over my shoulder. I didn't know why he was taking any
interest.

"New nozzle," I said as the lead in my pencil snapped.

While I sharpened the pencil with a plastic Hopalong Cassidy
sharpener, he picked up my drawing, frowned over it for a moment,
and then put it down. "Your lead is too soft," he said. "The thick-
ness of your lines should be consistent." He pointed at the edge of
the nozzle. "See how the line gets wider as you draw it? That's not
professional."

"Yes, sir," I said, withdrawing my pencil from the sharpener
and blowing the carbon dust from its tip.

"Here," he said, taking the pencil. He put its point down on
another sheet of paper and turned it back and forth a few times,
then showed it to me. "See how that rounds the point? The line
will stay the same width longer that way."

He handed me the pencil and then left, heading for bed. I
inspected the point and then put it to paper. He was right. The line
was steady and strong. Not for the first time, I wondered what
Dad might be able to teach me if only he took the time. I got out
the list I was making of things that were bothering me. *Pencils,* I
wrote just below *Poppy, Leaving Coalwood, 11 East,* and *Quentin.* As
an afterthought, I wrote down *Girls,* too, but then I thought—no,
that was too general a category. I crossed it out, but it was still
there where I could see it.

AT Quentin's insistence, I scheduled an official Big Creek Missile
Agency meeting on the Saturday before Thanksgiving. Quentin,
Roy Lee, Sherman, O'Dell, and I gathered in my room. O'Dell
reported that Billy couldn't make it. He had something he had to
do at his house.

Chipper was hanging upside down on the window curtains, watching us intently, and every few seconds irritably flipping his half of a tail. Chipper had half of a tail because he had caught it in the exercise wheel Mr. McDuff, the mine carpenter, had made for him as a gift to my mom. The wheel had chopped Chipper's tail off clean as a razor, but Chipper never seemed to mind. He loved his little wheel. I'd wake up sometimes at night and hear it churning downstairs. Mom said Chipper might not be going anywhere but he was getting there fast.

I could tell Chipper was thinking about jumping down on Roy Lee, a favorite target, and causing confusion, which was about all he was good for, except for eating up the Hickam family Bible. He'd done a fair job of that, shredding generations of Hickam genealogy for all time. When I pointed him out, Roy Lee frowned over his shoulder at the little gray squirrel. "I'm going to kill him if he jumps on my hair again," he said, smoothing the slick sides of his DA with both his hands. I didn't take the threat seriously. Roy Lee would have to deal with my mom if he got after Chipper and he knew it.

It had snowed overnight, and the temperature plummeted. Winter, always long and tenacious in Coalwood, had arrived. Still, it was stifling hot in my room. Mom had gone down to the basement and really stoked the furnace. It was chugging. Sweat was streaming down our faces. "Let's open the window," Roy Lee said, pointing at the fogged-up window that faced the tipple.

"Not with Chipper in the room," I said. "He might decide to get out. My mom would kill all of us."

"I hate that squirrel," Roy Lee said. I didn't hear anybody argue with him, although I could have, a little. I'd always admired Chipper mainly because, for some reason, he seemed to have it in for my brother. Before Jim had gone off to college, Chipper had made a habit of ambushing him on a regular basis. His primary technique was to hang on a curtain and leap on Jim as he went by. A quick bite on my brother's neck and then a run for Mom completed the squirrel's modus operandi. Jim might sputter and swear but he knew better than to harm one gray hair on Chipper's bony head. One time when Jim was asleep on the couch in front of the television, Chipper sneaked up and bit him on the earlobe. That had to hurt. Jim came flying off the couch like a devil had stuck a pitchfork in his britches. I saw the whole thing develop from start to finish, but when Jim looked at me, I was all wide-eyed innocence. It made me ashamed to remember it, which I did, often.

Quentin started off our meeting with a harangue about the new nozzle. "Now is the time for greater strides," he said. He was sitting on the bed. The other boys were arranged around the room in chairs or on the floor. "I should like an immediate test of the heat-sink ceramic liner that Roy Lee proposed. I have repeatedly suggested to Sonny that he begin the process." Quentin gave me the sly eye and then continued. "If the test is successful and I'm confident it will be, we should then construct a rocket of an order of magnitude greater than our present dimensional constructs and proceed to gross elevations and ultimate recognition of our rigor at the national level."

The other boys looked at each other with puzzled expressions. I translated the Quentinese. "He wants us to test a new nozzle based on calculations according to Miss Riley's book" (I pointed out the *Principles of Guided Missile Design* on top of my dresser) "and then also coat it with water putty. Two pretty big chores," I said grumpily, "and he wants us to do it yesterday. Then he wants us to build a great big rocket, fly it to the moon, and win the national science fair."

"Precisely so," Quentin said, "your satirical commentary notwithstanding."

I took up for myself. "I've got the water putty. You know I've worked the calculations. I'm doing the drawings the best I can."

Quentin gritted his teeth and looked at the floor in the manner he had when he was disappointed with me. "And why is your work incomplete?"

"I have to sleep sometimes," I said. "And study."

"Sleep?" Quentin sniffed. "My dear Sonny, there will be time for sleep when we work for NASA. But to get there, we must win the science fairs, beginning at the local level. Miss Riley insists that we have a full body of knowledge before we attempt them this spring. To date, we have something quite a bit less than that."

"I'm working as fast as I can, Quentin," I said, my blood rising.

Quentin laid his arm across his eyes. It was a Hollywood kind of dramatic gesture. Quentin didn't get to go to too many movies, but he paid attention to the ones he saw. "Sonny, will you never take our enterprise seriously?" he said beneath his arm. "Perhaps it doesn't mean much to you whether we do well in these science fairs, you being the superintendent's son who will undoubtedly be able to afford to go to college, but it makes a great difference to me. My hopes for college depend on these contests!"

I started to remind Quentin that, to my knowledge, no scholarships were handed out in any science fair, including the nationals, but O'Dell, Sherman, and Roy Lee all chimed in, agreeing with Quentin. "You can get the machine shop going on Monday," O'Dell said. "Why, I bet we can test the nozzle by next weekend if you'd just get on with it."

"Why don't *you* do it, O'Dell?" I demanded.

O'Dell looked puzzled. "Since when am I allowed to go down to the machine shop and tell them to do anything?"

I got up on my high horse. "I don't *tell* them. I ask them."

Roy Lee saw through my posturing. "So ask them. What's the big deal?"

"The big deal is that I have other things to do."

"You do, indeed," he said, giving me the Big Creek lovemaster grin.

"Be sure to run your drawings by me before you give them to the machinists," Quentin reminded me. "I must ensure their accuracy."

"Yes, your eggheadedness," I said. There was no use trying to argue with him and everybody else, so I gave up. It didn't mean I was going to do what they wanted me to do, but it did mean I was tired of talking about it.

"That's the style," Quentin said.

I heard Mom calling me. I held up my hand for Quentin to hold his thought (he always had another one) and then went downstairs to see what Mom wanted. She asked me if the boys wanted cookies and milk. If so, she was prepared to bring up a tray. "No, thanks," I said. "I don't think they're staying long." It was my hope, in any case.

"I thought I'd ask them to help out on the Christmas Pageant," she said.

"I'll send them down to you," I promised. She looked disappointed I hadn't said I'd changed my mind about helping her, but I still wasn't ready to tell her that, even if it was true. It was the West Virginia stubborn streak in me, I supposed.

I went back to my room and was slapped in the face by a gale of frigid air blasting through a wide-open window. The boys gave me a sheepish look, the boys who were in the room, that is. I poked my head outside and saw Roy Lee on the roof, looking over the edge. "What in the world, Roy Lee?"

Roy Lee turned around, and I could see his hair was messed up. O'Dell climbed out beside me. "He let Chipper out," he said, pointing at Roy Lee and summing up the disaster.

Roy Lee patted his hair. "Damned thing attacked me."

Nobody needed to say a thing more. I knew what had happened. Roy Lee had opened the window to cool things down, Chipper had sneak-attacked Roy Lee's hair. Then Roy Lee had chased him and Chipper had become the prodigal squirrel of Coalwood, going out the window into the big bad world to have himself a nice little adventure that would probably end up killing him—and me. "Did you see where he went?" I asked, desperation seeping into my voice.

"I did," Sherman said, climbing out of the window. He pointed at the mountain behind the house. "He jumped in the maple tree and ran across your yard, through your mom's rose garden, over the fence, and across the back alley."

Quentin leaned out the window. "It was interesting watching Chipper make up his mind," he said. "He looked at the open window for a long time before he decided to go off on his escapade."

"Why didn't you stop him?" I demanded.

"I felt a certain mammalian connection with his desire for freedom," Quentin replied archly.

At that moment, I felt a certain mammalian desire to kick Quentin in the seat of his pants, but what was done was done. There was a creek between the back alley and the mountain. I had a rush of hope. *Maybe that would stop Chipper!* I ducked back into the window, and all the boys followed me as I ran down the stairs and through the front door to avoid Mom in the kitchen. I didn't have any shoes on and I got my socks wet running through the snow in the yard, but I didn't care. Retrieving our shoes on the back stoop, we ran across the back alley. I spotted Chipper up a tree that leaned over the creek. There was another tree on the opposite side that was leaning toward it, making sort of a natural limb bridge. "Roy Lee, get on the other side," I said. "We've got to keep him from jumping across."

"Right!" Roy Lee hopped across the creek from rock to rock. He'd just reached the far bank when Chipper made a big leap across from one tree to the other. Then he jumped to another tree and then another and kept going up the mountain until I couldn't see him anymore.

"He is joining his fellows up there," Quentin said admiringly. Then, as ever, he turned the moment into an intellectual exercise. "I wonder what more than one squirrel is called? For instance, more than one cat is a clowder. Then there's a murder of crows, and also an exaltation of larks."

"It's a disaster of squirrels, thanks to you and Roy Lee," I growled before inviting Quentin to shut up. I was feeling a knot forming in my stomach. Even though he had a brain about as big as a pea, Chipper was part of our family and Mom surely loved him as much as she loved anything in the world. I had no choice but to carry the unhappy news to her.

"Do you want us to go with you?" Roy Lee asked in a tone of voice that clearly hoped for a negative reply.

I didn't see any reason for it. Roy Lee had let Chipper out, but I was the one who was going to get the blame. I figured I might as well get it over with. The BCMA meeting was called off on account of disaster, the boys scattering. I trudged alone up the back porch steps and into the kitchen, found Mom working on her mural, and confessed the entire thing.

"Where did he go?" Mom cried.

I told her and Mom threw her brush down and, coatless, ran outside and across the back alley to the creek. I slogged along behind. "Chipper!" she yelled up into the woods. The woods remained silent. "Why is it," she demanded, "I can't have at least one thing in my house I love?" She made no attempt to wipe away the tear that followed. She wanted me to see her misery, I guess. "He's got no nest. He'll die up there, cold as it is." She turned on me. "You've killed my squirrel!"

I stammered an apology, but she abruptly held up her hand. "Don't bother. I've heard it all before." She wrapped her arms around herself and stalked back to the house.

I had no coat on and my feet were wet, but I splashed through the creek and scrambled up into the snowy woods. I was going to climb every tree in the woods if that was what it took to find Chipper and bring him home. It was a fool's errand, but I was a fool and it was fine by me. I thought I heard, way up on the mountain ridge, a mocking chirp.

It was past dark when I came back down the mountain, defeated and chilled to the bone. Mom had retreated to her room. Dad was still at the mine. The cats and dogs were in the basement, huddled near the furnace. I sat alone in the empty, dead living room. Without Chipper in the house, it seemed suddenly larger and colder. I got up and went out on the Captain's porch and stared for the longest time at Chipper's wheel. It made me think of Reverend Richard's story of the potter and the wheel, but it gave me no comfort. Not much did these days, it seemed. I allowed myself a little self-pity and it felt pretty good. I thought to myself: *I guess that's why some people get so addicted to it.* I couldn't do it for long, though. Self-pity wasn't going to get Chipper back. For that, I needed a miracle.

12

JAKE'S PRESENT

THE MIRACLE I hoped for that would quickly bring Chipper home didn't happen. Instead, as Thanksgiving approached, a bitter cold wind came sweeping down on us out of the north, bringing with it an accumulation of ice and snow on the mountains that made it even more unlikely that he had survived. O'Dell said a squirrel that hadn't hidden itself a cache of nuts would starve pretty quickly in the winter, especially when there was a lot of snow. Still, I kept looking. As soon as I got home from school every evening, I climbed the mountain and searched, calling out Chipper's name and peering into the trees. I spotted a skinny squirrel or two, but they all had full tails. I came across a doe once, too, and wondered if it was one of the deer I'd seen at the filling station. It looked at me and took off. It was so thin I was sorry to make it work so hard to run away.

For a while, I reported my lack of progress on finding Chipper to Mom, and every time she said nearly the same thing in response. "Chipper was raised in the house, Sonny. Likely he didn't even make it through the first night without a nest to sleep in. I miss him, I surely do, but he's gone. You don't have to look for him anymore." She had put his things up. His wheel was in the basement. I could see it when I came down to work on my rockets, a constant reminder of how I'd messed up.

"How about we trap her another squirrel?" O'Dell suggested when I asked him what I should do.

"She doesn't want another squirrel," I said. "She wants Chipper."

He shrugged. "You know, I never could figure out how he survived in a house full of cats, anyway."

Neither did I, exactly, other than he was one blamed lucky squirrel. He'd used to be, anyway. It looked like he'd finally run out his streak.

OF all the problems that had so far arrived in a season of problems, none surprised me more than the one that arrived at a Monday-night supper table. That was when Mom chose to make an announcement: "I'm going to go to Myrtle Beach this Christmas," she said.

Dad held his spoonful of beans in midair. "What are you talking about, Elsie?"

"Mr. Peabody says I can work real estate with him and his wife. It's one of their busiest seasons and they can use all the help they can get. I'll stay in a room in the back of their place. I'll just be gone for a week. You'll hardly miss me."

Dad put his spoon down and seemed to organize his response. "Elsie, I forbid it."

Mom's eyebrows lifted. "Forbid?"

"You know what I mean," Dad said, rapidly backpedaling. "You can't be gone at Christmas. The family is supposed to be together." Dad gave me a hard look. "Isn't that right, Sonny?"

I looked back in surprise. Why was he dragging me into their argument? I was just trying to eat my supper.

He shifted his gaze back to Mom. "Wait a minute. Is this because of that blamed squirrel?" I kept my mouth shut. Silence is the best defense of the guilty, I reasoned.

"It has nothing to do with Chipper," Mom said, the corners of her mouth turned down. "Well, maybe. But that was just the final straw." She gave me a look and I slid down in my chair. I eyed the basement door with longing. If I jumped up and ran for it, I could be through it before they could stop me. It was an idle thought, but I think Mom caught me at it. She shook her head at me and then went back after Dad.

"The fact is I'm going, Homer, and I've got good cause, the same one I've been harping about ever since they found that spot on your lungs. When Coalwood finally knocks you down so far you can't get up again, I'm going to know how to do real estate and have us a place where we can go."

Dad looked at his plate and then picked up his spoon again. He shoveled his beans into his mouth and sat there, thoughtfully chewing. "For better or for worse," he said finally.

Tears had formed, despite herself, and she wiped them with the back of her hand. "Your better, my worse," Mom said, and the conversation was done. She left the table.

Dad pondered me and I wilted under his eyes. "Dad, I'm making all A's this semester," I said. It was a preemptive strike to avoid him talking about how I'd lost Chipper.

"Are you taking easy subjects?" he asked.

"Yes, sir," I said. "Every one of them is a snap."

He nodded and went back to eating. I felt like I'd been kicked in the stomach. I couldn't wait to put this one down on my list. But when I got to it, I was stumped. What was I to write? I finally settled on *Making straight A's*. I also remembered to add *Mom going to Myrtle Beach*. If this kept up, I was going to need another sheet of paper.

ALTHOUGH nobody talked to me directly about it, seeing as how I was who I was, I kept hearing snippets of conversations on the school bus from students whose fathers were working in 11 East. The Germans were in there doing something with their machinery, but nobody knew what. One Coalwood crew was trying to get through a big rock header while two other crews were driving entries into the coal on either side of it. Nobody could figure out why that was being done, even the men who were doing it. Every day there were fence-line bulletins about something bad that had happened on 11 East—rockfalls, trams jumping the track, seeping methane, even flooding. The pumps had failed once, O'Dell's cousin Jackie Carroll said, and men were up to their knees in cold black water within minutes. They'd been lucky they hadn't drowned. Roy Lee confirmed all the stories. His coal miner brother kept him apprised.

I could easily pick out 11 East men when I saw them walking down the road after work. Instead of being black with coal dust, they were brown, coated with the powder from the rock they were trying to batter through. When we passed the tipple in the morning on the school bus, nearly everybody cast a worried glance in its direction. Our driver, Jack Martin, tooted the horn, but only a few miners raised their hands in greeting. They looked as if they were about to go to war, and I guess, in a way, they were. The shaft's mouth lay yawning before them, a column of dirty mist rising from it. It was as if 11 East was a black-hearted dragon, ready to swallow them.

I couldn't escape 11 East even at Dr. Hale's office when I went to get my teeth cleaned. Coalwood's dandy dentist had just spent a week playing golf in Florida and, to celebrate it, was still wearing his golf duds at the office. He was a sight in a pair of knee-length knickerbockers, gaudy plaid knee-high socks, white shirt, black bow tie, and a slouchy hat. He was, as my mom would say, the cat's meow. "So, Sonny," he said as he probed my teeth with his cold steel implements, "what's the news on 11 East?"

With my mouth wide open and filled with his hands and dental gear, the best I could do was make a noise that had the cadence of "I don't know." It made him laugh.

One night, I was in the living room reading when I heard Dad talking on the black phone about how the evening and hoot-owl shifts on 11 East were "dragging their feet." I listened up, hoping for some details, but none came. Then Ted Keneda, the husband of Mom's best friend, was taken off the day shift and put on the evening shift so he could work the section. "Naomi wants Ted back on the day shift," Mom reported to Dad at the supper table.

"She's mad at you and she's mad at me about it and I don't much blame her. Ted worked hard to get that day-shift position."

Dad was silent for a moment. I think he was thinking about not saying anything, but then he apparently thought better of it. "Ted's one of my best foremen," he said softly. "I need him where I put him. He hasn't complained."

"Naomi's my friend, Homer," Mom replied. "As you know, I have precious few."

Dad chewed on a chicken leg for a little while and then said, "Ted will be back on his old section next week."

Mom gave him a nearly imperceptible nod and then looked over the lip of her coffee cup at the bird feeder in the window behind me. "The birds sure are hungry," she said, deftly changing the subject, since she had gotten what she wanted. I admired her technique. "I can't keep enough seeds in the pan."

"The deer are hungry, too," Dad replied, obviously just as pleased to talk about something else. "There was a buck, some does, and a couple of fawns in the tipple yard yesterday. They were pretty skinny so I heard."

I remembered the deer I'd seen out my window over by the filling station. I wondered if it was the same bunch. "What happened to them?" I asked Dad.

He shrugged. "I had them chased off the grounds. I guess they went back up in the mountains."

"Couldn't you feed them?" I wondered.

"I should have had them shot," Dad said without hesitation. "They don't have enough to eat up in the mountains this year. I guess because it's been so cold. The hunters say the hunting season was too short so there's too many of them, too. It wouldn't be right to feed them, Sonny. The strong will get through. The rest won't. That's nature's way."

Dad's answer didn't sit well with me. I thought somebody ought to come up with a plan to get more for the deer to eat. It wasn't the first time my ideas conflicted with the natural order of things and I guessed it wouldn't be the last. It wasn't nature's way to blast rockets off into the sky, either.

———

THEN it happened, what everybody feared: Somebody got hurt on 11 East. I saw the ambulance at the man-hoist when I came home from school. Mr. Sheets, a member of the header crew, had an arm broken by a rock that had slipped out from beneath a roof bolt. The next day, Mr. Crow snapped his ankle getting out of the way of more falling rock. The black phone rang constantly, and Dad kept yelling into it and then grabbing his hat and coat and heading up to the mine. Sherman told me on the school bus that he'd heard that the union was writing up all the articles it would need to call a general strike because of the "unsafe working conditions" on 11 East. Mom would make no comment on 11 East except to say, "One part of that old mine is as bad as another."

I'D had my share of problems with the Mallett boys, the sons of Leo and Cleo Mallett, over the years, especially during strikes. There were three brothers, Rodney and Siebert, both overgrown brutes, and little Germy. Germy's real name was Jeremy but it had always been pronounced Germy. The nickname suited him. Germy was too little to try to beat me up over 11 East, but he could throw a mean rock. He caught me on a Saturday just after I'd gotten a haircut in the little shop behind the post office. "Hey boss's boy," he squeaked. "You think you're a big shot, don't you? Your old man's stupid going down 11 East!"

When I ignored him and started to get on my bike, he threw his rock. He was a good pitcher, and it hit me square in the back. It hurt and I knew I was going to have a bruise. I decided to teach the little rat a lesson. Germy took off running, and I dropped my bike and went running after him. He ran up the alley beside the creek, cut through Buford Manning's yard, and then into a group of boys playing touch football on the road between the Community Church and the Club House. Rodney and Siebert were among them. Germy went screaming to them and pointed back at me. "He slugged me, boss's boy did!"

I skidded to a halt. "Germy hit me with a rock," I said.

Rodney and Siebert both looked at each other and then plodded in my direction, their hands balled into fists. They were vocational-school boys and had arms the size of telephone poles. I stood my ground. If I was going to get pounded, I'd get in a few punches of my own, but there was no way I was going to run from a Mallett or even a trio of them.

"You need some help?" a familiar voice asked behind me.

I couldn't believe my ears. "Jake!"

Jake Mosby had on a suit and a tie, so I guessed he'd just arrived in town. I looked past him and there it was, his bright cherry-red Corvette. It was the most wonderful car I'd ever seen in my life because it had brought Jake back to Coalwood.

The two Mallett hulks stopped. Siebert managed a thought. "His daddy's gonna kill our daddy down 11 East." His tiny eyes were nearly crossed he was concentrating so hard.

"What are you doing here?" I asked Jake. "Are you back to stay?"

Jake took off his suit jacket and pitched it down on the sidewalk. "For now, anyway. You know your dad couldn't run that mine without me. You ready to take these two on?"

"No. I'm going to get destroyed, but what else is new?" I pointed at Siebert. "One at a time," I said. "You're chicken if both of you come at me at once."

"We ain't fightin'," Siebert said, suddenly abashed. Seeing Jake beside me, even if I wouldn't let him help, had taken the fight out of him. I knew from the start neither boy really wanted to fight, anyway. I'd been attacked by enough union boys over the years to be able to see the glint in their eyes when they were really after me. Jake had given Rodney and Siebert the excuse they wanted. They went back to their football game, but I noticed Rodney give Germy a cuff on the side of the head and he went off bawling toward home.

I helped Jake carry his luggage up to his old room in the Club House and then filled him in on all the news I could think of. He sat on the edge of the bed and sipped from a hip flask and listened. Then he said, "To tell you the truth, I'm back in Coalwood to look over your dad's shoulder."

"Because of 11 East?" I asked.

Jake smiled. "So how's Miss Riley?" he asked.

Miss Riley was fine, or nearly so. It seemed to me that she looked tired these days, or maybe like she was fighting off something.

I reported what I noticed about Miss Riley, and Jake frowned. "Has there ever been a better looking, smarter, and nicer woman than Freida Riley?" he asked rhetorically.

I didn't guess there had. I thought to stir the pot a bit. "I think she'd like to see you, Jake." They'd dated a few times before Jake had gone back to Ohio. But Jake was known for his high-living ways, where Miss Riley was quiet and respectable. They seemed to be too different to enjoy each other's company but apparently they had, at least for a while.

"I'd like to see her, too," Jake said. "Tell her I'm back, will you?"

I promised I would.

Jake opened his suitcase and drew out a small package. "I got this present for you."

I took it from him. It was wrapped in brown paper. There wasn't a bow or ribbon or anything on it, but it didn't matter. I wasn't used to getting presents. "Thanks, Jake!"

"Go ahead, open it."

I pulled the paper off. It was a book titled *A Complete Guide to the Heavens*. On its cover was a drawing of a spiral galaxy and also Saturn with its big rings. "Wow" was all I could say.

"You been using my telescope?"

"Every chance I get."

He took a long drag off his flask and whistled out a breath. "This will help you figure out what you're looking at."

"This is great, Jake. I'll study up on it." I just had to add: "I'm getting all A's in my classes so far this semester."

He perked up. "Are you now?" He stuck out his hand. "Shake, you bastard. Attaboy!"

I shook his hand and basked in his glow.

————

BEING around Jake always gave me a sense of optimism. That night, I looked over my list of problems. Now that Jake had put me in a happier state of mind, the last item, *Mom going to Myrtle Beach,* could be pretty easily fixed, I thought. I resolved myself to it, prepared myself a little argument in my mind, and went looking for her. I found her at the kitchen table with a self-teaching real estate book. "Mom, here's the situation," I said cheerfully. "You're right and I'm wrong—about everything. Therefore, I've decided I'll help you with the Christmas Pageant." I laid a big satisfied grin on her like ol' Dr. Sonny had arrived with the cure.

She looked up from her book and regarded me through narrowed eyes. "Didn't you hear me when I said I was going to Myrtle Beach for Christmas?"

It was exactly what I thought she'd say. It was time for part two of my argument. "Yes, ma'am, I sure did, but here's the thing. You said you didn't want to be remembered for losing the float contest and then not putting on the pageant. So, see, you can't go to Myrtle Beach. You've got to put on the pageant. Just tell me what you want me to do first."

She shook her head. "When I said that, I meant it. But I've changed my mind. It's too late."

"No, it's not!" I exclaimed. My cocky grin evaporated. "Come on. Think up something for me to do. I'll get right on it!"

She tapped her book as I had done when she'd come up to my room asking for my help. "I'll be in Myrtle Beach. If there's a Christmas Pageant, I guess it will be put on by Cleo Mallett and her bunch."

She was referring to the new women's organization in town. For some time, Mrs. Mallett had attempted to organize a rival club to the Coalwood Women's Club but got few takers. After the Veterans Day float debacle, she saw her opening and announced the Coalwood Organization of Women was hereby established. Roy Lee was the first to note that its initials pretty much described its membership.

My logical attack on Mom's unhappy mood had been repulsed,

so I did the only thing I could do. I launched an illogical counter-attack. "Come on, Mom," I said. "You can't go to Myrtle Beach for Christmas. You just can't!"

"Oh, yes, I can," she said firmly. "Anyway, why do you care if I'm here or not? You don't much like Christmas. That's what you said. Don't you remember?"

She had me there. I'd dug myself a hole and crawled right into it. My mom wasn't above throwing a shovelful of dirt in behind me, either. I slunk off. I had been so confident, I'd already crossed *Mom going to Myrtle Beach* off my list. Now I had to add it again.

MISS Riley called me up to her desk after physics class a couple of days after Jake returned. She waved my most recent test under my nose. It had a big red 86 circled on it. "You've got an A going in this class but you're not going to keep it with this kind of work, Sonny. Why didn't you do better?"

"Because your test was too hard?" I guessed.

Miss Riley leaned her head on her hand, out of fatigue or exasperation, I wasn't sure. "Wrong answer. Because you didn't study hard enough or studied the wrong thing. Look here." She held up a test with a 96 in a circle. It was O'Dell's. "You can do as well as O'Dell, of that I'm certain."

She hadn't shown me Quentin's test or Billy Rose's, either. I figured they'd each made a hundred. I guess she didn't want me aiming too high. "What did Sherman make?" I asked.

"A ninety-eight."

"How about Roy Lee?"

Miss Riley sighed. "You and Roy Lee have the same tendency to let your minds wander in class. You, I suspect, are dreaming of your rockets. Roy Lee's mind doesn't much travel past the first pretty girl it lights on. I also plan on having a little talk with him."

"I'll do better."

"See that you do. Are you going to enter the science fair this spring?"

"Maybe."

"Quentin says you've been loitering." She eyed me speculatively. "That was his exact word. Loitering."

"I'll work harder."

"I suggest you do if you want to go to Cape Canaveral."

"I'm going there, Miss Riley."

She smiled. "I hope you'll have your old broken-down physics teacher come visit from time to time." She was, at the time, all of twenty-one years old. She looked past me, out the windows where there was nothing but gray skies. "I'd like to walk on the beach, be in the sun a bit."

"Yes, ma'am. You're invited anytime."

"I count on you, Sonny." She held up my test again. "Do better. Work harder."

"Yes, ma'am. Do you want to see a present I got?"

"Sure."

I showed her my book on the stars and planets. "Jake gave it to me. He's back. He said to tell you hello."

She lifted her head and her eyes sparkled. "Did he now? Well, please give Mr. Mosby my regards and remind him that I suspect he still knows where I live."

I promised her that I would. She looked happier than I'd seen her in weeks.

13

JIM'S DECISION

BIG CREEK'S PRINCIPAL, Mr. R. L. Turner, accosted me in the hall the day before Thanksgiving while I was on my way to class.

"Wait up, Mr. Hickam," he said from the door of his office. As he walked toward me, the sea of students in the hall parted like the Red Sea before Moses. "Did I hear correctly that you boys have recently put up a rocket as high as a mile?" he asked.

Nervously, I considered my possible responses and lit on honesty. "That's true, sir," I said, one foot sliding down the hall in case I needed to make a run for it. "We did it last summer."

"And how did you measure the altitude of this device?" Mr. Turner asked dubiously, his eyes narrowing.

"We used trigonometry, sir. We built two of what Quentin calls theodolites to determine the angles."

His eyebrows turned down into a V. "But you didn't start trigonometry classes until this fall," he pointed out.

"We taught trig to ourselves," I said. I barely managed to keep from sounding puffed up.

Mr. Turner studied me for a period of time that seemed to last about a century. "I'm impressed by your tenacity," he finally allowed, "even though you boys still strike me as little better than a demolition squad." He pursed his lips. "Why don't we visit for a minute in my office, hmm?"

I followed, certain that I was doomed in some way. He sat at his desk but didn't invite me to sit in one of his chairs. "What I want to know from you, Mr. Hickam, is why Billy Rose is quitting school and joining the navy?" I think my face told him my astonishment. "Mr. Rose is a member of your, ah, group, is he not?"

"Y-yes, sir," I stammered, "but I don't know anything about this!"

Frowning deeply, he drummed his fingers on his desk. "You know, Mr. Hickam, a man should take care to observe his friends lest they be needful."

I just stood there, trying to keep my mouth closed.

"This is to go no further," he said, pressing his index finger down on the desk to indicate he meant nowhere outside his office.

"Yes, sir," I said, and left at his curt dismissal. That evening, I surreptitiously watched Billy sitting up front on the school bus. I ached to find out everything that he planned, but I was boxed in by my promise to Mr. Turner. He'd said not to talk to anybody about Billy quitting school, and I guessed that included Billy. I cast around for another way to satisfy my curiosity. Then I had it! I would talk to O'Dell. O'Dell was as close to Billy as anybody. He'd know all about Billy's plans. And O'Dell could no more keep a secret than a cat in a sack. I'd figure out a way to steer the conversation to Billy with O'Dell and he'd tell me everything. I mentally patted myself on my back. I could get pretty clever when I had to. I figured to put *Billy* on my list that very night. I figured to, but the truth is I forgot.

To celebrate Thanksgiving, the War Grade School class came and played Pilgrims and Indians for the Big Creek High School assembly. My former beloved Dorothy Plunk sat two rows down and three to the right of me. She was sporting a poodle skirt and a tight blue sweater with a white collar and was also wearing her hair in a new style, her usual ponytail traded in for a long Veronica Lake look. Her lipstick was a new shade of pink, too. Not that I noticed, of course. She looked over her shoulder when she sat down and gave me a friendly smile. I studied the air above her. She tried to catch my eye again when we all stood to sing "My Country 'Tis of Thee," but I pretended I was too busy singing to pay any note. I thought it was interesting that we had stolen the music from England's "God Save the Queen" for our own patriotic hymn, so I sang extra loud. If Dorothy heard me, I guess I couldn't help it. "Gol, boy," O'Dell, who was sitting beside me, complained. "You couldn't carry a tune in a bucket." Then he said, "You want to come ride the ponies this weekend?" O'Dell was talking about the ponies his dad kept in the barn behind their house. I agreed. It would also give me a chance to ask him about Billy.

After the program, I watched Dorothy out of the corner of my eye as a couple of boys escorted her up the aisle. She gaily chatted with them, then giggled when one of them whispered something in her ear. I figured she would have laughed harder if she hadn't been so worried about me ignoring her. Roy Lee caught me at it. "Mooning over Dorothy," he accused, clucking his tongue. Then he said, "Melba June Monroe."

Roy Lee pointed her out as she went up the aisle, her bottom sashaying within a tight navy-blue skirt. She had lots of curves, all in the right places, and she was fine, indeed. He raised his eyebrows at me. "Sonny, there are girls and then there are girls. But that girl there is a woman! Don't ever get them confused. A woman can teach you things you can't even imagine."

I admired Melba June a little longer, and he nodded approvingly. "She'll go with you to the Christmas Formal if you ask her."

"How do you know?"

Roy Lee leaned in close. "Because I'm the Big Creek lovemaster, boy. Do I have to keep explaining that to you?"

I spotted Ginger going up the aisle. She gave me a shy smile and said "hi" with her lips, then kept on going. I made up my mind. "Well, Mr. Big Creek lovemaster, I thank you for all your help but I'm going to ask Ginger to the Christmas Formal and that's it."

Roy Lee let out a long, exasperated breath. "Why I even bother with you is beyond me."

"Well, it's beyond me, too, Roy Lee," I said.

He shook his head. "I'm telling you those Cape Canaveral women are going to put you through the grinder. Melba June is the only chance you've got to practice up."

I ignored him and wormed my way through the other students to catch up with Ginger. When I couldn't find her, I figured to see her on the school bus. To my disappointment, she wasn't there. I squirmed my way through the other students so I could sit beside Betty Jane Laphew, one of Ginger's sophomore friends. About halfway across War Mountain, I finally got up the nerve to ask her why Ginger wasn't on the bus. "She's going with her mother to New York," Betty Jane said. "She's visiting Juilliard's." When I looked blank, she said, "The music school. She's thinking about going there."

"Oh," I said, disappointed that I had missed her and that she was going to be gone for so long.

Betty Jane appraised me. My disappointment must have been transparent because she said, "Cheer up. Ginger likes you."

"She does?"

"Well, I definitely remember just the other day she said she thought you were pretty cute. Do you like her?"

Betty Jane had put the question to me plain and simple. Whatever I said in reply, no matter what it was, would get back to Ginger the next time the two girls were together. I was trapped. The answer I wanted to give stuck in my throat. "She's okay," I said, shrugging with feigned disinterest.

"She'll be thrilled to hear of your high opinion," Betty Jane said sarcastically, and left it at that. I felt pretty much like a flat tire.

WHEN I got home, I discovered my brother Jim was there, come home from college. I spied his bulk as soon as I came through the front gate, mainly because he was standing at the glass storm door and had to move out of the way to let me through. We didn't speak, just gave each other the eye. I thought he looked tired. When I got to the top of the steps, I turned around, having thought of a zinger to aim at him. I was far enough away to keep him from grabbing me. "So what's it like to be a Hokie?" I was going to ask, that being the nickname for students at the Virginia Polytechnic Institute where Jim had gone to play football. It was a funny name and I figured to get a rise out of him about it. But I never asked my question because all of a sudden I was worried about him. I didn't know why but I was. There was something not right about him. He kept staring through the storm door. There wasn't anything to see outside except the street and the mountain that rose above it. He seemed to be just soaking Coalwood in. Then I dismissed the idea. He was a college boy, gone to the great world beyond. Why would he care about this old place?

That night, Jim borrowed the Buick, bound for an unknown destination and an unknown purpose. At least, they were unknown to me. I suppose he had confided his plans to Mom. As always, he was splendidly dressed. His pants were draped and pegged, his shirt crisp, pressed, and pink, his sweater white, fluffy, and cashmere. His penny loafers gleamed. I could smell the cologne on him as he went past my room after a considerable time in the bathroom. I figured he had himself a new girlfriend. Curious as to where he was headed, I looked through my room window and watched him drive the Buick past the tipple, heading toward Coalwood Mountain. There were a lot of towns on the other side of that mountain, any of which could contain a new girlfriend for Jim. I tried not to be jealous but I was. I just couldn't figure out why Jim had such an easy time with the girls. True, he was a smooth talker, and he usually had a little money in his pocket. He also had ready access to a car and dressed better than Elvis Presley. He was also handsome, in a square-jawed, blond-hair, blue-eyed sort of way, and I guess it was fair to say he had himself a pretty bright future with his college scholarship and all. Otherwise, I couldn't imagine the attraction.

While I was puzzling over Jim, I saw Dad coming down the path from the mine. By the way he had his shoulders hunched, I could tell he wasn't happy. As soon as he got home, he looked for Mom, finding her on the Captain's porch with her real estate book.

I came down the steps to hear what he had to say. Orders had come from the steel company to cut off twelve men, he told her, and he had done it as always, calling the chosen men aside as they came off the lift after their shift. Dad was a bit shaken by what had happened. One of the men, he said, had cried. "I never had a man cry on me before, Elsie," he said plaintively. "He told me about his baby. What was I supposed to do about his baby?"

Mom listened, but there was little she could say and nothing she could do. A dozen more Coalwood men and their families were without jobs on this, our Thanksgiving Day.

JIM ate Thanksgiving dinner like he'd been starving for a month. Mom wasn't known for her fine cooking skills. In fact, if I'd made a list of the best cooks in town, Mom wouldn't have even been in the top ten. Sherman's mom would have been number one. Not that Mom wasn't pretty good at the basics—fried chicken, mashed potatoes, potato cakes, pork chops, brown beans, biscuits, and corn bread. And she didn't do too bad with the turkey she fixed every Thanksgiving, either. Jim devoured everything he could reach. Mom kept sliding the dishes and bowls in his direction.

We were eating at Mom's prized cherry wood dining room table. Jim and I had had a fight a few years before and had used one of her chairs to hit each other until we'd managed to break off a leg. We had glued it back, and as far as I knew, Mom never found out. I picked that chair as I always did when we ate in the dining room at Thanksgiving and Christmas. I eased myself in and out of it, testing its strength. Mom looked at me one time and said, "You'd think you were *glued* to that chair or something, Sonny." I was not certain if that meant she knew of its past or not, but I made no response. Red Carroll used to say never wake a dog up unless you wanted to get bit.

Mom had set a good table, putting on a lacy tablecloth and cloth napkins. She'd gotten out the real silverware (a carving knife had a navy insignia on it, I noted) and the fancy china that usually hid in the hutch cabinet. When she was getting the finery out, she discovered Chipper had chewed a hole in the base of the cabinet and used her prized mahogany napkin rings for teething rings. She went down in her mouth when she saw them. "Poor little boy," she said, holding the mangled rings in her hand. "He had to work so hard to keep his teeth pared down."

"But you loved those napkin rings," I said.

"This is Chipper I'm talking about," she answered forlornly. "You know, my squirrel you killed."

"Roy Lee let him out."

"It was your responsibility."

She had me there.

She had cooked a good turkey, too, although she had to use her old oven when her new turkey roaster had failed her, not even coming on when she plugged it in. Of course, I knew the reason for that was because its electrical guts were down at Cape Coalwood in our rocket-ignition system. She didn't ask me about it, so I just played dumb. Did failure to volunteer information count as a lie? I didn't think it did even though I wouldn't have wanted to put that question to a preacher. It was my experience that preachers could get snagged on the details and miss the big picture entirely.

I watched Jim out of the corner of my eye, astonished at the amount of food he was packing away. There was something strange going on with him, but I couldn't imagine what it might be. During Jim's years in high school, the supper-table conversation was usually dominated by Dad and Jim talking football. Dad kept looking Jim's way but kept his peace. Finally, unable to stand the silence a moment longer, I lobbed in a question, figuring to stir things up. "So are you going to be on first string next year?" I asked Jim, as innocently as you please.

Jim chose to ignore my question—it was only me asking, after all—and just kept silently eating everything but the tablecloth. But my words were still hanging in the air, accomplishing their purpose. "Do you think you'll play, Jim?" Dad asked. I felt the contentment of the natural-born agitator.

Jim took a big swig of iced tea. He looked down at his plate. "I could," he allowed, and then scooped up a mound of peas on his fork. I pushed the pea bowl closer to him. I thought to save time maybe he should just eat right out of it.

Dad frowned. "Well, what does Coach Claiborne say?"

Jim hunched his shoulders. "He doesn't say much."

"Will you play offense or defense?"

Jim stabbed a slice of turkey. "I played mostly defense on the freshman team," he said.

"So you're going to be a defensive lineman," Dad said. "You'll be the best one VPI ever had."

Mom shifted in her chair, giving me a look I couldn't decipher. Then the black phone rang and Dad went after it, his napkin barely hitting the chair before he had the receiver in his hand even though the telephone stand was twenty feet away. "Keep going!" he said after a moment of listening.

"Can't you ever do anything without stirring up trouble?" Mom hissed in my direction. The doorbell rang while I puzzled over her accusation. Mom went to answer it, and Jim threw down his napkin and got up, following her. I just sat there, mystified. Me? Stirring up trouble?

It was Woodrow and Mildred Duncan. Woodrow was the town plumber, and he and Mildred had always been good friends of my parents. For some reason, they were about the only adults I could call by their first names. Mildred was an energetic woman, always with tales to tell. "Gawdalmighty, Woodrow, looky here!" she declared when she saw Jim. She grabbed Jim around the waist. "Jimmie Hickam, ain't you turned into a good-looking man! That college food been going to all the right places!"

Jim said a few words to them and then excused himself to go up to his room. This was no surprise. Jim wasn't much for socializing with people who came to the house. His attitude always disappointed Dad. I suspected he liked to show Jim off. I went in to see the Duncans, offering myself as a consolation prize. Mildred patted me on the cheek, and Woodrow gave me a friendly grin, but I was otherwise of little interest to them. I guess they already knew all there was to know about me.

After the Duncans had finished their visit and gone, and after I had silently helped Mom clear the table, my curiosity got the best of me. I knocked once on Jim's door and then cracked it open. "What's with you?" I said straight out.

Jim was sitting on his bed. He'd put on his green Big Creek letter sweater. "Go away," he grunted.

I brazenly stepped in and closed the door behind me. "There's something going on with you. What is it?"

Jim looked at the mirror on his wall. It was a full-length mirror, but since he'd gone away, Mom had moved a storage cabinet in and blocked the bottom half of it. If he needed it, it was a reminder that it wasn't completely his room anymore. I had a flash of intuition. "Are you homesick?"

"I'm leaving college," he said.

I was so thunderstruck by Jim's announcement that it took a moment before my brain could begin its usual sifting. How could Jim leave VPI? He had a football scholarship, the one thing Dad was forever bragging about. Then I thought, *Dad doesn't know.* "Why are you leaving college?" I asked, striving to keep my voice casual. I sensed if I pushed too hard, Jim would clam up.

To my surprise, he seemed eager to talk. "Because it's too big," he said.

"But you said you wanted to go to a big school," I said, remembering back to when all the colleges had tried to recruit him.

He shrugged. "Well, I was wrong. In a big school, the coaches don't pay much attention to you. They just use you. I need to go somewhere where the coaches take care of their players, teach them stuff."

"Where would that be?" I wondered.

I had never seen him so talkative, at least to me. "When we played Wake Forest, I met their freshman coach, Beattie Feathers. He told me I was good enough to play pro ball but only if I got the right kind of coaching. He said if I transferred down there, he'd make sure I got it. So that's where I'm going. Wake Forest. I'll have to go out as a walk-on, but I know I can make their team, no sweat."

I didn't know who Beattie Feathers was and I didn't care.

"You're going to lose your scholarship," I said, surprised that it bothered me. I guess, deep down, I'd been a little proud of Jim's scholarship, too.

Jim just looked at me, and for the first time in the history of my entire life, I almost felt sorry for him. It was a novel emotion, not entirely unpleasant, although I didn't much think it would last. "When are you going to tell Dad?" I asked.

I had landed on a tough question. He looked away. "Soon."

As I had predicted to myself not more than a few seconds before, my sympathy for my brother wafted away to be replaced by a sense of satisfaction over the entire matter. All that bragging Dad had done over the years about Jim and none about me was going to come back at both of them now. "Dad's going to have a cow," I said. And then, even though I wished I could have avoided it, I smirked. "You're going to finally know how it feels."

A crack like that was usually enough to make Jim jump up and try to break my neck. I tensed, ready for action, but he just sat there, looking vulnerable. I couldn't stand it. I was back to feeling sorry for him again. I wanted my big brother back, no matter how obnoxious he was!

"Just go away, Sonny," Jim said miserably.

I moved my hands around in little mixing motions like I was going to box with him, but it did no good. Jim just wasn't interested in fighting with me. He was through talking to me, too. I gave up and went to my room. Mom soon visited me. She opened the door. "Leave your brother alone," she said. Then she closed the door. A second later, she opened it again. "And I want my turkey roaster operational in one week." She closed the door again.

After she left, I got my list out. *Jim quitting college,* I wrote. Then I wrote, *Fix Mom's turkey roaster.* I contemplated that one and then crossed it out. I figured Mom would forget her roaster until she needed to cook another turkey. I didn't see that happening real soon.

1 4

SNAKEROOT HOLLOW

WE FLEW *Auk XXIII* the weekend after Thanksgiving using a De Laval nozzle based on the calculations Quentin and I had made. It didn't have a ceramic liner. Mr. Caton and I hadn't been able to figure out how to layer the water putty inside the nozzle. The problem was the stuff was sticky and tended to clump up. Mr. Caton tried using one of his wife's butter knives to smooth it, but it still made a mess. Nothing else he tried worked any better. Until we solved this problem, we would have to continue to use nozzles built of raw steel.

Since we wanted to see how well the new "scientific" De Laval nozzle worked, we decided to go ahead and test, putty or no putty. *Auk XXIII* tore off the pad, then streaked out of sight in a few seconds while we danced beneath it. As elated as I was at the success of the new nozzle, I was deflated when I figured out the rocket's altitude, much less than my calculations predicted. Our inspection revealed that nozzle erosion was even worse with the new design. Somehow, we had to get the putty to work.

"Sonny, you must pursue this!" Quentin moaned. "Tell me you will!" I told him I would, but I was discouraged. Maybe we just didn't have the knowledge to defeat erosion in our nozzles. That meant we would never have a "great" rocket. Since it was automatically scientific and logical by definition, I had resisted putting a rocket problem down on my list. I did now. *Erosion!* Maybe, I thought, I had a mental barrier to overcome before the solution for erosion could be found.

It would be December 7, 1959, Pearl Harbor Day, before I got to look through Jake's telescope again. Actually, I had hoped to see Jake at the Club House, but when I came down from the roof, Mrs. Davenport, the housekeeper, cook, and manager, informed me that he was rarely in his room. "The boy spends all his time up at the mine," she said. "I swear, Sonny, he's starting to act more like your daddy every day. I say that with no lack of respect for Homer, of course, but—say, why don't you just eat with us tonight? I'll call on the black phone, let your mom know where you are."

I thanked her and, after I heard what was on the menu, gratefully agreed. Mrs. Davenport made the best stuffed pork chops, mashed potatoes, and gravy in town. The Hickam kitchen table wasn't much fun these days, anyway. Dad was rarely home for supper and Mom didn't even bother to set a place for herself. I ate alone, mostly. Sometimes, against strict Elsie Hickam rules, I would let Daisy Mae get up on the table and eat her food out of a bowl while I ate. She loved being there. After she finished eating, she could crouch down and watch the birds at Mom's kitchen window feeder. I kept an ear cocked for Mom's footsteps. Cats didn't belong on the kitchen table in her universe. They could get up on the dining-room table and lounge around all day, but they were never, ever allowed on the kitchen table. It was just her way.

In the big, high-ceilinged dining room of the Club House, I sat down to a table of two junior engineers. I anticipated some entertaining conversation. Coalwood's junior engineers, sent down by the steel company to get a little seasoning, were usually an interesting bunch. Mom said their tour of duty in town was about the last time they would ever get to kick up their heels. After their excursion with us, she said, they had to go back to the steel company, get married, have children, learn the business of draining West Virginia of all our money, and never ever have any kind of fun again.

The way I heard it, Dad tried to keep them from having any fun in Coalwood, too. He made sure their initial week in Coalwood was hell. The first day in the mine for a junior engineer meant trudging behind Dad for miles under a low roof. That could kill even the youngest back. During the journey, Dad yelled out coal mining lore over the roar of machinery. They poked into every crevice in the mine. The first day usually lasted sixteen hours.

The next day he jolted their already sprained backs in his truck at breakneck speed over fire roads through the hollows, visiting every slack dump, ventilation hole, and fan that belonged to the company, all the while barraging them with facts and figures they were expected to repeat back to him anytime he asked. Another sixteen-hour day.

The third day was used to visit the preparation plant in Caretta, where the men who ran it gave the junior engineers a thorough description of everything they did. They were shown how to mix up the chemicals and "wash coal" to see how much rock was in it. If it floated in the solution, the coal was pure. If it sank, it had too much rock and was pushed to the side to be dumped at one of the slack dumps. Another two-shift day.

The next two days were spent in the offices with the engineers learning how the mine was laid out, how the maps were made, and something of continuous mining strategy. Dad picked them up as they came out of the office at the end of the day shift and sent them into the mine to follow a foreman around during the two night shifts. These were twenty-four-hour days.

By the weekend, a junior engineer was either going to stick it out or not. The ones that stayed had at least a chance of becoming decent mining engineers, and Dad farmed them out to his foremen to use as they saw fit. The ones who couldn't take it went back to Ohio with their tails well tucked. What happened to them, I didn't know. What does any engineer do who fails? Maybe they become lawyers.

I was jolted from my ponderings about the fate of junior engineers in general when I realized the two at the table were staring at me. One of them was named Rollie and the other was named

Frank. Coalwood gossip had informed me that Frank was an Ohio boy. He looked about my age but he had to be older, having graduated from college. Rollie was a big, heavyset young man, originally from Kentucky. He had round, rosy cheeks and an earnest look about him. I figured him for the type who'd break wind in a scout camp at night and think it was funny. I'd seen both of them around town, but they'd apparently missed my shining face.

"Which one of the Hickam boys are you?" Frank asked. Mrs. Davenport had apparently informed them that the boss's boy was going to be in attendance.

"I'm the one who plays football," I said smartly. "I'm just home from college to rest up for the day." Besides being clever with the junior engineer, I didn't "sir" him. Junior engineers didn't rate a "sir" from anybody in Coalwood, even me.

Frank looked at me and said, "Your father . . . your father . . ."

"I know," I said. "He's tough as a tank."

"He sure is," Rollie said, whistling. "I never seen a man move so fast in a crouch. That day I followed him around, I bumped my head on the roof so many times my ears didn't stop ringing for a week."

"You're not really the football player, are you?" Frank asked suspiciously.

Seeing as how I was only about five feet, nine inches tall, weighed on the light side of 140 pounds, and was wearing thick glasses, even a junior engineer could eventually put two and two together, given time. "No," I confessed. "I'm the Rocket Boy."

"I heard about that!" Frank cried. "Rollie and I would like to build rockets, too! Could you show us how?"

"That depends," I said. "How much money do you have?"

"We're pretty tapped out," Rollie said sadly. "We were at Cinder Bottom last weekend."

"Cinder Bottom" was the notorious row of houses of ill repute in the town of Keystone, four mountains away from Coalwood past Welch. Coalwood's junior engineers often made pilgrimages to see the girls there, or so I'd heard. I'd also heard that the women of Coalwood considered such sojourns a blessing and a protection to their daughters.

"Those sweeties sure know how to go through a wallet," Frank added, sounding every bit as remorseful as a drunk at a revival.

"Then I guess you're out of luck," I said. I was actually relieved. I didn't see either of these two nitwits as rocket builders.

Before we could discuss my dad, rockets, or fallen women anymore, we were joined by Gerhard and Dieter, obviously released from 11 East duty for the evening. I noted they wore the same garb as the junior engineers: khaki shirts and pants tucked into high-top brown lace-up hard-toe leather mining boots. I wondered if Dad had put them through his grueling school of mining, too. They looked tough enough to take it.

Mrs. Davenport, a plump and pleasant-faced widow, brought in plates of food, piping hot, and then bustled back into the kitchen for more. She was pretty much a one-woman show. It wasn't long before the four young men had piled up what looked like miniature Mount Everests of pork chops, potatoes, and green beans on their plates. I had created a little mound myself. During the whole time we were stacking up our plates, Frank couldn't keep his eyes off Gerhard and Dieter. "Well, boys," he said finally. "This is the first time I have had the pleasure of sharing supper with you. What brings you to this fair town, eh?"

"A contract," Dieter said, holding his knife in his right hand and his fork upside down in his left. I'd never seen the like but it seemed to work just fine. I watched as he cut a piece of pork chop and then jabbed the piece with his fork, ready for eating. His method looked efficient. I couldn't wait to try it out. I wondered if Quentin knew about it.

"A contract for what?" Frank asked suspiciously, gnawing on a pork chop bone. He wiped his greasy fingers on his pants.

"I think it more proper for the company to say," Dieter responded discreetly.

"Aw, Frank," Rollie said. "These two old boys been working down on 11 East. You know, where we ain't allowed to go." He eyed Gerhard. "Why ain't *you* talking?"

Dieter looked at Gerhard and shrugged. "His English is not so good," Dieter said.

"You boys ever get a chance to travel around the county, see the other sights?" Frank asked.

Dieter managed a curt *"Nein."*

Rollie raised his eyebrows and elbowed Frank. "So, I guess that means you've never been to Cinder Bottom, eh?"

Dieter took the bait. "What is Cinder Bottom?" he asked.

Frank and Rollie grinned. I allowed a smile myself. After looking around to make sure Mrs. Davenport wasn't in the room, Rollie enthusiastically described the houses in Keystone and their purpose while piling up more pork chops and mashed potatoes on his plate. He picked up a big serving bowl of thick, brown pork gravy, pondered the spoon in it, shrugged, and then tipped the whole bowl to pour a lake of gravy over everything. His plate almost brimmed over. "Frank and I would be happy to escort you boys over to the Bottom any old time," he said, his eyes sliding toward Frank, who gave him a surreptitious nod. "I don't think them girls would hold it against you much, you being foreigners and all. They might charge you a little bit more, that's all. Of course, what you might do is let us hold your money. Then we could make sure you didn't pay too much."

Dieter frowned. "We would give you our money?"

Frank leaned forward. His face had taken on a feral look. "Just to make sure you got a fair deal," he said wolfishly.

Dieter's frown went deeper. "We would give you our money?" It was as if he had to say it twice, the concept being so utterly alien to him. It was clear he hadn't been born yesterday. Frank and Rollie I wasn't so sure about.

Rollie put his hand on his cheek, as if he'd suddenly remembered something. "My God, boys. You know what? I'd almost forgotten. We got to celebrate today which, by God, is Pearl Harbor Day!"

"What is that?" Dieter politely questioned.

Rollie looked shocked, in a theatrical way. "Why, it's a celebration of when the damn Japs came over and bombed the hell out of us Americans, that's what!"

"You celebrate getting bombed?" Dieter asked.

Frank put in his two cents worth. "Hell yes, we do and we got to celebrate it in style! Why, it would be a crime to let it slide by without making some kind of fuss. We're all veterans at this table, ain't we? I, for instance, am a corporal in the Ohio National Guard."

Rollie stuck out his chest. "Two years in the University of Kentucky ROT and C."

"I never knew that, Rollie!" Frank exclaimed. "You're nearly an officer!"

Rollie looked embarrassed. "I got above average in leadership potential," he said modestly.

Frank took on the Germans. "How about you boys? You veterans?"

Dieter said something to Gerhard and then both men nodded. "*Ja*. We served our country!"

"Damn!" Frank blurted. "You boys weren't Nazis, were you?"

Dieter looked indignant. "We served in the West German Army! Gerhard and I were *Maschinengewehrschützen*." To our blank looks, he made two fists and swiveled an imaginary machine gun around the table. "At-at-at-at-at!" he mimicked.

"My daddy kicked your daddies' tails in the war," Rollie said, apparently offended by Dieter's mock attack.

Dieter shrugged. "Our papas are dead," he said sadly. "The Russian front."

"Well, those damned commies!" Rollie fairly shouted, and then pounded the table with his fist for emphasis. I was trying out my new way of holding my knife and fork, and his outburst surprised me enough that I dropped my fork. It clattered on my plate. After a bemused glance in my direction, Rollie continued, "Well, I say you're veterans, by damn, and worthy of celebrating Pearl Harbor Day." He looked around the table. Nobody else had arrived, but it didn't keep Rollie from voicing a dire threat, just in case. "Anybody who says otherwise can just come and duke it out with me!" The Germans looked grateful at being defended, even if it was from nobody.

The junior engineers turned their attention to me. I picked up my fork and gave them a weak grin. "I say Sonny here's a veteran, too," Frank said, as if there was a big argument about it. "What I know of his rockets down at Cape Coalwood, he's seen more action than Audie Murphy."

Rollie took a long sip of iced tea. "It's a done deal, then. We're all veterans and that means we gotta celebrate." He gave the sly eye to Frank. "Now, I wonder how we oughta do that."

Frank seemed to be in deep thought. Finally, he said, "I'll tell you what we need to do, every single swinging Richard Nixon at this table. After supper, we need to go up to John Eye Blevins's establishment, get ourselves properly prepared, and then head on over to Cinder Bottom. We'll show them damn Japs they can't blow us up more'n once a century!"

Rollie looked at Frank with abject admiration. "Oh, lordy, what bliss!" he said.

When the Germans showed interest, Frank took me on. "You're with us, right?"

"I could use some alcohol," I said. It was an innocent remark. I meant I could use some alcohol from John Eye as a zincoshine ingredient, but my comment was misunderstood, of course, and got a round of hoots and hollers from Frank and Rollie.

"We could use some alcohol, too, boy!" Rollie roared. "Especially when your old man's draggin' our tails around his mine! How about Cinder Bottom? You game for that, too?"

"Not if I want to keep breathing," I said. "My mom would murder me."

"How would she know?" Frank demanded.

I almost laughed but I didn't. "My mom probably knows we're talking about it this minute," I said.

The junior engineers' faces went blank. "How would she know that?" Rollie wondered.

"This is Coalwood," I said, and left it at that. If you didn't live here, it was too hard to explain.

As soon as supper was done, Frank and Rollie led the way outside to Frank's ancient DeSoto. It was missing its rear bumper, and its right front fender was severely dented. Its paint job was dull and faded. It was hard to tell what color it had been originally, but in the light that reached the street from the Club House porch lamp, it looked sort of more or less gray. I clambered into the backseat with Dieter and Gerhard. Frank hung a right at the Community Church and sped up the road, slowing at the unpaved dirt road that marked the entrance to Snakeroot Hollow. The DeSoto chugged happily, although its gears tended to grind. I suspected that was more from Frank not being able to drive a straight stick than the quality of the DeSoto's transmission.

The little white houses in the hollow looked snug and warm, the windows glowing. No one was out. It was too cold. Snakeroot was one of Coalwood's two colored sections—Mudhole being the other—but I knew just about everybody who lived there, at least for the first half mile or so. After that, there was a long stretch of dark woods and then another settlement began, this one made up of older, dilapidated houses that included John Eye Blevins's place. John Eye had lost a foot in the mine a long time ago, but for some reason the company had allowed him to stay in town. He sold his own brand of homemade liquor, ran poker games, and would take bets on just about anything, including Big Creek football games. I never heard a word against John Eye from anybody. I guess he was doing something the company and the town wanted him to do. It was another of Coalwood's quirks.

With Dieter, Gerhard, and me following, Frank and Rollie stomped up onto John Eye's porch and pounded on the door. They acted like they were half drunk already but I guess it was just typical junior engineer excess. Mrs. Blevins, a mountain of a woman, answered the door, frowning at the sight of us. "John Eye," she called over her shoulder in a surprisingly sweet voice, "Frank and Rollie are here, honey. Sonny Hickam, too. And a couple of krauts, from the look of 'em."

Mrs. Blevins wore a yellow dress covered with green fringe. Every time she moved, it looked like wind blowing across tall grass. She opened the door wider and we all walked inside. It was a tiny house that I knew well. An old, broken-down couch sat near the front door. A couple of sagging easy chairs were against the far wall. An ancient record player was in a dark corner playing some kind of music with horns and drums that didn't have much melody to it that I took to be jazz. John Eye's huge bulk pushed through the beads that I knew led into his kitchen. I just got a glimpse of the poker game that never seemed to end back there. I saw four men, one of them white. I couldn't see who the white man was. The cards covered his face.

"Sonny boy!" John Eye boomed at me in his deep bass. "You after rocket fuel this time of night?"

"He's celebrating Pearl Harbor Day," Frank said delicately. "We're all veterans, you see."

John Eye ignored him. I guess I was the steadier customer. "I got three jars of your special stuff all brewed," he said. "Get it for you if you want it."

"Yes, sir!" I always wanted it. Then I remembered I didn't have any money with me. "Can I pay you next week?"

"We'll pay for it!" Rollie boomed, his hand slapping his back pocket. "If we can drink one jar."

John Eye gave him a narrow look. "Sonny's stuff's pure alkyhol, not a drop of cut in it," he said. "It'll melt your innards."

"Just our style!" Rollie said bravely. The innocent of pain are so often brave.

John Eye rolled his eyes but thumped on his wooden foot into the back and returned with a paper sack. Inside it were three big fruit jars of my zincoshine alcohol. Rollie and Frank made a big display of rummaging through their wallets but failed to come up with the cash to pay him. They looked at the Germans. Dieter got the message and dug into his pocket and came up with some scrip, company coins. John Eye took them, counted out the cost—six scrip dollars, total—and handed the rest of the coins back. Mrs. Blevins brought in a tray with some tiny crystal glasses on it. Frank did the honors, pouring each of us a drink. I confessed I couldn't have any of it. "Get the boy some water," Frank said, and I knew I was off the hook. I guess he was afraid of my mother.

I'd had some of the zincoshine drink before, the first time Roy Lee had carried me to John Eye's to buy some, and I knew it was lethal. It was 100 percent pure alcohol and went straight from your stomach to your brain where it started killing cells by the handful. I worried a little for Frank and Rollie. They didn't seem to have all that many brain cells to lose.

Frank raised his glass. "Here's to all the dead men at Pearl Harbor and every man who ever fought America's wars," he said solemnly. Then he added, "And Germany's, too, except for them damn Nazis, not counting Dieter and Gerhard's daddies."

"*Prost!*" cried the Germans. They downed their brew together and immediately started coughing and wheezing and eye-watering, the standard response to zincoshine juice. Frank and Rollie watched and then did the same with exactly the same result. I knew what they were feeling. It was like drinking liquid fire.

Rollie gasped and then bent over and made a long, strangled exhalation. Frank pounded him on the back. "Attaboy, Rollie!" he yelled. "Give them Japs hell!"

Three more rounds left the four young men dazed. That's when Frank started to cry. "Wha's wrong, Frank?" Rollie asked solicitously. "Tell ol' Rollie."

"It's a woman, what else?" he wept. With the zincoshine juice under his belt, he had turned desolate.

"There, there," Rollie said.

The two Germans, their faces flushed and their eyes nearly crossed, looked at the two Americans with what I took to be abject admiration for the deep conversation they were having. "There, there," Dieter said, and Gerhard said it, too, although from him it sounded more like "*Der, der.*"

Frank stood up, swaying. "A woman is a precious thing," he groaned. He dropped his glass. It bounced and rolled on the floor. Frank watched it with glazed eyes. "But damn them!" he cried. "Damn them all to hell!"

"You got that right, Frank!" Rollie said, staggering off the couch and putting his arm around Frank.

The Germans just watched, their jaws unhinged.

Tears flowed down Frank's rosy cheeks. "I havta have her, Rollie," Frank slurred.

"Who's her?" Rollie cried. "Tell me and I'll go get her so you can have her right here on this floor!"

The Germans were mesmerized by the two junior engineers. "Hear him," Dieter said, looking into his empty glass, then licking the rim.

Frank moaned. "She's in Cinder Bottom. You know her, Rollie. What's-her-name!"

Rollie's brow furrowed. Obviously, he was deep in thought. "The girl with the glass eye?"

"The very one!" Frank wept. "What's-her-name."

"Velma," Rollie said.

"Velma! God, how I love that girl!"

"But didn't she kick you out of her room, said you tried to cheat her?"

"Yeah! That's the one!" Frank cried out. "And I did, too. I tried to pay her with a two-dollar bill. Figured she'd think it was a twenty. Now I got to go tell Velma how sorry I am, show her how much I love her. If I just had twenty bucks."

Dieter wiped away a tear and pulled out his wallet. He contemplated it. Rollie saw it and snatched it from him. "Here, Dieter, you want to make a contribution, right?"

"I don't know that I have twenty bucks," Dieter said. "What is a bucks?"

Rollie fumbled through his wallet. "Naw, you don't. You got three tens, though." He withdrew them from Dieter's flattened wallet and offered them to Frank. "Will they do?"

Frank peered at the bills. "Well, it ain't twenty bucks," he said, grabbing them, "but it might do if I beg a little." He stuffed the money into his pocket. "I'm going to go find out right now!" He lurched to the door.

Rollie staggered after Frank but fell on his face. "I'll go with you," he told the floor.

Frank barged outside and then disappeared into the darkness. Dieter and Gerhard sagged back on the couch and studied the ceiling. There were some cobwebs up there, but otherwise it didn't

seem to me all that interesting. A cold wind blew through the door
Frank had left open.

The poker game murmured on in the kitchen behind the beads.
I went out on the porch to see how far Frank had gotten. He was
on the hood of his car. It looked like he was taking a nap. I came
back, carefully closed the door against the chill, and prepared to
wait until somebody got sober enough to drive me out of the
hollow. I didn't relish walking in the cold. I suppose I could have
waited all night, but the beads swept back and none other than Tag
Farmer walked out. He didn't have his uniform on, just a plaid
shirt and khaki pants. I realized he had been the white man in the
back playing poker. He looked over the scene. "Come on, Sonny,"
Tag said. "Let's get you and these boys home."

I went with Tag to get his car, which had been discreetly parked
in a grove of trees around a curve. John Eye and one of his fellows dumped Frank, Rollie, Gerhard, and Dieter in the backseat.
Legs and arms went in all directions. I climbed in the front and
Tag drove us down the hollow. It would have been dangerous to
strike a match in the car, considering the combined alcohol breath
of the unconscious men in the back. I clutched my paper sack
with the two precious fruit jars of zincoshine juice in it. Tag didn't
have anything to say except "I never met the first junior engineer
who ever had an ounce of common sense."

"Two of them are Germans," I said.

"A goose is still a goose," Tag replied. "Don't matter where it
flies in from."

15

A CUTE COUPLE

Tag helped Frank and I helped Rollie inside the Club House. Dieter and Gerhard helped each other. Mrs. Davenport was waiting up for Frank and Rollie as if it was a nightly duty for her, which it probably was. "Those boys," she said, with nearly a mother's pride. "Almost every night, they plan to go to Cinder Bottom, but I think they've actually made it only once."

She led the way up to the second floor and unlocked their rooms with a skeleton key she carried on a loop of string around her wrist. Each room had a bed, a table, and two straight-backed chairs. The toilet was down the hall. I thought they were the loneliest rooms I'd ever seen, and it made me glad I wasn't a junior engineer. The Germans' rooms were no better.

I went down the hall to visit the toilet. When I came back, Tag had already gone. I went outside to get my bike, but before I could leave, a woman came up the porch steps. I recognized her even though she had her coat pulled tight around her throat and a scarf on her head. It was Dreama Jenkins. She was holding a red bandanna to her mouth.

When the porch lamp hit on her face, I saw that it wasn't a red bandanna at all but a white handkerchief soaked in blood. A big purple welt had closed her left eye, too. Mrs. Davenport met her at the door. "Lord, girl, what happened to you?" She pulled back the kerchief and inspected Dreama's face. Then, she caught sight of me, standing to one side. "Sonny, call Doc Lassiter. Quick, now."

"Just need a room. Don't need no doctor," Dreama said through her swollen lips.

"Well, you're gonna get one, honey, and Tag Farmer, too. What's this?" She inspected Dreama's mouth. "Lord, you've lost a front tooth."

Dreama pushed the bloody cloth to her mouth. Her tears started flowing. "Yes'm," she mumbled.

"You need Doc Hale, too," she said. "He ought to be home soon." Doctor Hale, the company dentist, lived in the Club House in one of the fancy apartments on the main floor.

I followed them inside. Mrs. Davenport took Dreama into the parlor and sat her down in one of the plush, wing-backed chairs. There was a black phone in a well under the stairs. I went to it and dialed 226, Doc Lassiter's number. It was busy. Then I dialed 555. Tag's mother said she'd tell him to come back down to the Club House as soon as he got home.

When I told Mrs. Davenport that Tag would be along but Doc's line was busy, she said, "Run on down to Doc Lassiter's house. Tell him to get off the phone and get on up here and hurry his backside doing it."

Doc's house was about a half a mile from the Club House. I tore down the street, turning the corner at the Dantzler house and then past the apartments, running all the way. Doc had been on the phone, he said. He grabbed his black bag and we headed out together. It wasn't far enough for him to drive. When we got to the Dantzler house, Ginger came out, wearing her Big Creek jacket. "Mrs. Davenport called to see if Doctor Hale was visiting my folks," she said. "Then I saw you going by with Doc. What's wrong?"

I stopped while Doc went on. I explained to Ginger what had happened. "I'll go with you," she said.

"I don't think you should," I said. "She's pretty beat up."

"Oh, Sonny, don't be silly. Of course I'll go. I know Dreama. Come on!"

We walked quickly toward the Club House. "How was New York?" I asked.

"It was wonderful. Have you ever been?"

"I've been to Myrtle Beach," I said.

She laughed and took my arm as we went up the Club House steps. I felt my face flush at her touch. "Sonny, it just felt so alive! All those people going somewhere, all so busy, all so smart. I went ice skating at Rockefeller Center, too. You should have seen me! I only fell down once!"

"I bet you were the prettiest girl there," I said, and then gulped at my forwardness.

But Ginger just said, "Thank you, sir."

I saw that my message to Tag had been delivered. His car was parked outside the Club House. Mrs. Davenport had Dreama on the couch in the parlor. Ginger and I waited discreetly in the hall until Doc finished. "I've cleaned her up," Doc said to Tag and Mrs. Davenport. "That's about all I can do. I can tell her to put ice on her lips and her eye but I know she won't. She doesn't need any sutures. Time will heal her now as much as anything."

"What about her tooth?" Mrs. Davenport demanded.

"That would be Eddie Hale's department," Doc said. "She'll need some pretty expensive work. Eddie only works on Coalwood people, though, and she's not from here." He regarded Mrs. Davenport's disapproving look. "I don't like it any better than you, Helen, but that's the rule. If she's not married, she's not a Coalwood woman. It doesn't matter whose bed she sleeps in."

Tag looked at Dreama while Doc packed his bag. "Cuke do this, ma'am?" She turned away. Tag glanced at Ginger and me. "I got to ask her some more questions ain't fit for Ginger to hear, Sonny."

I nodded understanding and took Ginger inside the dining room. The polished wooden floor creaked under our feet. It was a huge room with a fireplace at one end. There was a piano in the corner. The Club House dining room was also where the company parties were held. One time, Jake and a secretary had done a dirty dance at a Christmas party and had fallen into a table filled with desserts. My dad had him pitched out in the snow. I guess he would have frozen to death out there except his blood was full of John Eye's antifreeze, and also because Jim and I had hauled him up to his room. I told Ginger the story. She laughed and clapped her hands. "I wish I'd seen it!"

I started to ask her why she hadn't, but then I remembered that this was Ginger's first year in high school. You had to be old enough to be in high school to come to a company party. "How old are you, Ginger?" My voice echoed in the big room.

"I'll be fifteen in January," she said. "Why?" Then she teased, "Are you afraid of robbing the cradle?"

"Oh, I was just wondering," I said even though that wasn't entirely true. The truth was I was suddenly very interested in everything about Ginger Dantzler. "Tell me more about New York."

She grinned and twirled around with her arms outstretched. "They told me I had talent. All I need is a little coaching. Mom says I can go to any college I pick and study voice! I'm going to learn everything!"

The insight hit me like a brick. "You're a Rocket Girl," I said.

She stopped turning and wrapped her arms around herself. "I'm a what?"

"You're a rocket girl. I mean, like I'm a Rocket Boy with a plan to go to college and learn everything I can about rockets and then go to Cape Canaveral. You're just like that except you're going to learn all about your music and then go off to New York or Atlanta or maybe even Hollywood. You're a singing Rocket Girl."

There was no mistaking the delight on her face. "I guess I am!" She looked around the hall, and then her eyes lit on the old upright piano in the corner. "Can you still play?"

"I doubt it."

"Oh, you can, I know it. My mom's too good a teacher for you to forget." She tugged my arm to the piano bench and pushed me down on it, sitting beside me. "I always enjoyed your recitals. You always seemed to play with so much spirit."

"I played fast. I just wanted to get it over with."

"Play for me," she said.

I put my hands on the keys. My right hand automatically moved to place my thumb on middle C and my little finger on A above it. The middle finger of my left hand touched F one octave down. "I think I remember 'All I Do Is Dream,'" I said. The song of the Cape.

"Then play it for me, Sonny," Ginger said softly. I turned and looked into her eyes. "Please," she said.

I played but stumbled after the first few bars. "Here," she said, and scooted in close. "Put your hands on top of mine." I did, feeling their velvety strength. She played the song through, touching each key with precision. I could smell her, a heady mixture of young girl and rose petals. My heart was slugging my chest. She finished the piece and then took her hands back. "Now, play it all the way."

In a trance, I did as she ordered. I didn't miss a note. And then she sang. Her voice made me think of a necklace, each note a round and smooth and delicate pearl.

Dream, dream, dream . . .
Only trouble is, gee whiz, I'm dreaming my life away . . .

I finished and Ginger held the last note and then her voice died away in an echo. I turned to her. I was going to do it. I didn't care what the Big Creek lovemaster thought about it. I was going to ask Ginger Dantzler to the Christmas Formal. I opened my mouth, but before I got a word out, she said, "You know what? You and I would make a cute couple."

My heart sang. "I feel the same way," I said enthusiastically. "Ginger, would you . . . ?"

"Stuart can be so moody," she said.

"Ginger, would you go to . . ." I stopped, her words sinking in. "Who's Stuart?"

She blinked her big browns. "He's the boy I date over in Welch." After a moment of hesitation, she added the second of her one-two punch: "His dad owns a car dealership."

A car dealership! My heart, singing only a moment before, sank down around my ankles. I knew I'd already been skunked before I'd gotten started. There was no way I could compete against a boy from Welch whose dad also owned a car dealership! That meant he was surely rich, probably had his own car, maybe a chauffeur! Then I latched on to the rest of what she had said and the careful way she had put it. Quentin had called me an "infernal optimist" more than once and I guess he was right. Ginger, I told myself, hadn't said "Stuart" was her boyfriend. He was "the boy I date." A subtle but important difference. There was hope! I was about to explore that difference when I heard a commotion in the foyer. Ginger got up. "What is it?" she called.

I followed her into the foyer to find Cuke Snoddy standing in the hallway. Mrs. Davenport blocked his way. "You're not welcome here, Cuke," she said.

Cuke looked past her into the parlor. "Dreama, I want you to come home right now," he said.

Dreama, lying on the couch, shook her head and turned away.

Tag came out into the foyer. "Cuke, you go home. I'll deal with you later."

"I ain't done nuthin'," he said defiantly. "Tell 'em, Dreama! You fell down the steps, didn't you?"

Dreama nodded. "Yes, Cuke. I fell down." Her voice was thick.

"Damn old clumsy girl," Cuke said.

Mrs. Davenport pushed Cuke in his chest. "Get out of my Club House, Cuke, or I swear I'll get my pistol and shoot you right here in front of Tag and God and everybody else. She didn't fall down. You knocked her down."

Cuke sneered. "You shoot me, you go to Moundsville for the rest of your life."

Tag laughed. "If she shot you, likely she'd get a medal, Cuke. You go on now. Do like I told you. Don't make me have to knock you around. I'll do it if I have to."

Tag Farmer didn't make threats. He made promises. Cuke turned and fled. Tag looked after him and shook his head and then went back into the parlor. Mrs. Davenport followed him.

After conferring again with Tag, Doc came out into the foyer. His eyes shifted from Ginger to me. "How's your folks?" he asked me.

"They're fine, sir."

He gave me a disbelieving look. "About the only way I see Homer and Elsie is they have to be pretty much dead. You keep an eye on them, Sonny Hickam. Hear me, boy? And what are you doing out so late on a school night, Miss Ginger?" He had one eyebrow raised so high it looked like it was going to jump right off his forehead. "Come along, dear. I'll walk you home."

Ginger touched my arm. "I had a wonderful time."

"I did, too," I replied, and then Doc shepherded her along. *He's the boy I date.* I had to think about that. I wished I could ask Roy Lee about it, but, of course, the Big Creek lovemaster had his own thoughts about my love life and they didn't include Ginger. Maybe I could disguise my situation. *Roy Lee, I know this boy, see . . .* I shook my head. It was hopeless.

Tag came out into the foyer with Dreama and Mrs. Davenport. Dreama kept her head down so I couldn't see her face. Then the two women walked past me, going outside. "Where are they going?" I asked Tag.

Tag yawned and stretched. "They're going out to my car and have some woman talk, I hope. After that, I'll take her on up the road."

"Where's she going?" I asked.

He shrugged. "She wants to go home."

I was incredulous. "To Cuke Snoddy's?"

"Yep."

"After he beat her up?"

Tag shrugged. "Let me tell you something, Sonny. There ain't no figuring a woman's heart. They get it in their head about a man, sometimes it takes more than a busted tooth to change their minds. Cuke's her connection to Coalwood, too, and she's got some fancy ideas about this place, like maybe it's special. She wants to be part of our town, that's the long and short of it, and Cuke's the only one letting her be."

I couldn't figure it. "You mean she's willing to get beat up just to stay in Coalwood?"

Tag shrugged. "Maybe you got to come from somewhere else to see it the way she does. Anyway, Cleo Mallett's already come to me, asked me to run the girl off. I'm not going to do it, but Cleo and her bunch will, one way or the other."

"Why do they hate her so much?"

He yawned. "Maybe they won't, now that she's got a tooth knocked out. She'll look as common as them." He looked at his wristwatch. "You want a ride home?"

"I have my bike."

He nodded. "One thing, Sonny."

"Sir?"

"I don't think it's a good idea for you to hang out with the junior engineers."

"Yes, sir."

He pondered me. "You and Ginger make a cute couple," he said.

"We're just friends," I replied, jamming my hands into the pockets of my jeans.

Tag smiled. "Yeah, I can tell," he said.

16

ROY LEE'S LAMENT

I WOKE TO hear voices downstairs the next morning. I got dressed and sneaked down the steps to see who it was. I was born curious. One time Mom caught me reading a love letter from one of Jim's girlfriends and said, "Curiosity killed the cat."

"That's true," I said, still reading as fast as I could go, "but satisfaction brought it back."

She said, "If a certain cat I know doesn't stop smart-mouthing his mother and put that letter up where he found it, it'll take a lot more than satisfaction to bring him back."

I said, "Yes, ma'am," even though I was just getting to the gushy part.

I peeked into the living room and saw Dad with one of his foremen, Woody Blankenship. Both of their faces were drawn. I wondered when they'd slept last. Mr. Blankenship was sitting leaning forward with a clipboard on his knee, a pencil poised, while Dad read from a small brown book that I recognized as his daily mine diary. I noticed both Dad and Mr. Blankenship were in their sock feet. Mom might let her ladies come in wearing their heels, but she protected her hardwood floors from Rocket Boys and mine foremen.

"Yesterday, the gearbox on the north face continuous miner burned up," Dad read, then rubbed his eyes.

Mr. Blankenship nodded, saying, "Treadwell's scared. Every time he takes a deep cut, his crews back out as fast as they can. That's why he's burning up his gears."

Dad pondered his notebook as if Mr. Treadwell was going to pop out of it and give him an explanation. "Hmm," he grunted, and then yawned. He made me sleepy just looking at him.

"Dubonnet came to me while I was fire-bossing his section," Mr. Blankenship went on, "said he'd talked to the miners on 11 East and we ought to pull out."

Dad scowled. "Remind John Dubonnet next time that I run this mine, not him. And keep him off that section. I don't want him to know what we're doing there."

Mr. Blankenship made a note. Dad must have sensed my presence. He turned in my direction for a blink but then just as quickly looked back at his diary. Mr. Blankenship smiled shyly in my direction. I nodded to him. Dad snapped his diary shut, regaining his attention. "I'm going to change out Treadwell. Woody, the north face on 11 East is yours. You pick your best crew, take 'em in first thing tomorrow. I know you're not a section foreman anymore. This is just temporary to get us past this rough patch. You let Treadwell know he's out, but keep him with you for a while, teach him how to boss. Far as I can tell, he doesn't know anything about ventilation, either. Teach him that, too."

Mr. Blankenship wrote Dad's directives down, his expression impassive. Then Dad got off onto the number of tons he wanted loaded out of other sections in the mine and I lost interest, but I'd also learned something, too: 11 East was eating up Dad's foremen, one by one.

In the kitchen, I found Mom at the kitchen table, staring out the window. The percolator was bubbling on the stove. I fixed myself some hot chocolate and toast and sat down opposite her. There was a nuthatch pecking at one of Mom's feeders. A curl of frost clung to the window. Old Jack Frost had been painting overnight, I thought. Then I took a look at the *Bluefield Telegraph*. There was some bad news right on the front page. "Oh, no!" I exclaimed.

"What?" Mom asked, startled.

NASA had launched a rocket to the moon but it had exploded before it had gotten more than a mile off the pad. Mom didn't seem too impressed. "You boys are flying that high, aren't you?"

"Higher," I said, my eyes glued to the report. "Look, it says NASA used an air force Atlas rocket, not one of Wernher von Braun's. That must be the problem."

She didn't seem to care. "Are you going to get the Christmas greens this Saturday?"

Christmas greens were what people in Coalwood called the pine boughs and rhododendron leaves they used as decorations around their windows and doors, sometimes with colored electrical lights woven through them. Coalwoodians who didn't decorate for Christmas were considered pretty loutish. Even if Mom was going to Myrtle Beach, she couldn't risk that. "Yes, ma'am," I told her. "Sherman's going with me."

Mom nodded, sighed, and then had another sip of coffee. She looked beaten down. She raised her eyes to her mural. I could see where she'd painted over a spot in the sky. "What do you know about seagulls?" she asked.

I sorted through my brain. "They fly and they live by the ocean."

"Thank you, Professor Audubon," she sniffed. "I was thinking more about the shape of their wings."

"I could ask Quentin," I said. Quentin had read nearly every book in the McDowell County Library. I was certain he'd run across one about seabirds.

"It would be much appreciated if you did," she said, and then regarded me with a knowing eye. "I hear you were up at John Eye's last night. And then I heard you and Ginger participated in some excitement at the Club House with Cuke's woman."

"Everything I did, I was forced to do by my elders," I said, wriggling on her hook.

She smirked. "I'm sure. But this house stinks of moonshine. I wish you'd find a better way to store that stuff."

"I'll look into it," I promised, but I didn't know anything except John Eye's glass jars that could hold up to zincoshine juice.

"I also heard so far you have A's in all your classes."

"Yes, ma'am. I've got to get through exams, though."

"Attaboy."

"Did Dad tell you about my grades?"

"I heard it over the fence. Your dad is otherwise occupied these days, as you well know."

"Yes, ma'am," I said. I resisted telling her I'd told Dad about my grades and he'd made fun of me.

"You're late for the school bus," she said laconically.

I "yes ma'amed" her and then I remembered Dreama. "Mom, do you think Doctor Hale could work on Dreama's tooth? She had a pretty smile. I think she was proud of it."

"Why do you care?" she asked.

"I don't. I just wondered," I said. It wasn't exactly the truth. I did care. I didn't know why. I just did.

"Wonder about something else," Mom said. "She won't be around much longer. Cleo Mallett and her gals will see to that."

"Tag said Mrs. Mallett asked him to run her out of town."

"I'm not surprised," Mom said. "That girl came in here and started living with a man without so much as a 'how-do-you-do?' to anybody. I don't much like Cleo, but she's right about this one."

"But it's mean not to fix her tooth," I said glumly.

Mom nodded. "It is mean, I'll grant you that." I looked at her beseechingly. She got the drift of my look. "No," she said. "Now, get to school."

I made the bus but just barely. Jack, our often grumpy bus driver, regarded me with hooded eyes, an unlit stub of a cigar clamped between his teeth. "I swan, Sonny," he said, "you going to be late for your rocket to the moon, too?"

In the auditorium before classes, Roy Lee kept elbowing me while I was trying to catch up on my civics homework, a comparison of our constitutional form of government with the ancient Athenian model. "Look," he said, giving me the elbow every time

Melba June Monroe walked up or down the aisle. She seemed to be doing a lot of walking that morning. "Look." "Look." "Look."

"You elbow me one more time, I'm going to slug you, Roy Lee," I warned. "Do you think it's just a coincidence that a lot of the government buildings in Washington are built to look like Greek temples?"

"No. Yes. Who cares? Look!"

I looked. Melba June was a fine-looking girl, that was sure. She gave me a quick glance, her long lashes fluttering. Then she stopped to have a conversation with a football boy, Holder Wells. Holder had one eye that wandered. When you talked to him, you never quite knew where to stand so he was looking at you.

Roy Lee gave me another shot to the ribs. By then, they were aching. "There she is, Sonny! I've got her all primed. All you got to do is pop the question. Wouldn't surprise me if she laid a kiss on you right here in this auditorium."

Melba June had turned her profile to us. Her sweater looked like it had been painted on and she had some prodigious curves. "Look at her, Sonny," Roy Lee said. "She's ready and she wants *you*!" Then he started singing, to the tune of the popular song "Brazil." "Brassiere, you hold the things I love so dear, Brassiere, Brassiere, Brassiere . . ."

"I'm asking Ginger," I told him.

Roy Lee let his head drop. "If stupidity was money, you could buy this school," he lamented.

I pushed Roy Lee away and stood to look around for Ginger, spying her in a knot of other tenth-grade girls. It looked like they were doing homework, so I resolved to catch her later, maybe on the bus ride back to Coalwood. I decided to seek out Quentin, instead. I wanted to see what he knew about the ancient Athenians. I figured to ask him about Mom's seagull wings, too. "Look!" I heard Roy Lee slavering behind me as I made my way down the aisle.

That afternoon, Ginger wasn't on the bus. Betty Jane said Mrs. Dantzler had picked her up at school to go shopping. She was going to buy a dress for the Christmas Formal, Betty Jane said, studying my face. I couldn't help but let it sag a bit. "Who's she going with?" I asked acidly. "That guy from Welch?"

Betty Jane nodded. "You should have asked her. I think she'd have gone with you." She eyed me. Betty Jane was a pretty girl, too. What Coalwood girl wasn't? Her father was one of our machinists. Her mother worked as a nurse for Dr. Hale. "How's your brother?" she asked.

"I guess he's okay," I said. "Why?"

She smiled a faraway smile. "I wish he'd ask me to the formal."

I thought *You and about a million other girls* to myself but didn't say it. I was feeling too miserable to make anybody else feel that way. I said, instead, "He couldn't take a nicer girl," and meant it.

17

THE GATHERING OF THE GREENS

I GOT UP at sunrise on Saturday morning, ready to go get the greens. "I left the hatchet and bags for you on the back porch," Mom said, back at her kitchen-table station. Her real estate books were stacked by her arm along with her usual paint cans and brushes. I quickly finished my toast and hot chocolate and rose to go. "Did you ask Quentin about the shape of gull wings?" she asked.

"He said they were cantilevered airfoils," I reported.

"Oh, good," she said. "All my artistic problems are solved."

I washed my dishes and then went upstairs to my closet and dug out my miner's boots. I usually wore them up in the mountains. I tucked my pants into them. Then I pulled on Uncle Joe's old navy pea-coat, added a scarf, put on a pair of old leather miner's gloves, and I was ready to go.

As Mom had promised, a hatchet was on the back porch along with two big cloth cotton sacks. Everybody in Coalwood owned a hatchet to cut the kindling for starting the fires in the Warm Morning coal heaters. We boys also thought it was a wonderful tool to carry around the woods, especially if my friends and I were into one of our Indian warfare periods, pretending we were Coalhicans or some such made-up tribe and Jim and his older, bigger boys coming after us were the United States Cavalry or maybe another bunch of Indian warriors. Our hatchets were just for show. We never hit each other with them, at least not on purpose.

Sherman was just arriving, parking his bike by the garage. He had his mountain-climbing clothes on—jeans and a heavy woolen plaid jacket, making him look a little like a lumberjack. He was bareheaded, caps being out of style, his thin brown hair fluffed by the bitter breeze. Dandy, his stub tail wagging, stood beside him. Poteet ambled over, too. "You want to take the dogs?" he asked.

I sure did. Dandy and Poteet always enjoyed a romp in the mountains.

Before we could get going, a white Cadillac pulled in behind the house. It was Dr. Hale. When he got out, I saw that he was wearing a fur coat. I remembered that he owned a chinchilla farm somewhere in Virginia and wondered if that's what the fur was. "Hello, Sonny, Sherman," he greeted us. I unlatched the back gate for him. "Your folks home?" he asked me.

"My mom is," I told him.

Mom had come out on the back porch. "Hello, Eddie," she said.

He tipped his hat to her. "Elsie. Do you have a minute? I'd like to talk to you about something."

"Sure," she said, pushing the screen door open. "Come on in."

We watched Dr. Hale go inside. "I wonder what that's about?" Sherman wondered.

"Not a clue," I said, but I was already considering my tactics to get it out of Mom. "Let's go get us some greens."

I let the dogs out of the yard and we all headed up the street to Substation Row. There was a big stand of pine trees and a cluster of rhododendron on the mountain there that I thought would make easy pickings for our greens. I'd been raised in a house on Substation Row, one of the old bachelor boardinghouses that had been converted into duplexes. We'd start from there, where Mom had built a bridge over the creek.

As we walked, I saw coal smoke coming out of nearly every chimney. Since we sat on about a billion tons of pure bituminous coal, it was pretty cheap. When we went past Roy Lee's house, he was at his coalbox, shoveling coal into a shuttle bucket. When he spotted me, his lower lip went out about a foot. "Sometimes I just hate you," he said.

"Why?" I demanded.

He threw the shovel back into the coalbox and picked up the shuttle, carrying it to his front porch. He left it there and came to the fence. "Melba June's going with Holder to the Christmas Formal. She wanted to go with you, you freak, but old walleye finally wore her down. I hope you and little Miss Innocent Ginger are going to be very happy. Have you asked her to go with you, by the way?"

"She already has a date," I confessed. "Some boy from Welch."

Roy Lee rolled his eyes and then stomped inside, taking the shuttle with him. "Hopeless" was his final word before he shut his door.

There was no use dwelling on Ginger. Jake had once told me, "Until you get knocked down, you don't know how good it feels to stand." But just as soon as I gave myself a little pep talk, I got the blues. I checked myself as we walked. It wasn't about Ginger. It was something else. It was so close I could almost touch it. I tried to think of something to dispel the feeling and lit on my good grades. All A's. I was so proud I could bust. The odd feeling of being sad passed, but its mystery remained.

Dandy and Poteet raced ahead until Dandy skidded to a halt in front of what had once been our house. I guess he still remembered it. We cut through the yard to the creek. Mom's bridge over it was actually just a couple of thick planks thrown across a place where the creek narrowed. Roy Lee and I had done a lot of fishing in that old hole under Mom's bridge during our lazy summers. It was a good place for crawl-dads, too, especially the big red ones we liked to scare the girls with. I'd put one down Teresa Anello's back one time and, to return the favor, she'd pushed me into the water. Everybody said Teresa and I were destined to grow up and get married. Teresa had a football player for a boyfriend now, so things hadn't quite turned out as predicted.

Since I knew this mountain well—Mom called it Sis's Mountain after an old mama cat who liked to lie on a rock in the sun on it—I led the way up the trail. Dandy and Poteet angled on down the creek. I paid them no mind. They'd be back. Dandy couldn't stand to be away from a Hickam for long and he'd bring Poteet with him.

Although Sherman had to contend with a weak leg, he kept up. I'd hear him grunt as he worked hard to get his leg up over a rock, but he never complained. At the top of the clearing was the first major obstacle on the mountain, a crag of rocks we called Big Cliff. There was a path beside it that went up an easy slope to the top, but that was for girls and sissies. If a boy used it, he was immediately and forevermore a "sister." Sherman and I, of course, went up the hard way even though there was nobody there but us. Sherman had to use mostly his arms to pull himself up. It was amazing to watch him do it. He had the strongest arms of any boy I knew. At the top of Big Cliff, we caught our breath and turned to look down on Coalwood. The town was quiet, not even a car moving down the road. Sherman glanced up. "Look at that!"

I looked where he was looking and saw, miles above us, something marking a white line across the wispy blue of the sky. "It's a jet!" I said, marveling.

"I bet it's a bomber," Sherman said. "Strategic Air Command!"

I studied the contrail. It was thick, meaning it had to be more than one engine. That meant Sherman was probably right. It was most likely a multiengine jet nuclear bomber such as a B-52 or maybe a B-47. "Wonder where it's going?" I said more to myself than to Sherman, scarcely willing to breathe at the wonder and glory of it.

"Wonder where it's been?" Sherman replied.

"I'm going to ride in a jet someday," I said as sure of it as anything there was in the world.

"Me, too," Sherman said. "I might just own me one, too."

I couldn't top that, so I silently kept watching until the white streak had completely disappeared behind the edge of a fluffy cloud peeking over the mountains to the east. Luckily, only one jet flew over. If there had been more, likely Sherman and I would have sat down and watched every last one of them go past.

Above Big Cliff lay Picnic Rock, a natural stone formation that looked like a large flat table. Around it were perfectly spaced rock chairs. Several clefts behind it formed shelves. We boys could stay all day on the mountain without eating anything other than birch bark and teaberry grass, but we'd always stop and eat at Picnic Rock when girls brought us lunch. They'd bring real food—sandwiches and apples and bottles of pop. As a reward, sometimes we'd even let them join in our games. The only trouble was they took it all too seriously. To us boys, our mountain wars were fun. To girls, it was war, and they played too rough and held grudges.

Dandy and Poteet caught up with us at the top of the mountain where there was a ridge called Fort Hill. There, the remains of more than a dozen log forts attested to the multitude of battles fought among generations of Coalwood kids. Poteet spotted a rabbit and took off after it. It escaped when it zigged and Poteet zagged, losing her footing in a big pile of leaves. She climbed out, sneezing at the leaf sticking to her nose. Dandy trotted over and nuzzled her and Poteet grinned, even though she'd lost her rabbit. Snorting, she put her snout to the ground and started looking for something else to chase.

We moved close to the hollow I had in mind for our Christmas greens and went inside it. I knew the place well. I'd spent a lot of time there over the years, just sitting on a log and listening to nothing except my heartbeat. The old familiar pines arched around me and dusted me with their sharp, fresh perfume. I was looking up at them when I tripped over something in the leaves. It was a deer fawn lying on its side, its thin legs sprawled.

I stared at it and it looked back at me with one huge brown eye, the only one I could see since its head was on the ground. Its legs trembled, then stilled. The eye slowly closed, then opened again. I saw terror in it.

The dogs ran over, Poteet bounding with her tongue hanging out, Dandy waddling behind. They stopped short of the fawn and sat down and stared. Sherman caught up with me. "Poor thing," he said.

"What's wrong with it?" I asked, trying to find my breath.

Sherman shrugged. "Starved. Look at its ribs."

The little fawn was quivering. A small pink tongue hung from its mouth. A drop of saliva fell into the leaves. "We can't just let it suffer," Sherman said.

"I don't know what else we can do," I replied in a near whisper. My voice wasn't working right. I knelt beside the fawn and felt its neck. It trembled at my touch. "I don't think it's long for this world," I said.

"We can't just leave it," Sherman said. "It wouldn't be right."

"Why not?"

"You should never let anything die by itself. That's all I know."

I thought of Poppy and the night I ran from his death. "Okay, Sherman," I said. "We'll stay with it."

We took up station on a nearby log and watched the fawn and waited. It lay there, its big eye staring at the sky and occasionally blinking. It gulped a couple of times, too. After a while, Sherman got up and limped over to the fawn and draped his jacket over it. "What are you doing?"

"I think it's cold."

"So am I." I shivered. "You're going to freeze without your coat."

"I'll be okay," he said quietly, and sat back down on the log beside me. "I wish we could feed it."

I looked around. There was nothing, not even a blade of grass, just a sea of brown dead leaves and some moss on the rocks. "O'Dell said the drought this summer killed all the stuff the deer usually eat," I said. "I think this little guy's too far gone to eat, anyway."

We kept our vigil on the fawn. After a while, Sherman said, "I heard you have something bothering you and you can't figure out what it is."

It didn't surprise me that he knew. There were few secrets

between the rest of the Rocket Boys. I guess I was the one who tended to harbor mysteries. "Yeah. I've got part of it figured out now." I didn't go into the details. I got up and took off my pea-coat and covered the fawn's speckled head. "Maybe if it thinks it's night, it won't be so scared," I said.

"That's a good idea," Sherman said. Then he said, "I get scared sometimes, too. I get scared that maybe there's not going to be enough time in my life to do all the things I want to do, or go to all the places I want to go. I mean, my whole life I've hardly ever been out of Coalwood but I've read so many books and seen so many movies about other places and things, I just want to see them all before I die. I wake up sometimes and think about that. Do you ever do that, Sonny?"

"I guess so," I said. "Mostly when I wake up, it's because I hear Dad coming up the steps past midnight. The first thing I think about is 'I hope he doesn't start coughing!' He almost always does." I looked away from Sherman, embarrassed. I'd told a family secret.

We sat quietly, letting our thoughts wander. Sherman was in a philosophical mood. "I love Christmas," he said. "I just feel something in the air this time of year, a sort of resting up, kind of. Christmas really is a holy time."

It didn't surprise me to hear Sherman talking that way. He could get deep every so often if you didn't keep your eye on him. Still, I couldn't let his comment go by. "Mr. Jones in history class said Christmas is really a pagan winter festival. Jesus was probably born in the spring."

"I know," Sherman replied. "But I don't think God has to pay any attention to what really happened. He's bigger than history."

Sherman's thoughts wandered on. "You remember that time we got eraser-dusting duty in the third grade?"

I remembered. I'd just finished reading a book about George Washington and Thomas Jefferson and all the other men who got the U.S. of A. started and decided that having a powdered wig was what must have made them so smart. Sherman and I were outside to slap the erasers together to get the chalk dust out of them, and seeing all that white powder flying around gave me an idea. I talked him into letting me pat one of them on his hair. After I finished with him, he returned the favor. It was so much fun, we managed to dust ourselves white from head to toe. Then, one thing led to another, and we had an eraser fight, leaving a few of them a bit ragged. Mr. Likens, the school principal, made sure we understood that we had not performed our eraser-dusting duties in the proper manner. He had a paddle that could take the joy right out of you. It could take the powder off, too. A few swipes of it and his office turned into a chalk snowstorm. He might still be whacking us if he hadn't gotten into that sneezing fit.

"How about that time we were the only two boys left in the spelling bee?" Sherman asked.

"Second grade—Mrs. Brown's class!"

"Yep. She finally had to go into fifth-grade words to stump us."

"Stumped *you*," I said. "I won."

"No, Linda Bukovich won. We just tied for second."

We chuckled together. "I hope you get all the time you need, Sherman," I said.

He shrugged and I thought of Little Richard's wheel. It kept turning for all of us. Then Dandy made a long, low moaning sound and Poteet got up, turned around three times, and lay back down, her head on her paws. "I think the fawn just died," Sherman said.

We crept up to it and removed our coats. The fawn's eye was wide open, staring, covered by the dull film of death. "Should we bury it or something?" I whispered.

Sherman pondered. "No. There might be something up here that needs to eat it, a bobcat or something."

For the next hour, Sherman and I cut off low boughs on the pine trees, and leaves from the rhododendron until we had our sacks well filled. Then, the dogs cavorting around our legs, we headed down the mountain. Sherman took his sack and headed down Main Street for home while I went down into the basement to get the wire and pliers I would need to put the greens up. I bustled around looking for what I needed, but then I remembered the fawn. Without Sherman to make me stay brave, I leaned on the washing machine and held my face in my hands. I really felt bad about that little fawn.

I heard a soft thump on top of the washing machine. Old Lucifer, who usually made a habit of ignoring me and everybody else except when he was hungry, sat before me, cocking his head as if pondering my grief. He was a wreck of a cat. His broad nose was slashed with scars, and both his ears were split. One of them wouldn't stand up straight at all and just flopped over. Lucifer knew the mountains. He went up there all the time. What had he witnessed among the animals while we humans in the valley went about our lives? The rabbits Lucifer brought home weren't much more than fluff, grist, and marrow. He was a hunter and a killer, a warrior cat. "Good old Lucifer," I said, petting him. He purred, kind of a stuttering rumble, as if he wasn't sure it would work. I petted him some more, feeling the scars and scabs on his head. Then, as if he was satisfied with whatever he'd tried to convey, he jumped down and went back to his bed at the base of the stairs. What a mystery it all was.

I got the ladder and went to work, setting up under the kitchen windows to start. The first thing to be done when putting up your greens was stringing the wires around the window frames, then tucking in the pine boughs and rhododendron leaves under the wire to form a solid line. After that, you had to weave through the electric lights. It didn't take long before my hands were covered with sticky pine tar. It would stay on for days, no matter how hard I tried to scrub it off. I liked the smell of it, though. I moved to the living-room window and set the ladder up there.

I heard the back gate being unlatched and saw Dad coming in from the mine. He had on his old cowhide coat, his hat pulled down low on his head. He walked as if he was a hundred years old. "Where'd you get the Christmas greens?" he asked.

"Sis's Mountain," I replied, pulling another bough from my bag.

He yawned. "Where's that?"

I realized that I had never seen Dad up on Sis's Mountain.

Mom had been up there a bunch of times, but Dad had never climbed it. He'd just worn a groove back and forth to the mine. "Up there." I nodded vaguely across the creek.

He took a bough from my bag and held it up to his nose. "I used to get Christmas greens for our house in Gary. Emmett was working at the mine so I took little Clarence and up we'd go into the woods."

He was talking about my uncles, Clarence and Emmett. Clarence worked for Dad over at the Caretta mine. Emmett was at the Anawalt mine the last I'd heard. All three Hickam boys had gotten no farther than the mines, but Dad had managed to climb to the top of his profession, at least as far as they were going to let him go without a college degree. It was strange to think of Dad as a young boy, up in the mountains gathering greens for his family. I couldn't imagine him any other way than the way he was.

Dad handed the bough back and trudged off to the basement. I felt vaguely unhappy but didn't know why.

"Hey, little sister!" It was Roy Lee at the back gate. He had on his dancing clothes—a tight pair of black pants, a bright pink shirt, a sunshine-yellow jacket, and a black hat with a pink hat band and a feather in it. He gave me a knowing smile and looked at me out of the tops of his eyes.

"What?" I asked.

"Go get ready," he said. "You want Ginger Dantzler. All right. You're going to get Ginger Dantzler. I got her all scoped out."

"What do you mean?"

He grinned slyly. "She's going to be at the Dugout tonight. Betty Jane Laphew, Sue Burnett, Cheryl Ridenour, and none other than your sweet little Ginger are all going by their little sophomore selves, no dates with 'em. I got it straight from my mom and she got it from Betty Jane's mom. The field is wide open, Sonny. If you can't beat a Welch guy out, you're not half the boy I think you are. I still think you need to train for those Cape Canaveral women but, hell, you want little Miss Innocent, then what's the Big Creek lovemaster for?"

18

THE DUGOUT

"GOL, SONNY, DON'T you own anything besides overalls and flannel shirts?" Roy Lee asked. "You want Ginger to think you're a hillbilly? And what is that smell? You smell like a Christmas tree!" After rifling through my closet and dresser drawers, he had finally settled on a gray crew-neck sweater I'd gotten for my birthday last year and a pair of khaki pants. They had a hole in one of the back pockets, but he said if I pulled the sweater down low enough, nobody would notice. He also dragged out my penny loafers. "You ever hear of shoe polish?" he demanded, and then spit on them and gave them a polish with his handkerchief. Then he got the bottle of Aqua Velva Dad kept in the medicine cabinet and splashed it all over me. Added to the pine aroma on me already, I figured I smelled like a cemetery on the Fourth of July.

I probably could have borrowed the Buick, but Roy Lee insisted he wanted to be my chauffeur. "If things work out, you might need my backseat for some hot lovin'," he said. Then he caught himself. "Oh, yeah. I forgot. Miss Sweetcakes. Well, you could hold her hand back there, anyway." He shook his head, the Big Creek lovemaster foiled by the perception of innocence.

We descended the concrete steps to the Dugout. The Dugout was the place to be on a Saturday night if you were going to Big

Creek High. Ed Johnson, a janitor at Big Creek, had converted the basement of the Owl's Nest Restaurant, just across the river from the school, into high school heaven, a warm room festooned with crepe paper and dim lights and the best rock and roll to be found anywhere in America, all played over Ed's homemade sound system. There were benches around the walls of the basement, actually wooden pews from an old church he'd found somewhere. In the corner was a furnace and a pile of coal in front of it. You could tell how much you'd danced when you got home by the amount of coal dust stuck to your socks.

Ed had decorated for Christmas. There was a wreath hung on the door with a Big Creek owl doll attached to it. Inside, crepe paper, green and white for the school colors, red for Christmas, was wrapped around the support posts. Ed liked to play a medley of fast and slow songs, thoughtfully planned to get his dancers in a romantic mood. If you were having an argument with your girl-friend, an Ed Johnson dance was the perfect place to get her willing to climb in the backseat with you before the night was out. At least, that's what I'd heard. It had only worked for me once, last year with Valentine Carmina. Valentine was an older girl who had taken pity on me when Dorothy Plunk had thrown me over for my brother. It seemed like ancient history now. Valentine had gotten married as soon as she had graduated from high school, and then left to work in the Detroit car factories.

Shadows danced around me as I paid my quarter and entered the dance floor. The place was hopping. Gradually, my eyes adjusted and I started recognizing individuals. Emily Sue Buckberry twirled past, doing the chicken with Bobby Gray. Emily Sue was the girl I always turned to for advice. She called herself my "philosopher's stone." I took her word for it. Bobby was our band drum major. Ordinarily, those two couldn't be found anywhere near each other, but in the Dugout, it was almost like we became different people. Emily Sue spotted me and came over. "Who dressed you?" was what she wanted to know. Roy Lee volunteered that he'd done it. "Thought so," she said. "You got a date for the formal yet?"

"That's why we're here," Roy Lee said, craning his neck. "He's going to ask Ginger Dantzler out."

Emily Sue frowned behind her big, round glasses. "Ginger? I thought she had a boyfriend over in Welch."

"Look!" Roy Lee said, elbowing me and ignoring Emily Sue. "There's Ginger. Go after her, boy."

I had butterflies in my stomach. This was it. The big moment. All I had to do was walk across the dance floor and go up to Ginger, tap her on the shoulder, ask her to dance, and so charm her she'd throw over her rich Welch car-dealer boyfriend for me, even though she'd already bought a dress with the other boy in mind. Before I could take a step, a vision appeared in front of me. "Hi, Sonny." It was Dorothy Plunk.

My butterflies grew to small birds. "Let's dance," she said just as Ed began to play "All in the Game." All glory is shadows, so they say, and there is no armor against fate. It was pure chance Ed was playing what I had always considered *our* song, Dorothy's and mine, and then there she was, asking me to dance with her. She took my hand and led me out on the floor. I could almost hear Roy Lee's teeth grind behind me.

"There's been so much I've wanted to tell you," Dorothy said, settling into my arms. She looked at me with her wide, gorgeous, expressive, intelligent, seductive, heartbreaking, summer-sky blue eyes. I started to drown in them. "You've been the best part of my life at Big Creek," she whispered in my ear as the music played. "I know that you hate me now but I will always remember when we were friends. I'll never forget you—you sweet, wonderful person. I think you're wonderful. No, I'll tell you the truth, Sonny, although it scares me to say it. I love you."

I love you. I tried to reply, tried to get something out that made sense. Had I been able to take a full breath, I might have managed it. When the dance ended, I gulped about a dozen times, trying to get the dust out of my throat. "Dorothy, would you go to the Christmas Formal with me?" I croaked. Then I thought: *My God, what have I done?* I'd gone to the Dugout to fight for Ginger Dantzler and had ended up asking Dorothy Plunk to the formal! I was nearly certain I had lost my mind! The next words out of Dorothy's mouth took the "nearly" out of my equation.

She smiled sweetly. "Oh, Sonny," she said, lowering her eyes. "I already have a date."

My heart bottomed out around my ankles. "But—but you said . . ." I caught Ginger's eye. She was looking right at me, and I sensed she knew exactly what had just happened. She turned away.

"I said I love you," Dorothy said patiently. "And I do. Just like a brother."

Then Dorothy began dancing with another boy I couldn't see because I had closed my eyes hoping when I opened them I would be living in some other universe.

I felt Roy Lee's urgent hand on my arm. I opened my eyes. To my utter disappointment, I was still on Planet Earth, December 12, 1959. "Get over there, you fool!" He pushed me toward Ginger. Ed was playing a fast song now. I fought my heart back into my chest and tried to make a reasonable appearance. I'm certain my smile was crooked. The first thing Ginger said when I got to her was "Dorothy Plunk is sure a sweet girl."

"Yeah. Uh, Ginger . . . uh." I couldn't find the right words. Dorothy had knocked them right out of me. I kept trying. "I know you already have . . . uh . . . the Christmas Formal . . . uh . . . Look, I know you already . . . uh . . ." I couldn't make any sense out of anything.

Ginger smiled, but I detected pain in her eyes. "Sonny, let's dance. You look like you need to have a good time. I do, too. Just you and me. Come on."

We started to dance and just kept dancing, fast tunes, slow ones, ones in between. Gradually, I began to have fun. Ginger was a good dancer, rhythmic and smooth, her mother's daughter. She danced close during the slow tunes, but not too close. We chattered away. High school and Coalwood gossip. Dreama, 11 East, my mom, her mom, our dads, her sister Eleanor Marie at Duke University making straight A's, my brother Jim at Virginia Tech making the freshman football team, how much Betty Jane liked Jim and was going to someday pin him down. Finally, Ginger said,

"Let's get some air." I agreed. We grabbed our coats and walked out on the steel trestle bridge that went over the Dry Fork River just across from Big Creek High.

The air was bracing, and as we cooled off, Ginger huddled in closer to me. We stood in the middle of the bridge and contemplated the dark, gurgling river below. The Christmas lights from the Owl's Nest Restaurant sparkled merrily off the tumbling water. Just beyond, our old high school sat behind its manicured football field. A single light on its roof beneath a giant wooden owl was its only illumination. A chuffing coal train passed behind us, the coal cars clacking on the track. The locomotive called a warning into the darkness, its whistle a long, low moan. The old trestle bridge shook beneath our feet as the vibration from the tracks soaked through. "Bound for the steel mills," I said.

"You'd think the ground would fall out from under us," Ginger said, "with all the coal dug out."

I chuckled. "It doesn't work that way. The mine roofs are held up with posts or roof bolts when they take the coal out."

"I've lived here my whole life but I don't know a thing about the mines," she said. "Have you ever gone down in one?"

"Once," I said. "Dad took me."

"I'd like to go. It doesn't seem right, living here and not knowing what it's like down there. Do you worry about your dad when he's in the mine?"

"No," I said firmly. "Dad knows what he's doing."

The last coal car finally trundled past followed by its red caboose. A man on its back platform raised his hand to us. "Sonny, are you mad at me?" Ginger asked. "Betty Jane said you wanted to ask me to the Christmas Formal and, to tell you the truth, I would go with you if I could. But I can't. I promised Stuart I'd go to his formal at Welch High. It's on the same night as Big Creek's."

"I know," I said. "It's okay. I don't blame you."

"We'd have made a cute couple, though," she said playfully. She found my hand.

Her hand felt so small. "We would have, for sure."

"Sonny, we can still be friends, can't we? I know boys think that's a terrible thing to hear from a girl, to be just friends. But I've never had a friend who's a boy. Would you be mine? Look out for me maybe?"

I was in a fatalistic mood. "You ever want anything," I said, "just call on me. I'll be there like a rocket."

"I've got so many dreams. Could I just talk to you like we've been doing, share my dreams with you?"

"Anytime you want. Never doubt it."

Ginger stood on her tiptoes and kissed me on the cheek. "You ready to go back inside?"

"You go on," I said. "I'll catch up."

"Please do," she said. "I want to dance 'Goodnight My Love' with you." That was the record Ed played at the end of every one of his dances.

"I wouldn't miss it for the world," I said.

Ginger walked back toward the Owl's Nest and the Dugout. I watched her and then turned back to the Dry Fork River. I leaned on the bridge rail, listening to the low grumble of the coal train already miles down the valley. By now, I thought, it was probably passing Miss Riley's house. I hoped Jake was visiting her.

Roy Lee found me on the bridge. "How'd it go? Do you have a date?"

"Better," I said, falling in beside him and walking back to the Dugout to dance the last dance. I clapped him on his shoulder. "I have a friend."

19

TRIGGER AND CHAMPION

I DROVE MOM to church the next morning. Icicles hung from the roofs of the houses along Main Street Row, and I saw a thin layer of ice coating the creek when we went over the bridge that led to Coalwood Main. It didn't look like it was going to get much above freezing all day. Snow clouds hurried overhead, spitting occasional, indecisive flurries.

As soon as we walked into the church, I knew there was trouble brewing. A stranger to Coalwood would have never seen it. People coming early to the Coalwood Community Church tended to fill up the back pews first. Those coming in later sat in the middle. The latest had to settle for up front. Trouble, however, restacked the congregation. Mom took it all in as quickly as I did and said, "Oh, what a fine lot of Christians we have with us today!" Up front, the union families were clustered around Mr. Dubonnet and the Malletts. The foremen and their families were all in the back. When anyone came in, they immediately sorted themselves according to their loyalties. There was a no-man's-land in the middle where Doc Lassiter, his wife, and three young daughters took their ease. "11 East," Mom muttered. "It was only a matter of time before John Dubonnet started stirring his pot."

She passed up the foremen and walked up front and plunked herself down beside Mrs. Mallett. "Excuse me, Cleo," Mom said, wiggling to find a spot beside the wide-bottomed woman. Cleo huffed but made room. Mr. Dubonnet turned and nodded to Mom. He looked amused. Mom glared at him.

I sat with Sherman toward the middle where there were a lot of empty seats. The church was going through a series of trial preachers. The one before us, Reverend Schrieber, was a young man from somewhere up north. He had an accent that most of us found a little grating to our ears. When the choir finished with its opening hymns, he stood to deliver his sermon. It was based on the 49th Psalm, an obscure one to be sure, but acceptable. It could have been a pleasant little talk about being charitable, but, perhaps due to a mistaken belief that anybody in the church cared a thing about what he had to say, the boy preacher managed to turn it into a diatribe. "What about the starving people of Africa?" he cried out. "What about the starving people of Asia? How can it be that any one of us might have a dollar if our fellow man has none?"

I looked around and saw about half the people inspecting the ceiling and the rest the floor. The truth was Coalwood people didn't care a whit about anybody in Africa or Asia. What Reverend Schrieber's congregation cared about was 11 East. The silence of his audience screamed it at him. *11 East. 11 East.* But people ten thousand miles away who he'd never seen were so loud to Reverend Schrieber, he couldn't hear his own people just a few feet away. The young reverend kept swinging at air. When he finished, he could look out across his congregation and see a sea of nudging female elbows probing male ribs, heads rising and sleepy eyes blinking awake.

Perhaps finally sensing the futility of his sermon, Reverend Schrieber sat heavily in his chair behind the pulpit and waved at the choir to sing. They did so, happily, while the young man held his head. I noticed he was wearing tennis shoes, strange footwear for a man of God.

Ginger was in the choir and gave me a wink as she walked down the aisle after the service. She was cute in her maroon robe, I thought. Afterward, Sherman and I waited on the steps for Mom, who was having a word with Mrs. Dantzler and the teachers of the

Coalwood school. "Another man got hurt on 11 East yesterday," Sherman said.

I hadn't heard that. "Who?"

"Mr. Franklin. Broke a finger."

The Mallett boys swung by close. In a mocking voice directed at me, Germy sang, "We're going on strike. We're going on strike." I didn't hate that kid but I came close.

Mom was quiet on the way home. She was chewing on something, and it could have been anything. As we parked in the garage, she said, "I like Ginger, too." I had a hunch she could have told me how many times Ginger and I had danced at the Dugout if I'd asked her.

As we came into the kitchen, I remembered I wanted to know why Dr. Hale had visited her. "Was that a chinchilla coat Dr. Hale had on yesterday?" I asked, all innocence. I was just going to warm her up on the subject a little.

She inspected me for a moment and then said, "He wanted to know if your dad would give him permission to work on that girl's tooth." At my startled look, she continued, "I just thought I'd save us both some time. That's what you wanted to know, wasn't it?"

"Yes, ma'am, pretty much," I confessed. "Did Dad agree?"

"I haven't asked him," she said. "When do I see him to ask him anything?"

I didn't care to get off on that particular subject. "Can Dr. Hale really fix Dreama's tooth?" I wondered.

"He can put a crown on it, but it's expensive. He said he'd do his part for free, but since it was company equipment he'd be using, he needed company permission."

"I wonder what Dad will say."

Mom smiled and hung up her coat. She opened her pantry and considered what she had inside it. I hoped she was going to fix lunch. I was starving. A sermon, even a poor one, can leave you pretty hungry. "You know, Sonny," she said, "I don't know what your dad would say but I know what he should say so I said it for him."

"Dr. Hale's going to fix Dreama's tooth?"

"I reckon so," she said, selecting a can of tomato soup. "And I'd give a dollar to see Cleo Mallett's face when she finds out about it. Being the superintendent's wife isn't all it's cracked up to be, but it does have its moments." She chuckled. "It does have its moments, indeed."

IT was the day O'Dell had asked me to come ride the ponies with him. After a lunch of tomato soup and a fried baloney sandwich, I pedaled my bike down to Frog Level. Along the way, I plotted my strategy to find out what he knew about Billy. I'd have to be less obvious than I'd been with Mom about Dr. Hale. I figured to come at O'Dell about Billy from an acute angle. That way, I wouldn't have to break my promise to Mr. Turner to keep Billy's secret. Billy no longer showed up for any of our BCMA meetings in the auditorium in the morning, and his class participation had fallen off, too. He looked a bit worried and wide-eyed to me, as if he was staring into a firing squad. I guessed quitting school was sort of like that, anyway.

O'Dell and I saddled Trigger and Champion and got going. The ponies tossed their heads and stamped their feet, getting used to the snow. Steam erupted from their noses as we came down off the hill behind O'Dell's house. O'Dell was on Trigger, named after Roy Rogers's palomino trick horse. I was on Champion, named after Gene Autry's horse. Like his Hollywood namesake, Champion was a rich brown color with a white star on his forehead. He had a gentle way about him and was easy to ride. O'Dell inspected the sky. The clouds had blown away. "I was hoping we'd get more snow," he said. "Someday I'm going to live out in the Rocky Mountains. Every day there'll be snow. I'll even go skiing!"

"That I'd like to see," I laughed. "A Coalwood boy on skis. How do you figure to learn?"

"Nothing to it," O'Dell declared. "You just strap on barrel staves and aim downhill. It's just like sledding, only you stand up."

Our ponies clip-clopped up through Middletown, prancing when Margie Jones's dog barked at us as we went past her house.

Across the ball field, I saw some men in front of Little Richard's church. One of them was the reverend himself, dressed in his all-black Sunday frock. I turned Champion across the grass to have a word with him. Trigger and O'Dell followed.

A small stack of lumber sat in front of the church next to some glittering panes of glass. Two men stood in blue bib coveralls alongside Little. They seemed to be having an argument. "Hi, Reverend Richard," I said as I rode up to them.

Little lifted his hand. "Hidy, Sonny, O'Dell. Mighty fine fillies you got there."

"They're geldings," O'Dell said.

The reverend clucked his tongue. "Are they, now?"

"Working on a Sunday, Reverend?" O'Dell asked.

"Got my ox in a ditch, young man."

I recognized the men in the overalls. One was Mr. Willy Franklin. When I saw the splint on one of his fingers, I remembered Sherman telling me that Mr. Franklin had been in an accident at 11 East. The other man was Mr. Billy Joe Blevins, a shuttle-car operator and also John Eye's brother. "Hey, boy," Mr. Franklin said while Mr. Blevins nodded. Though they didn't call me by name, they knew who I was and I could sense their unease. I was the boss's son.

"The boys and I are just having a little discussion about our new church windows," Little said.

The two men were looking at a drawing on a piece of notebook paper. They turned it this way and then that. "We can do it, Reverend," Mr. Franklin said. "But it still ain't right."

"It's what I want," Little said, smiling. "And it is as right as heaven."

The men shrugged and went inside the church. "What kind of windows are you putting in?" I asked, the curious cat on a pony.

Little waved my question away. "So, lookit you and O'Dell, a couple of cowboys. Heh heh. My, oh my. I can remember when you used to ride your bicycles!"

So could I, since it had been earlier that same day and would probably be tomorrow, too. "I'm glad Dad sent you the stuff for your windows," I said.

"Ol' Homer usually comes through after some foot dragging just to show you he don't have to do it. Guess you know how that goes." A memory seemed to cross his face, "Say, you ever figure out that thing that was bothering you?"

"Not yet."

Little sat down on the steps of his church. "Did you pray on it?"

"Not exactly."

"God's wheel shaping you, praying or not, Sonny Hickam."

"Yessir."

"You ready for Christmas, Reverend?" O'Dell asked.

"I live for it, O'Dell. Best time of the year." Little got back to me. "Your granddaddy died last Christmas, didn't he?"

"Christmas Eve," I said.

"Mr. Benjamin Hickam," Little said. "I used to go over to War-riormine, sit on the porch with him, talk things over. He didn't care if you was colored or what—just come on over, Reverend, any old time you like. When he wasn't on the paregoric, he was interesting to talk to. Knew something on just about everything. Read a lot of books. I'll say a prayer for him tonight." He searched my face. "You been getting any hassle about 11 East?"

"Some."

"Been about all people care to talk about around here," he said, watching me carefully. " 'Cept maybe that woman who lives with Cuke."

I was surprised that the goings-on of a young white woman was gossip in the colored part of the camp. "Her name's Dreama," I said. I assumed he'd heard about her getting beat up. "Why do you think she stays with Cuke, Reverend?"

Little studied the sky for a bit and then said, "Well, Sonny, people do what they do. Man wants a woman, woman wants a man. That's the way the good Lord made us. So far as I know, nobody's seen fit to fix us like your poor ponies there." At the sound of splintering lumber, he called over his shoulder, "Easy, boys!" Then he said, "A man can't hit a woman and stay a man. He becomes a loathsome thing, even to himself. But the woman who stays with such a man panders to his darkness. They both risk their souls."

Mr. Franklin walked out on the church stoop. His black curly hair was sprinkled with sawdust. He was carrying a pry bar. I was surprised he could work with a broken finger. "This old place is hammered together pretty good, Reverend."

Little gave him his slow laugh. "There wasn't no shortage of nails when we built it, only boards."

"What kind of windows are you putting in?" I asked again.

Little shook his head. "Sometimes a thing can't stand to be talked about before it happens," he said mysteriously.

Mr. Franklin made a sour face. "It's durn crazy is what it is." He looked at his bandaged finger. Then he looked up at me. "Like 11 East."

Little gave Mr. Franklin a stern look. "Willy, I done told you why we're doing what we're doing. Don't you be calling it names, now. And don't be getting cute with Sonny. He didn't do 11 East and he can't undo it, either. Don't matter who his daddy is."

Mr. Franklin gave me a sheepish look and then joined Mr. Blevins. They began covering the front of the church with squares of canvas. "What's that for?" O'Dell asked.

"To keep your prying eyes away, O'Dell," Little said, smiling.

Trigger and Champion were getting restless, so we excused ourselves and pointed them up the road. "Ya'll be careful now," Little called after us as we waved.

We rode at a plodding pace past the old mule barn, long since emptied of the mules that had once hauled the coal out of the mine. Some of their old leather harnesses, moldy and falling away into dust, still hung inside. I always felt a bit forlorn when I passed that old barn, remembering the fate of the mules. After he'd automated his mine, Mr. Carter had kept the mules in the barn or pastured them around town. When he'd sold out, the mules had gone to the renderers the next day.

When we reached Sherman's house, just down the creek from the machine shops, he whooped at us from his porch. "Mr. Bolt said he'd like to see you," he said. I saw that he'd gotten his greens up. We waved and moved on.

We found Mr. Bolt and Mr. Caton at work on one of the benches in the rear of the machine shop. "Take a look at this," Mr. Bolt said proudly, holding a shiny object aloft. "Clinton did it for you last night. It's pretty much glorious."

The shiny object Mr. Bolt held up was indeed glorious. It was a perfectly crafted De Laval rocket nozzle, with an interior lining of hardened water putty. "I finally figured out how to make it smooth," Mr. Caton said of the putty. "I used a Popsicle stick dipped in lard."

The putty was as smooth as a sheet of paper. "It's just the thing!" I said happily. "We'll try it out next weekend."

"We'll be there," Mr. Bolt and Mr. Caton said in unison.

After O'Dell and I admired the nozzle some more, I put it in my jacket pocket for safekeeping. We said our good-byes to the machinists and went outside to swing back into our saddles. We took the road up past the Club House. Jake's Corvette was parked in front. Then I saw that the light was on in Dr. Hale's upstairs office in the post office building. He didn't see patients on Sunday, at least to my knowledge. I wondered if he was working on Dreama.

When we got opposite the Big Store, Ginger came out of the front door, turning to lock it. The Big Store was closed, but I guess she was allowed inside anyway, since she was the store manager's daughter. She was carrying a carton of milk. "Take me riding," she said with a grin and a cant of her head.

"Hop up," I said, patting Champion's rump.

She was in a skirt. "If I had my jeans on, I'd be there, boy, and don't think I wouldn't!"

We said good-bye and cantered on. O'Dell laughed. "That girl's got more spunk than any girl in Coalwood." He turned in his saddle to watch her as she walked down the street toward her house. "You ought to ask her out."

"I can't," I said sadly.

"Why not?" O'Dell demanded.

"Because I'm her friend."

O'Dell patted Trigger's neck. "Is that supposed to make sense?"

"No," I said. "Except to Ginger and me."

We were in front of Linda DeHaven's house when Jake sped past us in his Corvette. He jammed on the brakes and backed up. He had on his junior engineer uniform. "Hey, boys."

"Hey," we called back.

Jake tapped the steering wheel, his brow furrowed. "Listen, Sonny, you free next Saturday?"

"We're testing a new rocket nozzle."

"Launch your rocket in the morning, then meet me at the Club House around one o'clock. Wear your boots."

I said okay and started to ask him why, but before I could, Jake floored the Corvette and peeled rubber for at least fifty yards. I figured he probably wanted me to guide him on a hike. I'd done a fair amount of that when he'd brought weekend women to the Club House and was looking for something else to do with them. Then I thought maybe he wanted to gather some greens for his room at the Club House. Maybe Rollie and Frank would go along, too. If so, I hoped they'd all stay halfway sober. I didn't look forward to hauling the three of them out of the mountains.

Linda DeHaven came out on her porch, wrinkled her nose at the smell of burning tires, and waved at O'Dell and me. "Got a date for the Christmas Formal?" she asked. The big dance seemed to be on everybody's mind.

O'Dell took a moment to wax about the beauty of the girl he was taking, a sophomore who lived in Squire. Linda D., a classmate of ours, frowned at me when I confessed I was dateless. "You're too picky, Sonny Hickam," she said. "Always have been." Linda D. and I had known each other practically from the day we were born.

I laughed. "You go with me, then!"

She laughed back. "I already got a date, boy." Then she said,

"I'm having a pajama party on Christmas Formal night. A bunch of girls are going to stick around for Slug and Carol's wedding."

"Slug" was Linda's older brother, whose real name was Jimmy. Carol was Carol Todd, Ada and Ray Todd's daughter. Their wedding was already down as one of the biggest social events in Coalwood history.

"Who's coming?" O'Dell asked.

"Emily Sue, Tish, Tootsie, Patty, Linda B., Becky, and Dana." She waited a beat. "And Dorothy Plunk."

My heart did its usual flip-flop at the sound of Dorothy's name. There was no way I could control it.

Linda D., getting cold, went inside. We headed the ponies down the road, easing slowly past the houses on Main Street Row. I absorbed the concept that the exalted Dorothy Plunk would be sleeping in a house so close to my own. I would ignore her, of course, but I'd have to calculate how best to do it. Anything that had to do with Dorothy in my own personal universe took careful calculation, even when my plan was to do nothing.

I shook off Dorothy and focused on the passing houses. So much had changed since the houses had been sold. Instead of the solid company white, many of the houses had been painted different colors—greens and yellows, mostly, but one was a shade of pink. As we passed it, I noticed Cuke's house looked as nasty and gray as ever. It had been over a year since the company had pulled up the railroad tracks that went past his house, but it was still coated with a crusty layer of coal dust. It didn't look like anybody was home, although it was hard to tell with Cuke. I hoped Dreama was at Dr. Hale's office instead of being in there.

When we got up by the Coalwood school, I decided it was time to find out about Billy. "Billy seems kind of unhappy lately," I said.

It didn't usually take much more than the mention of a subject for O'Dell to tell you all he knew about it. But, in this case, he didn't. He just gave me an odd look and said, "Well, I guess he is. That's why he's joining the navy. Didn't he tell you?"

I pondered his question. Billy had been a member of the BCMA for nearly a year. He had come to the launches and put in his two cents worth and I had listened to his ideas, usually good ones, but beyond that, I couldn't remember when I had ever actually shared more than a few minutes of conversation with him. It was odd when I stopped to think about it. Billy Rose was one of my best friends, at least if anybody had asked me that's what I would have said, but I couldn't think of a single time in the entire history of my life when I had actually sat down and talked to him. That was pretty sad, now that I thought about it. "When did he tell you?" I asked.

"When I was at his house a couple weekends ago."

"I've never been to his house," I confessed. The truth was I wasn't even sure where it was. Somewhere up Six Hollow, that's all I knew.

We rode quietly on, O'Dell volunteering no more information on Billy. I guess there was little else to say about it, or maybe he didn't know any more. "It's hard to believe we're so close to graduating from high school," he said after a bit. "We've been in school twelve years. In a way, it seems like forever."

I smiled. "Do you remember your first day at school?"

"I sure do. I was in Mrs. Williams's class. She accused me of talking too much."

"She must've gotten you mixed up with somebody else," I said, laughing. "I'm sorry I missed it. Our class was so big, they split us in two. I was in Miss Stapleton's class, remember?"

"But we all took recess together," he said. "I didn't know any kids except the ones from Frog Level. I was kind of scared, meeting you kids from the main part of town. I remember you, though. You kept running into things. You also fell off the slide and bloodied your nose."

"That's because I was nearly blind. I didn't get my glasses until I was in the third grade."

We rode on. "Wonder where we'll be in twelve more years?" O'Dell asked.

"Cape Canaveral," I replied confidently.

O'Dell shook his head. "You maybe, but not me. Daddy says

he can't afford to send me to college. I'm thinking about the air force."

I took in O'Dell's unhappy news. I was sorry to hear it, but it put me in a ticklish position. Of all the Rocket Boys, it appeared I was the only one who was pretty sure he was going to college. I couldn't blame them if they resented me for that. "You can work on their rockets," I said, trying to find some light in his situation. "Then come on down to the Cape afterward."

"All I want out of the air force is the GI Bill," O'Dell replied morosely. "But I wish I could just go on to college and get it done."

"I do, too, O'Dell," I said.

"It's not your fault, Sonny," he replied, and pulled on Trigger's reins to turn him around.

"Thank you, O'Dell," I said, fully meaning it. I turned Champion around, too, and we headed back down the valley.

The sun was fading behind the mountains when we got to the barn built behind the Carrolls' house. Red had built the barn for the ponies the year before and it smelled of fresh lumber, hay, and horses. The Carrolls were an industrious family, given to country living. They raised pigs and, for a while, even kept a cow. There was a time when nearly every family in Coalwood raised some kind of animal for food, but the practice had dwindled as the pay at the mine had gone up and the houses were fenced and built closer together.

We unsaddled the ponies and groomed them. O'Dell said his dad wanted their stalls changed, so we shoveled the soiled straw into a wheelbarrow and dumped it behind the barn. Then we climbed into a loft full of baled hay and loose bedding straw. It looked to me like the Carrolls had enough hay and straw in their barn to last a lifetime. O'Dell laughed when I said so. "We've got even more bales of hay under a tarp outside," he said. "Daddy bought a bunch of it when it was real cheap. But now that we don't have a cow, it's probably going to go sour before the ponies can eat it. They prefer oats, anyway."

After we finished mucking out the stalls, put down fresh straw, and saw that Trigger and Champion had their bucketful of oats, O'Dell invited me inside his house. The Carrolls were about to have supper, and Red asked me if I wanted to join them. The smell of ham and butter beans got my stomach to growling so I quickly agreed. Riding a pony can build a powerful appetite. O'Dell had two younger brothers and a sister. Everybody bowed their heads and Red blessed the food. Then, after he said "Amen," he nodded to me and said, "Dig in, Sonny." I didn't need to be told twice.

Mrs. Carroll sat beside me. She had sewn our original BCMA flag, coming up with the design of an owl riding a rocket. "Sonny, O'Dell says your flag is getting kind of worn out," she said, and handed me a folded cloth square.

I unfolded the cloth. It was another flag, completely hand-stitched. "Thank you!" I said, searching for something more to say to express how I felt. I was just so grateful. Mrs. Carroll had a ton of work to do every day with all her kids and her house. Yet, she had taken the time to sew us up another flag. I settled on Quentin's vocabulary. "It's prodigious!"

"Is it worth a hug?" she asked.

It was. I kissed her cheek, too.

WHEN I got home, it was after dark. I found Dad dragging a huge Christmas tree through the back gate. He had his miner's lamp set on the fence so that he could see what he was doing. One of the branches had tipped off his hat and Poteet had picked it up. She sat, Dad's hat in her teeth, her tail wagging furiously. "Your mother always likes a big tree," Dad said, grunting with the effort. I hoped he wouldn't start coughing.

Together, we propped the big pine against the back porch near Mom's bird-feeding station. "She usually picks her Christmas trees out," Dad gasped. "I thought I'd do it for her this year." He gave a few coughs, as if testing his lungs, and then swallowed heavily. I didn't mention the obvious to him. With Mom heading for Myrtle Beach, she didn't need or want any tree.

Dad went back to the gate and held his hand out. Poteet trotted up to him with his hat. He took it, gathered up his miner's lamp, and got back in his truck, driving off, I presumed, to the mine.

I looked at the tree. If it was going to fit in the living room, it was going to need to be trimmed by several feet. Mom, probably hearing the commotion, came out on the back steps and pondered the tree in the glow of the porch light. "And there it shall remain," she said, and turned on her heel and went back inside.

It hurt my heart to hear her words. Never, in all my born days, had Mom ever been anything but completely, totally delighted with a Christmas tree. To my chagrin, I felt responsible for her new attitude. If only I had told her from the start I would work on her blamed Christmas Pageant, I thought. And maybe if only I hadn't given her such grief over her forcing me to be with Dad and Poppy last Christmas. Then I went further to think that if only I hadn't let Chipper out, then maybe . . .

But there was that blamed phrase. *If only*. I surely wished it could be banned from the English language.

I went upstairs and got out my list. I added *Mom and Christmas Tree* to it. It was an odd little list, no question about it, and it seemed to me that it was missing something very important, something so obvious that it should have just jumped out and hit me right between the eyes. Still, I believed that somewhere in that list, maybe actually in between the words, was the answer to that thing that, every so often, vexed me so. Then, finally, I remembered to put one more thing down. It was past time and I was proud that I did it: *Billy*.

2 0

SIX HOLLOW

I FOUND MOM looking at a suitcase on a chair in her bedroom. It was open but empty. "Can I borrow the car?" I asked. "I want to go up to Billy Rose's house."

She tore her eyes from the suitcase. "Why?"

"Because I've never been before," I said. Then I told her about Billy quitting school and joining the navy.

She didn't act surprised. "I've been hearing some bad things about Arnee Bee," she said darkly. Arnee Bee was Billy's dad. She pondered me. "What say I go with you? I could visit Henrietta Johnson. I haven't talked roses with her in a coon's age."

I wasn't sure who Henrietta Johnson was but I said okay. I aimed the Buick up the road past the mine and turned in at the Six company store. Mr. Dantzler had closed it the year before when many men up Six Hollow had lost their jobs and business had fallen off. The store's vacant, dirt-smeared windows stared at us. Somebody had finger-written GO OWLS on one of the windows. Another message said HICKAM GO TO HELL. "At least they spelled it right," Mom said grimly.

The road up the hollow had been built out of slack and cinders. It was potholed and rutted. We entered a row of sagging, dirty houses with peeling paint and knocked-out windows. "I don't remember it looking like this," Mom said. "Haven't been up here in a couple of years . . ." And then her voice trailed off as she turned her head to look at a house that had burned down. Charred boards stuck out in crazy angles where the roof had collapsed. There was a plastic doll without a head in the front yard.

Scrawny chickens pecked at pebbles along the road. Runny-nosed children, playing in yards stripped of grass, stopped and watched us with big eyes. Their coats were dirty and torn. "This is where the trick-or-treat children came from," Mom said. She seemed to be talking to herself. "I thought somebody had brought them in from some other town. . . ."

Every house seemed to get tireder and poorer as we drove farther up the hollow. Windows were busted out, fences drooped, trash lay in the ditches. I saw a rose trellis arching over a gate and it stirred a sudden memory. I remembered who Henrietta Johnson was. She was a colored lady who had helped Mom out when we'd lived up on Substation Row. It was when Dad had come down with cancer of the colon, and Mom was staying with him a lot at the hospital. She didn't want Jim and me to come home from school and find the house empty, so Mrs. Johnson had started coming by every day. Besides making sure we boys got supper, she also did some light housekeeping. Mom had planted one of her first rose gardens in the backyard about that time, and Mrs. Johnson came to admire it, so much so she had planted a rose garden at her own house. Every so often, Mom would want to go see Mrs. Johnson's roses, to admire them and have tea with a woman who had become her friend. I remembered the Johnson house being neat as a pin, its white paint gleaming, and the trellis covered with bright red roses. But now, as we passed it, I saw the trellis was broken down, a scraggly brown network of dead vines the only indication that anything had ever bloomed there. Mom looked at the sagging trellis and the ghostly house behind it. "Poor Henrietta," she said, her fingers at her mouth. "Why didn't she let me know she was leaving?"

I pulled up in front of the tiny crackerbox of a house O'Dell had described as being Billy's. The front yard was a strip of black slack dirt. The porch sagged on cinder blocks, and one of the windows had a pane missing. A piece of brown cardboard covered it. When I stopped, Mom stayed seated. "Are you coming in?" I asked her.

"Will you be long?"

"I don't think so. I just want to say good-bye. I'm not sure when he's leaving, so I thought I'd better catch him while I can."

"I'll wait for you," Mom said. "If you boys need to talk, you don't need me around."

"I'm sorry about Mrs. Johnson, Mom," I said.

She shook her head. "I still can't figure out why she didn't let me know she was leaving. We were friends."

"If Mr. Johnson got cut off, I guess Dad was the one who had to do it," I said. "Maybe she got mad at you over it."

"No better woman in Coalwood than Henrietta Johnson," Mom said. "I always meant to come visit her. I don't know why I didn't."

"Yes, ma'am," I said. I thought I understood how she felt. Neglecting a friend seemed the surest way to lose one.

When I got out of the car, I was hit by a foul odor coming from the ditch that ran in front of Billy's house. The coal company had installed indoor plumbing in all the houses in Coalwood, but when the houses had been sold off, the utilities had been sold, too. I wondered if Six Hollow was still connected to the sewer line. It didn't smell like it.

A flimsy board lay over the ditch. I walked across it and climbed up on the porch and knocked at the screen door. The door was ripped at the bottom, as if it had been kicked in. It took a couple of knocks before Billy answered. His forehead lifted at the sight of me. "Sonny?"

"I need to talk to you," I said.

Billy looked past me, saw Mom sitting in the Buick, and then opened the door. The odor of cigarette smoke filled the air. The door opened into the living room. There was a faded green sofa along the far wall, a wooden table sitting beside it holding a clear glass ashtray piled high with butts. A small, sour-looking man regarded me from the sofa. He was wearing a pair of old canvas pants and an undershirt. It was Arnee Bee Rose, Billy's dad. When he saw me come through the door, he nervously jerked the cigarette from his mouth as if I'd caught him smoking when he wasn't supposed to. He blew a purplish plume up at the ceiling, then narrowed his eyes at me. He slowly and painfully got to his feet, holding one shoulder higher than the other as if it hurt him to stand up straight. "Homer Hickam's boy," he said, by way of a greeting, and then glared at his son. "Billy, you comin' up in the world, ain't ya?" My eyes strayed to the couch where there was a big hole in one of the cushions. He saw where I was looking and said, "I fell asleep with a cig in my hand. Getting a new couch next week, all the way from Bluefield. Ain't we, Billy?"

Billy shifted his weight from foot to foot. "Come on," he said miserably, and led me to the back of the house. An open doorway led to a tiny kitchen, where two little girls sat at a card table, playing with some ragged dolls. They watched us go by but said nothing. There were three doors in the back. The one in the middle led to a tiny bathroom. As I went by, I could see there was no water in the toilet bowl. Billy opened the door to the left. "This is my room," he said.

It was a tiny room, its floor covered with a sickening shade of yellow linoleum. Blankets and pillows were scattered about. A kerosene lantern sat on a rough wooden table littered with school books. "I share it with my brothers and sisters," Billy said. He nodded toward the lantern. "The electricity got cut off last month."

I tried to imagine the room at night, when Billy slept there with six children. It was also where Billy studied and did his homework. Billy made almost straight A's every semester. I thought of my room in comparison and felt a twinge of shame. His father started to yell at someone, a stream of curses. Billy ignored it. "I still don't know why you're here," he said.

"I heard you were going to join the navy."

"That's right." He was subdued.

"Billy, I know you've been mad at me—"

"I'm not mad at you," Billy said. "I'm just tired of you."

I couldn't imagine what he meant. "Tired of me?"

Bill gazed through the grimy window. The light that pierced it looked cold and gray. "I'm tired of you talking about going down to Cape Canaveral and working for Wernher von Braun, tired of you building your rockets and people coming down and applauding you for doing it, tired of you being who you are and me being who I am."

"They don't applaud just me," I said. "It's for everybody in the BCMA. You, too."

"Me? What's my job with the BCMA? Did you ever invite me to help you calculate a nozzle? Or had me down to your house to help load a rocket? Not once. I chase after your rockets, find them for you. Hell, you could train a dog to do that."

"I never knew you wanted to do anything more," I said weakly.

He tucked his thumbs in the pockets of his faded jeans. "You never cared enough to know," he said. "Why are you really here?"

The truth was I really didn't know myself. "I guess I just wanted to see where you lived," I said. It was the best I could do.

He swept his hand around the room. "This is it," he said bitterly.

Mr. Rose was yelling at someone or something, or maybe he was just yelling to be yelling. A baby cried somewhere in the house. Billy grimaced when something crashed in the living room. It sounded like the ashtray. "Yeah, my daddy's a drunk," he said. "Guess he's got a right to be with his pelvis crushed and not healed right. But he's getting harder to control. . . . He hits my little sisters too hard sometimes and then he . . . I don't know what's going to happen. Only thing I know is the navy's got a place for me and I'm going."

"Billy, is there anything I can do?" I asked.

He shook his head. "You're a little late. I've already signed the papers. There's nothing anybody can do. It's just the way it is."

WHEN I came out of Billy's house, the Buick was empty. I found Mom down the road at the old rose trellis. She was fingering the dead vines. A couple of dirty kids stood watching her. One of them kept sniffling and then wiping his nose with the back of his hand.

"I asked"—she nodded toward the kids—"and they said the house has been empty for over a year."

"There was no way for you to know."

"Your dad had to know," she said more to herself than me. "He knows everything that happens in this town. But he didn't tell me. Maybe he didn't think I cared. I guess the way I go on about Coalwood, he has a right to think that."

It was getting dark. "We better get on home," I said.

"Do you know why your dad is in 11 East, Sonny?"

"No, ma'am."

"I heard you had a run-in with the Mallett boys because of it."

I shrugged. "Nothing I couldn't handle."

She nodded. I suspected she'd already gotten a complete description of what had happened. "What do you and Jake Mosby have cooked up next Saturday?"

"I think he wants me to take him hiking or get some greens or something," I said. "Why is Dad in 11 East, Mom?"

"Because he's trying to save the world, as usual." She fingered the old vines. "How's Billy?"

"He's signed the navy papers."

"I could hear Arnee Bee yelling."

"I don't know how Billy gets such good grades in that place."

"What else did Billy say?"

"He said he was tired of me."

She frowned. "What did he mean by that?"

"He thinks I've got the world on a string. He makes straight A's and nobody cares. I make an A in anything and everybody celebrates. That's the way he sees it."

"Maybe that's because that's the way you see it," she said, smiling. "You've been known to get full of yourself from time to time."

I was tempted to say that if that was so, I came by it honestly. Wisely, I stayed silent.

Mom's smile faded as she looked back up the hollow, toward Billy's house. She squared her shoulders. There were gears turning in her mind. I could see it in her eyes. But all she said was, "Gol, it stinks in this old place." And then, "Sonny, take me home."

21

A COALWOOD GIRL

IT WAS TIME for me to complete my Christmas shopping. I'd already gotten something for Jim and Dad. A subscription to *Argosy* was my gift to Jim. The only complication was whether to change his mailing address at Virginia Tech or wait to see where he was going. I dithered on it and then figured Jim would leave a forwarding address and the magazine could catch up with him. For Dad, I'd written to Charleston to see if I could get an autograph from Cecil Underwood, the state governor. Mom's letter to Wernher von Braun last year in my behalf had been my inspiration. Governor Underwood was the first Republican governor in West Virginia in about a thousand years, and Dad thought he was the best thing to ever hit the state. I didn't expect a reply but, to my amazement, the photograph arrived. I'd asked Mr. Varney, the postmaster, to keep an eye out for anything from the governor's office for me, and he'd done it, slipping a manila envelope with the governor's seal on it to me one day in the Big Store. Governor Underwood had written: *To Homer Hickam, the best (and maybe the only) Republican in McDowell County.* I knew Dad would love it.

For Mom, I had something really special picked out. My plan was to give it to her just before she left for Myrtle Beach. I'd gone to the ladies' department at the Big Store and found an enameled powder box that played "Love Me Tender" when you opened it. Mom always liked Elvis Presley's slow tunes, and I sensed I had a winner. The only problem was it cost seven dollars. It took me a while to get up the courage to spend that kind of money on a present. It wasn't that I didn't have it. I did, but only if I dipped into the rocket-propellant money I'd saved up by washing cars and selling ginseng. After having a long conversation with myself on the importance of giving, especially to one's only mother, and reminding myself that I'd gotten a free quantity of moonshine from the Germans, I decided to do it. I chose to slip on down to the Big Store to get Mom's present on a special day, the day Santa Claus was coming to town.

The Big Store had set up Santa's sleigh in the front near the drugstore counter. I recognized who was playing Santa despite his white whiskers and red suit. It was Mr. Clowers, a widower who lived up on Substation Row. Mr. Clowers, who was in charge of the bathhouse beside the man-hoist, had an ample belly and played the part well. He also had a bum leg, and the jolly old elf arrived with a noticeable limp. "Daddy, why is Santa limping?" a wide-eyed little boy asked worriedly. His father, a shuttle-car operator, said, "He's been working 11 East." It got a laugh and also reminded everybody how much the section was haunting all the thoughts of so many in Coalwood, even so near Christmas.

Santa settled into his sled, built by the company carpentry shop, and began to laugh the traditional ho-ho-ho with his stomach shaking like a bowlful of jelly. The children of Coalwood all lined up to give Santa their list and receive their baskets of fruits and nuts, gifts from the company.

Roy Lee had come along to help me make my purchase. I was too embarrassed to go into the ladies' department by myself. He was looking for something for his mom, too. We stopped to watch the excited children who were lined up for Santa. Some of them yelled bloody murder, fearful at the sight of Santa. Others cooed in wonder and willingly crawled up on him to state their Christmas list. I looked over and was surprised to see Dreama Jenkins also watching. She was wearing the same brown cloth coat I'd first seen her in down at the Cape. Her long red hair hung lifelessly, some stray strands over her eyes. She clutched a small brown leather bag with her chapped, pink hands. She looked not only lonely and forlorn but fragile. I thought she'd break if anybody hugged her. Not that there was any danger of that. People were keeping their distance. I decided to talk to her. "What for?" Roy Lee asked when I told him what I was going to do.

"I feel sorry for her," I said. "Don't you?"

Roy Lee shrugged. "I guess I do," he said reluctantly. "But she doesn't belong here. Don't you see that? Look around. Pay attention for once in your life."

I took his challenge and paid attention. I saw that nearly every one of the mothers filing past with their children were averting their eyes from her. I watched a little girl run over to Dreama when she held out her hand, and I saw the mother pull her daughter back. The little girl wailed, and Dreama blushed beneath her thick makeup. "I guess I see what you mean," I said.

"Let her be, Sonny."

Roy Lee was right and I knew it. Most people in Coalwood wanted Dreama Jenkins to leave. And the truth was it didn't matter much to me, one way or the other. I felt sorry for her, but that was about as far as it went.

At his urging, I followed Roy Lee past Dreama and the mothers and kids and Mr. Clowers to the ladies' department. I took him to the counter with the music box inside. Mrs. Anastopoulos waited on us. Her husband was a continuous miner operator. "It's really a pretty thing," she said, placing it on the glass counter. I agreed. It was shaped like a beehive, and on the top was a little painting of a bee. A clever, nearly invisible latch opened the lid to reveal a depression for the powder and puff. Mrs. Anastopoulos pushed the latch, the lid lifted, and "Love Me Tender" started playing in little tinkly notes.

"Nice," Roy Lee said. "You have two of them?"

I was incredulous at his audacity. "We can't give our mothers the same thing!"

"Why not? When do they ever powder their noses together?"

"We just have the one," Mrs. Anastopoulos said, heading off an argument. "But Roy Lee, your mother has looked at these hair combs more than once."

Roy Lee looked at the combs. He liked them well enough, and they were within his budget. We had our presents. Mrs. Anastopoulos even gift-wrapped them. I felt a surge of sheer exultation while she did it. I knew Mom was going to love her present. I imagined the moment when she first opened the lid of her new powder box and heard the little tune. It made me feel warm inside to just think about it. The Bible says it's more blessed to give than receive, and at that moment, I knew what it meant. I was so happy that I just felt like the world was a wonderful place, and so were all the people in it. I soared in the spirit of the moment. When I came down from my inner flight, Roy Lee was looking at me with worry in his eyes. "What?" I asked.

"Where do you go sometimes?" he wondered.

I told him to stop being an idiot. I didn't go anywhere but right where I was. It wasn't the truth, but I wasn't about to confess to anything else. I didn't want people to start saying I was a dreamer. I wasn't, not at all. I did things, launched rockets, played in the band, hiked the mountains, made things happen. Dreamers never got anything done, just mused away the day. A dreamer? Not me, boy.

On the way out with our presents, Roy Lee and I found Dreama still watching the line in front of Mr. Clowers. There were just a few mothers and kids left. I don't know why I did what I did. I guess I was still so filled with the warmth of the general good of all mankind I couldn't stand anymore to see her standing there so dismal. I broke away from Roy Lee without a word to him and went up to her. "Hello, Miss Jenkins," I said.

She looked at me with wide-eyed but delighted surprise. She let a grin peek through. I caught sight of her broken tooth, only it wasn't broken anymore. It was fixed, or nearly so. Something about it didn't look quite natural, though. She saw that I'd noticed. "It's a temporary crown," she said proudly. "Dr. Hale has ordered me a special one. And it's Dreama, remember?"

"Yes, ma'am."

"Isn't this fun?" she asked, nodding toward Santa Claus Clowers and the little boy on his knee.

"Yes, ma'am, it is."

"I never got to sit on Santa Claus's lap," she said wistfully. "They had him down at the Gary store but Mama, she wouldn't take us. I used to cry and beg but she never would. It took me a while to figure out why. She didn't want to get our hopes up, that we'd get much at Christmas."

The way she said it was most sad, and I wanted to say something comforting but couldn't imagine what it should be. So I just blurted the first thing that came to my mind, which was "I was always afraid when Mom brought me to see Santa Claus." That sounded sort of negative, so I tried to clarify the thought. "Of course, at the time I had Santa Claus and God mixed up. I guess I'd still be scared if that was God sitting there and not Mr. Clowers."

"Shhh," she hushed me. "The kids'll hear you. They need to believe as long as they can."

An idea popped into my head. "Why don't you get in line, Dreama? You could sit on Mr. Clowers's lap." Out of the corner of my eye, I caught sight of Roy Lee opening his mouth in dismay.

"I couldn't do that!" she said, but the way she said it, I knew she wanted to.

"Why not? I'll stand with you."

And I did. I coaxed her into the line and we stood at its end. Roy Lee came up and whispered in my ear. "Are you nuts?"

I excused myself from Dreama. "I'm trying to do a good thing," I told him over by the drugstore counter. "It's Christmas. You're supposed to be charitable."

"You moron. You're just going to get her in trouble."

"Don't be stupid, Roy Lee," I said, and left him fuming.

The room was emptied except for me, Dreama, Roy Lee, Mr. Clowers, and Junior, the drugstore clerk. Dreama hesitated when Mr. Clowers looked at her with round, surprised eyes. "I can't," she whispered to me.

Mr. Clowers got the idea. He was a kind man. "Come on, little lady." He patted his knee. "Ol' Santa's always got time for a pretty girl."

Dreama put her hand to her mouth, showing her uncertainty, but then she seemed to find courage and slid into the sleigh and onto Mr. Clowers's knee. She held her purse in both hands. "I don't really want nothing," she said to his question.

"Oh, come on, every girl wants something," Mr. Clowers said.

Roy Lee came and stood beside me. He released a quiet sigh.

Dreama shrugged her thin shoulders and turned her head, her whole body turning kind of into itself like some shy little girl. It seemed to me that she really was a little girl at that moment, that she was letting out who she had once been, or wanted to be. "I'd like a doll baby," she said in a voice that could have belonged to a six-year-old. "And a little bottle with a nipple so I can feed her."

"Well, I'll see what I can do," Mr. Clowers said. His eyes had turned misty. "Is that all?"

"Yes, sir."

"Have you been a good girl?"

"Yes, sir."

It seemed to me that a kind of magic had entered the store, that what I was seeing wasn't happening at all, except perhaps in a pretty girl's dream. The spell was shattered by a low, angry voice. "Jack Clowers, you are a dirty old man. See, Tag, see what I told you was going on? She's been in here, sizing up our kids, seeing who she was gonna grab or something. Now, she's even after Santa Claus."

Mrs. Mallett had come in, bringing Tag Farmer with her. His face had a pained look. He shot a glance at me and then Dreama and Mr. Clowers. Dreama hastily got up from the sleigh. "I didn't mean nothing," she said. "I just wanted to see the children have fun."

"Why did you want to see them?" Mrs. Mallett demanded. "You thinking about getting one of them for Cuke? We know what he did once with that baby girl. That's why he was in prison."

Tag said, "Now, Cleo, that girl was sixteen years old. It wasn't right what Cuke did, but it wasn't like she was a baby."

This was all news to me. I'd never heard the reason why Cuke had gone to prison. I still didn't understand exactly what it was.

Dreama hung her head. She mumbled something. "What's that, ma'am?" Tag asked.

She looked at him. "I just want . . ." Her voice dropped off so I couldn't hear what she said.

"Yes, ma'am, I know," Tag said. "But I guess it's best if you go on now."

"Ain't you gonna arrest her, Tag? You can see what she's doing." Mrs. Mallett looked at me and Roy Lee. "I bet she's after these boys, too."

Tag was clearly embarrassed. "Cleo, let it go."

Mrs. Mallett was never the type to let anything go, especially when she saw an opening to expound on her perceptions of sin and other human folly. "What kind of woman are you?" she demanded, while Dreama seemed to shrink before her. "You come in here from some stinking Gary hollow, shack up with Cuke, and think you're allowed to mix with decent folk? I'll tell you where you belong. You belong in Cinder Bottom, not in a respectable place like Coalwood."

"Mrs. Mallett!" It was Junior. Startled, Mrs. Mallett turned to look at him. The bespectacled clerk was leaning forward on his counter. His eyes said he was scared but he was mad, too. "Mrs. Mallett, I'll thank you to leave my customers alone. If you can't behave better than that, you should . . . well, you should just leave."

Mrs. Mallett regarded him. "A colored man could get himself in big trouble with talk like that, Junior."

"All right, all right," Tag said. "That's enough. I want everybody to go. That includes you, Cleo. You, too, Sonny and Roy Lee." He put his finger to the bill of his cap when he faced Dreama. "You too, ma'am. I'm sorry."

Just then, a mother and child arrived. "Ho-ho-ho!" Mr. Clowers cried in relief at the sight of them. "Merry Christmas!"

Dreama wrapped her arms around herself and walked quickly, her head down, through the door. Mrs. Mallett watched her, her fleshy arms crossed. Despite Tag's order, she didn't look like she planned on budging. "Tag, you're making a big mistake, I'm telling you." She looked around at all of us. "You think you're doing that woman a kindness, but I'm telling you she's up to purely no good."

Tag went over and leaned on the drugstore counter. He rubbed his face and took off his cap and laid it down. "What's the strongest thing you've got, Junior?" he asked grimly.

Junior gave it some thought. "Chocolate milk shake," he said at last.

"Make it a double," Tag said, slapping his scrip down. Then he looked around, his eyes falling on me and Roy Lee. Mrs. Mallett was squatted down beside the little girl, cooing, telling her how pretty she was while her mother beamed. He raised his eyebrows at us, and Roy Lee and I headed out the door.

On the drive back, we passed Dreama walking up the sidewalk toward Cuke's house. "We ought to stop, give her a ride," I said.

"Don't you know when to give up?" Roy Lee demanded. Just to show me, he pressed harder on the accelerator pedal, leaving her in a puff of blue exhaust. "Leave her alone. You can't help her."

Then I remembered what Mrs. Mallett had said about Cuke. "What do you guess Cuke did with that sixteen-year-old girl?" I asked.

Roy Lee huffed a joyless laugh. "He raped her. At least that's what he went to prison for. The way I heard it, she'd been raped by a lot of men in Bradshaw on pretty much a regular basis. Cuke got caught by her daddy and that got him shipped off to the state pen for a few years."

As we rattled up Main Street, I tried to get what had happened to Cuke settled in my mind. Men had a responsibility to women, no matter how old they were. I'd been taught that from practically the day I was born. I believed it, too, although the concept had been sorely tested a few times when Wanda Kirk used to beat me up at grade-school recess. But I figured a mature man had an even greater responsibility to a young girl. A man who crossed the line on that deserved everything more righteous men might give him. I was glad Cuke had gone to prison for what he'd done, and I was sorry he'd found another young girl in Dreama.

At my house, Roy Lee stopped to let me off. I had another question before I got out of his car. "What did she say, Roy Lee?" I asked. "Could you hear her?"

I guess Roy Lee was pretty much done with me for the day. "Who?" he snapped.

"Dreama. You know, when she told Tag—I just want . . . something—I couldn't hear her."

"My God, Sonny. Can't you just let it go?"

"I'm just asking," I explained. "Did you hear her?"

"Yes."

"What did she say?"

Despite himself, I think, Roy Lee's eyes betrayed a hint of sadness. "It was stupid." He turned his face away.

"Roy Lee, what did she say?"

He kept his expression hidden but his voice was glum. "She said she just wanted to be a Coalwood girl."

IT was the last week of classes before exams and the Christmas break, and there was barely contained excitement coursing through Big Creek's halls, bright with candy canes, red and green crepe paper, wreaths, and over nearly every door entrance, sprigs of mistletoe. Kisses were legal under mistletoe, and if you stood under a door long enough, some girl would give you a peck on the cheek if only to get you to move. Hand-painted posters from the various clubs wished everybody a Merry Christmas. Sandy Whitt and her Christmas Formal decorating committee had placed notices at strategic spots, reminding everybody of the big dance. The theme this year was "Let It Snow."

The week before, Sandy had snagged me in the hall between English lit and civics class. "I need help decorating," she said.

"I'm not going to the formal," I replied.

"How come?"

"I don't have a date."

"You don't? Well, that's crazy. You're the friendliest boy I know."

"Friendly and date material apparently don't go together," I said. Then I asked, "How about you?" I was going for a miracle. Sandy Whitt was the most popular girl in school.

"Silly. Dave and I have been going steady for a year."

I knew that. Dave Taylor was not only a star football player, he was just an all-round nice guy. Heavy competition. "When are you decorating?"

"All day Sunday after church until we're done."

"I'll come if I can." There was no use resisting once Sandy had you in her sights.

"Thanks, Sonny, I can always count on you," she said, and off she went, ponytail flying.

Ginger, Betty Jane, and Sue Burnett passed me going the other way while I hurried down the hall. The civics teacher, Mr. Short, was a placid man but he had a pet peeve. He didn't like anybody to be late for his class. Ginger broke off from the trio. "You look tired," she worried.

"I've been staying up late studying," I confessed. "I'm trying to get all A's this semester."

"That'll make two of us," she said.

"Well, at least you don't look tired." It was my clumsy way of paying her a compliment.

"That's because I don't go around trying to save the world all the time, Sonny Hickam," she said. "I heard how you took up for Dreama at the Big Store."

"I just got her in trouble," I replied miserably.

"That's not what Junior said." The bell rang and she headed down the hall to catch up with the other sophomores.

I looked after her. It was funny. Ginger had said the same thing about me that Mom had said about Dad. We were both trying to save the world. I sure hoped the world knew it.

"Coming to my class, Mr. Hickam?" Mr. Short called from his door. I expected trouble, but he only gave me a smile as I rushed past him into the classroom. I guess he'd already caught the Christmas spirit.

Mr. Short settled behind his desk, a huge slab of brown oak. He wore a charcoal-gray three-piece suit, and, in a splash of Christmas color, a green-and-red-striped tie. He had brown hair, combed straight back, but his Errol Flynn mustache was tinged with gray, as were his sideburns. He had a kind face and a soft voice, but most of us knew better than to mess with him. He was also the assistant principal, and that added an aura of extra authority about him.

Mrs. Turner appeared at the door. "Mr. Short, excuse me for interrupting, but I need Billy Rose," she said.

After Mr. Short had given him permission, Billy stood up, shoveled his books under his arm, and grimly followed her. "He's gone," Roy Lee said. "I saw the navy recruiter down at Mr. Turner's office."

"Would you like to share your information with the class, Mr. Cooke?" Mr. Short asked.

Roy Lee repeated what he'd told me. Mr. Short said, "Quitting school represents two failures: that of the teachers and that of the student. But Billy hasn't given up. If he's going in the navy, he's still trying to better himself. We need to remember that."

What Mr. Short had said was true to my way of thinking, but it didn't make me feel any better about it.

After civics, we moved to physics class. Miss Riley asked everybody to gather around her desk. Although her supply of chemicals and hardware was running on empty, her supply of creativity was always filled to the brim. She invited us to look at a razor blade floating on the surface of the water in a shallow pan. "What holds the blade up?" she asked. We all knew the answer and competed with each other to say it first: surface tension, the elastic property of the surface of liquids. Then she squirted some liquid detergent in the water and the razor blade sank. "How come?" she asked.

Roy Lee said, "Because it makes the razor blade so slippery it cuts through?" We just laughed at him, but we didn't know the answer any better than he.

Quentin piped up and said, "Is it not clear to you all that the detergent simply reduces the surface tension of the water such that it cannot hold the blade?"

Everybody went silent. Quentin, we were certain, had nailed it. "You've described *what* happened, Quentin," Miss Riley said gently. "But *why* did it happen? That's the more important question."

Quentin's eyes registered puzzlement. He licked his lips. She had him stumped. I had an idea. "Could it be," I said, "that the detergent molecules are so small they get in between the water molecules and that's what keeps them from clustering? If they did, the tension would be gone. It would be like knocking the legs out from under a table."

Quentin looked at me. "A rigorous thought, Sonny," he said.

I preened, just a little. Miss Riley smiled. Her experiments, no matter how simple, were to provoke our minds.

Miss Riley waved me up to her after class. She rested her cheek on her hand. "Can you tell Jake something for me?" I nodded, and she said, "Tell him I have received his message and will oblige."

I was happy to hear that she and Jake were communicating. She perused her grade book. "If you get an A on your exam," she said, "looks like you'll get an A in this class. I'd put that down as prodigious, as Quentin would say."

"I have a good chance of getting A's in all my classes," I reported, careful not to sound too proud.

"Why the turnaround?"

"My rockets," I said instantly. "Every class seems to have an application. Even speech class. I've been giving every one of my speeches on the space race."

Miss Riley worked her lips as if trying to keep them straight, but a crooked smile broke through. "I know. Miss Bryson said she'd like to see a little variety in your act."

"Well, I'm kind of interested in the Loch Ness monster," I confessed.

"You might want to use it as the subject for your final speech," she suggested.

Quentin was waiting for me outside the classroom. "I applaud you for your rigorous thought process on surface tension, Sonny," he prattled. "Roy Lee's idea of the razor blade becoming slippery was, of course, ludicrous, but you might be interested to know that I have been considering the entire concept of slipperiness lately, a subject profoundly ignored by most scientists. In fact, I believe that if I put my mind to it, I might be able to create the perfect slippery surface. The applications of that would be enormous! Frying pans, for instance. Would that not be prodigious, Sonny, my boy? Your mother with a frying pan whereby her eggs did not stick? A complex polymer will probably be the solution. I have been considering the chemistry of the banana to start . . ."

"Quentin, not now," I said. "I've got other things on my mind."

"Such as?"

"I have a list. It was your suggestion. You want to hear everything on it?"

"Not really," he confessed.

"Then how about your ceramic-lined nozzle? You want to hear about that? Mr. Caton finally figured out how to layer in the putty. And I got to tell you, it's prodigious!"

Quentin opened his mouth. I could tell he was about to say "Prodigious!" but since I'd already said it, I nearly had him at a loss for words. Finally, he said, "Stupendous!"

"Quentin?" I stopped him in his tracks. He raised his eyebrows. "Please don't start saying 'stupendous.' I don't think I could stand it."

He nodded, implying that he understood, although I knew he didn't.

WE walked down the hall past the principal's office. I was surprised when I glanced through the glass in his closed door and saw some familiar faces. I was most astonished to see my mother as well as Mr. and Mrs. Likens, the Coalwood school principal and his wife. In the corner of Mr. Turner's office was a man in a navy uniform. I didn't see Billy. "What do you make of it, Sonny?" Quentin asked.

A surge of hope passed through me. "Did I ever tell you the navy occupied Coalwood one time, Q?"

Quentin scratched his head. "No. Why did they do that?"

"Because they wanted something we had." I looked into the office again. Mrs. Turner spotted me and closed the door to the outer office but not before I saw Mrs. Likens shaking her finger at the navy man. I laughed. "I think the tables just got turned."

That evening, Billy wasn't on the school bus back to Coalwood. The next morning, he wasn't at the Six bus stop, either, but he did turn up in our first class. Mom had already given me the good news the night before. Mr. Turner was going to keep Billy at his house through exam week and even the Christmas holidays. He could stay there the rest of the school year if he needed to. The navy had been sent packing. "You and Mr. and Mrs. Likens did a good thing, Mom," I said.

Mom was sitting on the top of her ladder, concentrating on the wispy clouds in the sky of her painting. "It saves him for now," she said. "We'll keep our fingers crossed that he can get through the rest of the year."

I didn't try to compliment her anymore. Sometimes just doing something is praise enough.

EVERY time I went past the union hall, I saw more activity. Hand-lettered signs were stacked out front. One of them said HICKMAN IS A RAT. Another one said HICKHAM AGAINST THE WORKING MAN. The signs didn't bother me. Every time there was a strike, I'd seen them like that, or worse. What I wondered was how many years we'd have to live in Coalwood before people figured out how to spell our simple name.

Roy Lee, who kept his finger on the union pulse through his brother, said Mr. Dubonnet and Mr. Mallett were primed to take their men out on strike during Christmas week. All they needed was the approval of UMWA headquarters in Charleston. "Your dad can kiss 11 East good-bye if they do," Roy Lee said. "It's going to be one of their main gripes. They're going to shut that section down for good. You ever find out what he's doing in there?"

"No."

Roy Lee was driving me down to the machine shop to get Mr. Caton to take another turn on the nozzle he'd built. I had found it to be just a shade too large for the rocket casement it was supposed to fit within. It was probably because of me trying to design with a fat lead pencil and a large-scale ruler.

As we drove past the Club House, we saw Mrs. Mallett and some of the other women in her new club. They were supervising their husbands who were putting up plywood camels, sheep, and other Christmas cutouts on the Club House lawn. One of the Wise Men held a sign that said THIS DISPLAY ERECTED BY THE C.O.W. LADIES.

I tried not to care but I did. Coalwood was just going to have this blighted little display this year and, in a way, it was my fault. If I'd jumped in and written the pageant script for Mom way back when she'd first asked me, it might have given her the momentum she needed to make it happen, despite the company's abandonment of it along with everything else. I shook my head, sighing. "Shut up," Roy Lee said before I could open my mouth. "It's not your fault."

"You're a good guy, Roy Lee," I said.

He hunched his shoulders. "Well, keep it to yourself. I have a bad reputation to defend."

MY brain was crammed full. I had to let it get out on paper before it fell out of my ears. Exam day had struck at Big Creek High School, and I had studied all I could study. I gave my speech on the Loch Ness monster and got a thumbs-up from Miss Bryson. I was on a roll. Civics, English literature, typing, physics, and trigonometry all went by, one exam after the other. When I finished, I knew I'd done well. I could just feel it. I was going to get all A's. I allowed myself a small grin, then wiped it off lest someone see me being proud.

2 2

BACK TO THE DRAWING BOARD

"WHAT DO YOU think?" Quentin asked nervously. It was the third time within the last minute he'd asked the same question. We were standing at the launchpad. *Auk XXIII-A,* with Mr. Caton's proud putty-lined De Laval nozzle, was ready to go. Dean Crabtree, an auxiliary Rocket Boy, had come over from Caretta to help Roy Lee get the pad ready. But after I had pressed the cork holding the nichrome hot wire into the nozzle, I saw Billy emerging from the fog, loping across the slack. He came straight to me. "I'm back," he said.

I felt like hugging him. Instead, I balled up my fist and hit him on the shoulder, though not too hard. "What happened? I thought you were staying with Mr. Turner clear on the other side of the county."

The other boys came running. Billy gave them all a small, embarrassed grin. "Tell you what," he said. "I've said my share of bad things about Mr. Turner but never again. You know why he's so hard on us? It's because he cares."

"Yeah, yeah," O'Dell said impatiently. "But why are you here?"

Billy shrugged, his smile lost. "I decided to just come on home and stick it out. I need to watch after my brothers and sisters, anyway. And just knowing that I have a place to go when things get too rough helps out a lot."

"Anytime you like, you come stay with me," Sherman said. Except for Quentin, we all echoed the sentiment for our own homes.

Billy drew me aside. "Tell your mom thanks for me. I don't know how, but I'm going to pay her back."

"She doesn't expect anything, Billy."

"I'll figure it out," he said, going over to the pad to help Roy Lee and Dean.

The sun was taking its time burning off the mists swirling around Rocket Mountain. If we launched through the fog, we had a good chance of losing the rocket. If we lost it, then we couldn't inspect the nozzle, the real purpose of the launch. We just had to wait, as hard as that was. Quentin came over, and we went over our checklist again. "I think it's going to be a great rocket," I said. I had designed this one to reach an altitude of precisely two miles. Included in my calculations was a half-pound payload of smoke-producing, high-sulfur, low-grade zincoshine. This was to help us track the rocket better. When the fog lifted, I hoped for either a high solid cloud layer or blue sky. Both were good for tracking because we could see the casements silhouetted against a solid background, clear or cloudy.

"I should have checked your calculations," Quentin said, still worrying. "Lord knows you have your problems with logarithms."

"Did I tell you I got all A's this semester?" I asked serenely. I was watching Billy show Dean how to set up the launch rod. Nothing was going to dent my good mood.

"About a thousand times," he said. "It is a depressing statistic, is it not? Once out of how many semesters? Five in high school so far! That means you have failed to reach your potential during eighty percent of your academic career."

"You're a pal, Quentin," I said. "By the way, what kind of grades did you get?"

He frowned. "If Coach Mams had an ounce of fairness in his bones, I would've had all A's, too. Once more, I've been unfairly graded a B in phys ed."

"You know, Q, you might want to actually come to his class

once in a while," I suggested. "I'm not sure, but doing something physical in physical education is probably a good idea if you want an A."

"Can I help it if I often experience a headache at that precise time of day? Do you think it's easy to tote around all these brains?" He tapped his noggin.

"Are you ever going to set up the theodolite stations?" I wondered. It was the square on my checklist still unchecked.

"When my assistants arrive," he said haughtily.

"Your what?"

"My assistants. Ah, there they are. Over here, my good men!"

I looked and spied Tug and Hug Yates strolling across the slack. I knew them well. Tug and Hug were twins who worked on the hoot-owl shift. When my class reached the fifth grade, we'd found Tug and Hug patiently waiting for us to catch up with them. As a matter of fact, they had been patiently waiting in Mrs. Mary Alice Cox's class for nearly four years. It was their final stand at the Coalwood school. Mr. Likens, the Coalwood school principal, figured if Mrs. Cox couldn't educate them, nobody could. Mrs. Cox had given it her best, but it had turned out to be hopeless. The thing about Tug and Hug was that they were not the least bit disruptive in class, just uninterested. They sat in the back and read when they were asked to read, or wrote when they were asked to write, and took tests when they were given them to take, none of which they ever passed or even came close. They were marking time until Mr. Likens let them loose to go to work in the mine.

When my class moved on to the sixth grade, we left Tug and Hug holding down their two desks in Mrs. Cox's class. That's when Mr. Likens finally gave up. He came into their classroom and said, "Boys, we've done all we can do for you. You are free to go." With a whoop, they had bounded from their desks and run down to the bridge that crossed from the school over the railroad tracks. Tug was so excited, he vaulted off the bridge into a full coal car passing below. Hug did the same, not noticing that Tug had caught the last coal car. The next one was the caboose. Hug bounced off the top of it, breaking both his legs. That mishap had delayed the two boys getting their job at the mine but not by much. They had become two perpetually cheerful employees of Olga Coal Company, assigned more or less permanently to the hoot-owl shift by my father, who liked the two boys and used their intellectual limitations to the company's best advantage as well as their own. Tug and Hug were their own best friends. I often heard their distinctive braying laughter at night from my room as they walked in the long line of hoot-owl-shift miners going to work. Everybody in town thought the world of Tug and Hug. "Ready to go to work, Cap'n," they saluted Quentin.

"What's the deal, Q?" I demanded.

"The deal is this telephone wire is heavy and I need help. These two fine gentlemen have volunteered to assist me. In return, I have made them honorary members of the BCMA."

Tug and Hug grinned. "We like being Rocket Boys," they said. They proceeded to shoulder the telephone wire and Quentin's theodolite and head downrange.

I grabbed Quentin before he could follow them. "They can't be part of the BCMA!"

Quentin pulled away. "Why not? They seem like good old boys to me."

"You want a club full of good old boys or Rocket Boys? Seems to me it has to be one way or the other."

Quentin looked down his long nose at me, his crisp blue eyes crinkling along the edges. "It never occurred to me until this moment that you are quite the prig, Sonny Hickam. Without a doubt, the result of your privileged life as a mine superintendent's son."

I sputtered, searching for a comeback but couldn't find one. "Quentin, just tell me you aren't going to recruit any more fifth-grade dropouts into the BCMA."

Quentin shrugged and stalked off, shaking his head. "Quite the prig," he said over his shoulder.

I looked downrange. Tug and Hug already had the telephone wire and theodolite station set up. It would have taken Quentin another hour at the rate he usually went. Maybe the boy was on to something, I didn't know. But—me, a *prig*? I struck the accusation from my mind as unworthy and went to the blockhouse. "All ready, Sherman?"

Sherman patted the firing box. "Roger that. How's the audience?"

I went back outside to see. There were about a hundred spectators, I estimated. I saw Basil Oglethorpe pull up in his purple Studebaker. He got out, his notepad at the ready. He was wearing a fur coat that went all the way down to his ankles, and on his head was a straw boater with a red ribbon around the crown. A few of the miners who had never seen him before gave him second and then third looks. "Hey, Basil," I called.

A big grin split his narrow face. "Ah, Sonny. A delightful day to continue the adventures of the Rocket Boys, eh? I shall be pleased to continue to make you famous. Someone told me you were thinking about entering a science fair. Is that so?"

"I guess it is," I said. "If we can solve our nozzle-erosion problem. We're trying out an ablative ceramic coating today."

Basil kept his pencil poised. "I'd prefer that quote to be a little snappier," he said.

"We're going for it," I said.

"Ah." Basil scribbled it down. "Going . . . for . . . it! *Excellentay!*"

I excused myself from Basil when I saw Ginger drive up in her parents' Buick. She was alone. "Have you seen those awful plywood things the COW ladies put up on the Club House lawn?" she demanded as soon as I got within range. "Are those not the tackiest things you've ever seen?" She put her hands on her hips. "So what are we going to do about it?"

"I can't do anything about it," I said. "I'm in charge of the BCMA, not Christmas. Anyway, remember you said I shouldn't try to save the world."

"No, I didn't. I just noticed that that's what you do."

Sherman came up. "Hi, Ginger."

Ginger apprised Sherman of the "awful plywood things."

"I know," he said. "I hate them, too."

Billy and Roy Lee and Dean, seeing that Sherman and I had stopped working to talk to Ginger, strolled over. "There's not going to be a Christmas Pageant this year?" Billy asked. When told it had been canceled, he didn't try to hide his disappointment. "You know, I really loved going to those things."

"Well, I say there's got to be a Christmas Pageant for Billy's sake, if for no other reason," Sherman said. "Anyway, it's our last Christmas here. That's a reason right there."

I had to challenge him. "Come on, Sherman. You don't think you'll come back to visit your parents at Christmas?"

"Sure I will," he said, "but I won't be a Coalwood boy. You know how it is. When somebody leaves here, they can come back but they're not part of the town anymore, not really. This is our last Christmas."

Roy Lee piped up. "Hell, if we can build a rocket, we can put on some little Christmas Pageant."

"Is that right, Roy Lee?" I asked, taken aback that he, of all people, wanted to do this thing. "And how do you propose that we do it?"

"You can do it, Sonny," Sherman said. "You have a talent for planning."

I had sensed that was coming. "No way," I said. "You're not going to put this on me."

"I'll help and so will my mom," Ginger said as if I hadn't said a word. "The teachers will pitch in, they always do. And we can get the Community Church choir."

O'Dell came over, Quentin with him. Tug and Hug brought up the rear. "Heck, yes," O'Dell said when Sherman told him what we were talking about. "It wouldn't seem like Christmas without a pageant, would it?"

"What are you talking about?" Quentin asked. Since he wasn't a Coalwood boy, he'd never seen one of our pageants.

"We sing carols!" Sherman said.

"There's a manger scene," Billy said.

"Everybody plays a role like an angel or something," Roy Lee said. "Hey, can I be an angel?"

"How can the Big Creek lovemaster be an angel?" I asked sarcastically.

Roy Lee looked hurt. "We're talking about *acting*, Sonny."

"It sounds prodigious!" Quentin fairly exploded. "Can I help?"

"No, you can't," I said, "because there's not going to be any pageant. Like I said, to pull one of these things off takes company support. I mean the Club House lawn is company property, for one thing."

"So's Cape Coalwood," O'Dell said. "It hasn't stopped us from using it."

"We have permission, O'Dell," I said. "I'm the one who got it, remember?"

"So get it for the Club House."

"Another thing," I said. "It takes weeks to plan one of these things. Today's December 19. If we start tomorrow, we'd barely have five days."

"Then start today," Sherman said. "Plan it out, tell us what to do and we'll do it."

"The union's going out on strike," I said, still trying to head the thing off. "We get miners and foremen together, there'll be a riot, not a pageant."

I was wasting my breath. Sherman said, "All in favor say aye!"

"*Aye!*"

"Nays?" he asked.

"Nay," I said, but my heart wasn't into it. The truth was I was starting to catch some of their enthusiasm, but I wasn't about to admit it. For one thing, Mom wouldn't be around to see our pageant, and that would be pretty sad. For another, I truly doubted our ability to pull such a thing off in the short amount of time we had. I didn't want to get excited over nothing.

"The ayes have it," Sherman said smugly.

Ginger laughed. "This is going to be so much fun!"

I sincerely doubted the accuracy of her statement but kept my opinion to myself. "Can we just launch our rocket now?" I asked the assembly instead.

———

I stabbed the launch button and *Auk XXIII-A* took off smoothly, climbing swiftly on a towering funnel of zincoshine smoke. Our audience applauded and hooted with joy. Zincoshine-propelled rockets seemed to have that effect on most people. They were exuberant rockets, and they brought out exuberance in everybody who watched them go.

After it hit downrange, we stampeded over to the Auk. A quick calculation revealed that we'd flown under my altitude projection by a thousand feet. I rolled the casement over a couple of times with a stick to help it cool. When it did, I turned it on its end and peered inside the nozzle. "Not as much erosion," I reported, "but we've still got some and it's at the worst place. Right at the throat."

Quentin groaned. "If we don't solve this puzzle, we can just kiss the science fair—and our futures—good-bye."

Dean put his finger inside the nozzle and swiped it around, his finger coming out covered with metal filings and soot. "Maybe this edge right at the throat is so sharp the putty can't stick to it very well."

Mr. Bolt and Mr. Caton came walking up. Mr. Caton inspected the results. "I think Dean's right," he said. "That edge is probably a hot spot, too. How about I smooth it out, make it curved rather than have that sharp angle?"

"Better hurry," Mr. Bolt said. "I hear the strike's not more than a day or two away. A strike will close the machine shop, too."

"I'll get right on it," Mr. Caton said. "If Sonny will get me a drawing."

"Sure," I said. "Back to the drawing board. What else do I have to do besides plan a Christmas Pageant? It's a good thing I'm not going to the Christmas Formal."

"I am!" Quentin said, to my surprise.

Roy Lee raised his eyebrows. "Too bad," he said. "I was going to suggest you and Sonny go together."

"Who are you going with, Quentin?" Dean asked.

"Mary Kay Yates."

"Tug and Hug's sister?" Roy Lee whooped.

Now I understood the new honorary members of the BCMA. "I hope you have fun, Quentin," I said sourly.

Roy Lee's eyes were aglow. "With Mary Kay Yates, he's going to have trouble mostly keeping his pants on."

Quentin blushed severely. Tug and Hug grinned proudly. I thought of my lack of a date and the Christmas Pageant that had been dumped on me and my list and everything else. Then I recalled the snow goose that had accidentally landed on Cape Coalwood so many months before. She'd looked around, then spread her wings and taken off for a better clime. Overwhelmed and oddly disheartened, I wished with all my heart I could do the same.

23

THE LONG WALL

I REPORTED TO Jake on the Club House porch at 1:00 P.M. that afternoon as directed. I gave him Miss Riley's message. "Good deal," he said. He threw me a pair of coveralls and a miner's helmet. "Put these on."

"I thought we were going hiking in the mountains."

"Nope. Whole different direction."

I did as I was told. "Where are we going?" I asked while I laced up my hard-toe boots. I'd tucked my coverall pants in them as all Coalwood men did.

Jake ignored my question and walked toward his Corvette and I followed, but we didn't get in. Instead, he went to a red Jeep on the other side of the street. OLGA COAL COMPANY was painted on its hood and rear hatch. "Get in the back," he said. "We've got another passenger."

"Jake, what's going on?"

"Company business," he said brusquely. He didn't sound like the old Jake, the happy, carefree Jake. This Jake was all business. Trained to obey adults at least until I could see what direction they were going, I subsided into the back of the Jeep and waited to see what I would see. That proved to be none other than one Mr. John Dubonnet.

Mr. Dubonnet came out of the union hall, dressed in mine

clothes. He climbed in the passenger seat of the Jeep. "Jake," he greeted. He looked over his shoulder at me. "Sonny." He looked questioningly at Jake.

"Because," Jake said, throwing the Jeep in gear. We sped up Main Street until we reached the mine. We walked up to the cage, and the lamp-house attendant brought out lamps for our helmets. Jake and Mr. Dubonnet picked up their identification tags, circles of brass with a number stamped on it. "I can't do this," I said when the attendant handed me my own tag. "Mom will kill me. You too, Jake."

"This is not a time to worry about your mother," Jake said grimly.

"Where are we going?" I asked anew.

"11 East. I thought you should know why everybody wants to beat you up." He looked at Mr. Dubonnet. "And why some people want to cut and run."

"This better be good, Jake," Mr. Dubonnet growled.

Jake pushed the warning bell at the lift gate. "It won't be good. It'll be business. Let's go."

The rock walls crept by as we descended down the shaft. Layer after layer passed, whole geological ages, millions of years of sediment. Jake and Mr. Dubonnet were silent, lost in their own thoughts and purposes. The rectangular opening at the top of the shaft gradually shrank until it was just a twinkling star. Then it disappeared altogether. We were at the bottom of the shaft.

"Turn your light on, boy," Mr. Dubonnet said, and I reached up to my helmet and clicked the battery-driven lamp on. We stepped off the lift, the operator swinging open the gate for us. A train of cars waited, a motorman squatting on the locomotive in front. I recognized him as Mr. Bradley, the father of Miss Liberty on the Veterans Day float. We crawled into a man-trip. Jake slapped the top of the car. "Let's go," he gruffly ordered Mr. Bradley.

The locomotive lurched forward with a shriek, found its traction on the rails, and began to pick up speed. Soon, timbers and cribs on the main line were blurring past. The walls were white, thoroughly dusted down by the rock-dust crews on the hoot-owl shift.

"You're not afraid, are you, Sonny?" Mr. Dubonnet asked over the rush of air past the man-trip and the anguished wail of the steel wheels on the track. "A West Virginia boy is born for these deep places. There's something that just feels right about being here for us. I guess it shouldn't surprise me that even a Rocket Boy would like it."

"I wouldn't say I like it, sir," I told him, feeling suddenly vulnerable to his thoughts. "But I'm not afraid."

He pondered me. "When he took you down here, what all did your daddy say to you?"

I recalled that Mr. Dubonnet had seen us on that day last spring. Of course, it was none of his business what Dad had said, but it irritated me enough—Mr. Dubonnet trying to wheedle personal stuff out of me—that I gave it to him both barrels. "He said he knew the mine like he knew a man. He said he knew it because he came down here every day, breathed the air, felt it on his face, went back into the gob and poked around. He said if he didn't come down here, men might get hurt or the coal wouldn't get loaded. He said coal is the lifeblood of the country, and if coal failed, steel failed, and then the country failed. That's what he said."

Jake was grinning, about what I didn't know. That irritated me, too. Mr. Dubonnet fell silent, then turned out his lamp and settled down, apparently for a nap. I knew I'd gotten his goat but I didn't know how. The man-trip rattled on, deeper into the bowels of the vast mine.

Many minutes later, nearly an hour, I estimated, the man-trip finally slowed and stopped. Jake aimed his light out the side hatch. "This is it," he grunted, and climbed out. Mr. Dubonnet switched his lamp back on and climbed out behind him. I clambered out, too, and stood up, cracking my helmet against the roof, jamming it nearly down around my ears. Jake, Mr. Dubonnet, and Mr. Bradley all laughed. "I been trying to make that old roof higher for a long time myself, Sonny boy," Mr. Bradley said.

I lurched into a piece of machinery, cracking my shins. I shined my light on it. It was a conveyor belt. "The coal will come out here," Jake said, pointing at the end of the belt. He waved us on. Mr. Dubonnet hesitated, had a word with Mr. Bradley, and then followed.

The roof of the tunnel we were walking through kept getting lower. I kept trying to straighten up, but my helmet would hit the rock and knock me back down. We had nearly been forced into a duckwalk when the tunnel suddenly opened into a large room. I shined my light on the roof, a rough dome, and saw it was studded with roof bolts. The room was stacked with equipment, yellow devices that looked like huge car jacks. "This is the staging area," Jake said.

Mr. Dubonnet swung his light around. "Long wall," he said. "So that's the big secret. I thought so but I couldn't tell for sure by the reports from my men. Jake, this is a violation of the union agreement."

"That could be debated, John," Jake said, "and I guess it will be, if it comes to that."

"It won't come to that," he growled. "I got strike approval from headquarters this morning. I'm going to shut this operation down."

Jake made no reply, just waved us on. There were three tunnels leading off from the domed room. He chose the center one. "This is where the advance will begin," he said. "If we can get through the header."

We walked for some time. I lost track. The tunnel seemed to slope downward, and my ears kept popping, the air getting heavier. A breeze touched my face. Lights flashed far ahead. A conveyor belt along the sides of the tunnel was running continuously. It was carrying chunks of rock, not coal. We emerged in another domed room with more stacks of equipment. A huge rock slide blocked our way, but a dozen men swarmed over it, hand-loading rock on the belt. Four men stood watching them, holding massive drills attached to what I took to be pneumatic hoses. An electric compressor whined nearby. "The header," Jake said. "We get through there, we can start the advance."

Mr. Dubonnet swung his light around the pile of rock. "You'll never get through it. The Captain couldn't do it and neither can Homer Hickam."

At the mention of his name, I anxiously looked around for Dad, but there was no sign of him. Then an ugly, bewhiskered face suddenly appeared in the spot of my light. It was Cuke Snoddy, grinning. He shined his light in my eyes, and I put up my hand to shield the glare. "Well, well, little Sonny the Rocket Boy. Haw, haw! You kind of lost, ain't ya?"

His breath stunk of tobacco. There was a big lump in his cheek and brown trails of chew spit and rock dust ran down from the corners of his mouth. He kept grinning at me, as if trying to figure me out. I didn't say anything, lest I provoke him in some way. Jake and Mr. Dubonnet shined their lights on Cuke. "You gonna be ready, Cuke?" Jake asked.

"You get me up to it, I'll have that header moved, Mr. Jake. Don't you no never mind," Cuke said.

"Cuke's our powder man," Jake said to Mr. Dubonnet. "The best one Olga's got."

"You're going to blast in here? You can't do that in this mine. It'll blow the whole place up."

Jake shook his head. "You feel that air pressure when you came in? This is a pressure mine, John, and we've got this whole area with more holes in it than a pincushion. We're blowing the methane right up to the surface."

"You hope you are, you mean," Mr. Dubonnet said. "This coal is so gassy you could get a pocket of methane and never know it. You can't blast."

"I'll do it, slick as chicken shit, Johnny boy," Cuke interjected, and then spat a huge stream of juice in between Mr. Dubonnet's boots. "Ain't nobody better with powder than ol' Cuke and I can sniff out the black damp." He tapped his nose. Black damp was what the miners called methane.

"You'll do what I tell you to do, Cuke," Mr. Dubonnet shot back. "You're going out on strike with everybody else."

Jake pointed up at the overhead dome. "See the roof? Thin-bedded. Perfect for long wall, John."

"It's weak is what it is," Mr. Dubonnet grumped. "This whole section is a death trap. It always has been."

"Long-wall mining is the future," Jake said.

"That may be, but not in this mine," Mr. Dubonnet spat.

"What's long-wall mining?" I asked, but Mr. Dubonnet tramped off, going back down the tunnel. Jake hurried to catch him. Not wanting to stay alone in the company of Cuke, I charged off behind them. Jake and Mr. Dubonnet had some words I couldn't hear and then turned into an entry I hadn't seen on the way down. I struggled to keep up with them. They were moving fast, bent almost double. My neck was killing me, trying to hold it up at an awkward angle to keep my light on them. If I lost them, I was certain I would wander around for the rest of my short life, lost under Coalwood Mountain.

I saw lights up ahead and heard the guttural howl of a great beast, apparently being tortured. When I rounded a curve, I saw it was a continuous mining machine, tearing away at a coal face. The roof had gradually risen until I could stand up with my helmet barely scraping it. I put my fist in my back, rubbing. I was sixteen years old, but miners twice, three times my age could take the low roof better than I could. It was a matter of practice, I guessed.

Some men were watching near a pillar of coal. One of them came over. His face was coated with black dust. It was Dieter the German. *"Guten Tag,"* he said to each of us in turn. "Ah, Sonny the telescope boy."

"Hi, Dieter," I said as he grinned at me, his teeth showing white through his coal-black lips.

Apparently, Dieter knew he was supposed to inform Mr. Dubonnet of what was going on. "Here we drive one of two head entries," he explained. "Gerhard is supervising the bleeder and panel entries across the way."

Mr. Dubonnet took a moment to look around. "Why are you bothering with the rock header?" he asked.

Dieter reached up under his helmet to scratch his head. "We believe on the other side is the high coal. If it is there, it will be our primary face. Within days, we will be loading twice as much coal out of 11 East than any other section."

"You're gambling," Mr. Dubonnet said.

Dieter shrugged. "It is where I was told to begin the long-wall mining."

"What is long-wall mining?" I asked again.

Jake answered. "You cut a wide face or wall between entries and then you mine across the entire wall, letting the roof fall in behind you as you back out. Retreat mining, some people call it. The coal comes out either end, is put on conveyor belts, and dumped into cars to be hauled out. It's quick and it's efficient. Germany's pioneered the method, and Dieter and Gerhard are here to show us how to use the equipment we bought from their company."

"Don't let Jake fool you, Sonny," Mr. Dubonnet interrupted. "It's not that simple. First off, you've got to hope the roof caves in the way you want it to. Secondly, mountain bumps—they call it rock bursts in this kind of mining—can be huge. Thirdly, you'd better ventilate the hell out of your mine. With that long face, methane comes out in buckets."

Jake said, "There's problems, sure, but they're manageable."

"The UMWA hasn't signed up to it yet, Jake," Mr. Dubonnet said. "We'd like to study it some more."

"Study it to death, you mean," Jake said hotly. "Meanwhile the whole world mines coal cheaper while West Virginia falls behind."

One of the men in the group by the pillar detached from it and came over. It was Dad. His light shined in my face. "What in the ever-loving hell are you doing here?" he demanded.

Jake said calmly, "I brought him, Homer."

Dad's spot of light hit Jake in the face and then came back to me. He pulled me out of the other men's lights. "Sometimes you confound me."

I didn't know if that was a compliment or an accusation. "Jake made me come," I said, just in case it was the latter.

"Did Jake put a gun to your head?" When I didn't answer, he

said, "I didn't think so." He kept his light in my face for a moment longer. "If you don't tell your mother, I won't, either," he said, and then his light flashed away.

Jake and Mr. Dubonnet broke off from Dieter. Jake motioned for me to follow. We headed back to the man-trip. Jake slapped the top and off we went. I presumed we were heading out. Jake put his light in my eyes. "Sorry if I got you in trouble with your dad," he said.

"You haven't seen anything. When Mom hears about this, she's going to kill me and then come after you."

"What if you don't get through that header?" Mr. Dubonnet suddenly asked.

"Then we're sunk," Jake said. He leaned over, his hands on his knees, and looked Mr. Dubonnet in the eye. "John, I'm going to level with you. The steel company's already ordered me to shut down 11 East. That's why I was sent back to Coalwood, to pull the plug on it."

"Then why didn't you?"

"Because I believe in long-wall mining. And because I don't like spending a bunch of money for nothing. We made a major capital investment in this operation, John. *Major.* If we quit now, Olga Coal Company is going to take a financial bath and the steel company is, too. I'm not sure we'll survive it. We either make this long-wall conversion work or we'll be selling this mine within a few months. After that, who knows? Whoever buys it could shut it down, sell it off for scrap."

Mr. Dubonnet looked dubious. "If that's so, why did they tell you to shut down 11 East? Wouldn't it make more sense to keep going?"

Jake studied his hands. "Because the steel company managers are scared. They want to stop Olga's bleeding before it breaks them, too. I was supposed to be their messenger boy, but when I got down here and saw what Homer was doing, I told him to keep going. He's close, John. Real close."

"You're crazy."

"I'm a capitalist, John. Come from a long line of them. I want my company to make money so it can keep on doing what it does. You're a union man. You want to keep your members working. If we work together on this, everybody is going to win. You go out on strike, it's all over, for me as well as for you."

Mr. Dubonnet scratched his nose. "Maybe you'll sell Olga to somebody better, somebody more friendly to the union."

"You heard what Sonny told you, John. You know it's the truth. You won't find a better man than Homer. He's hard but he knows what he's doing and he looks out for his men."

"They're *my* men!" Mr. Dubonnet shouted over the shriek of the man-trip's wheels as we took a curve.

Jake shouted back. "They're Homer's men, John. You're kidding yourself if you think anything else!" The wheels quieted to a low rumble as we trundled down a straight stretch of track. Jake lowered his voice to match. "You tell them what to do when they're at the union hall. Homer tells them what to do in the mine. That's the difference. Coalwood men are coal miners, first and always, not union stiffs." Jake shined his light outside the man-trip, flashing it down other entries as we rattled by. "You want to gamble on somebody else coming in, go ahead."

For a while, Mr. Dubonnet watched the timbers blur past. Then he turned off his lamp and crossed his arms and lowered his head.

At the surface, Mr. Dubonnet stalked into the bathhouse without another word. I stayed back with Jake. "Why did you make me go with you?" I asked.

Jake smiled. "John Dubonnet is so jealous of your dad I kind of figured he'd get you off talking about him. What you told him about your dad was better than anything I could have said."

So Jake had used me. I started to say so but then decided it wasn't worth the effort. Instead, I asked, "Why is Mr. Dubonnet jealous of my dad?"

Jake laughed. "Because he's in love with your mother. He always has been. Since high school, I think."

I considered and dismissed Jake's comment. Such a thing was

beyond my imagination. I just wanted to know one thing that Jake Mosby could tell me. "How is it that you've changed so much? You seem different, somehow."

"Grown up, you mean?"

There it was. "Yes." It was an accusation.

He took off his helmet and ran his hand through his dirty brown hair. "I don't know. It had to happen sometime." He smiled his old Jake smile but then fell into contemplation, his eyes traversing the mountain behind the mine as if it held the answer he was looking for. "I'll tell you," he said after a bit. "My parents didn't do it, Korea didn't even do it. It was your dad who did it. He got to me."

I wasn't expecting that answer. "How?" I demanded.

Jake plopped his helmet back on and shrugged. "He kept after me, making me learn even when I didn't want to. He ground me down, I guess you might say."

"Like a wheel," I said, Reverend Richard's Bible story popping into my mind.

Jake pondered. "Yeah, I'd say so. Like a wheel."

I turned away and began walking home. "Hey, Sonny," Jake called, "aren't you going to wash up?"

I ignored him and kept walking. I had decided Mom would see me the way I was, my face as black as the deep pit she hated. There was no use hiding it from her. Coalwood would tell her, anyway. All the way home, I kept thinking about Jake. Some wheels are used to shape, some are for grinding. My father was a grinding wheel and he'd ground down my friend, turned him into somebody I hardly knew.

24

THE STARVATION ARMY

WHEN I GOT home, it was no surprise at all that Mom was standing on the back porch waiting for me. "Well, well," she said, "my son the coal miner returneth. If there is so much as an atom of coal dirt on you in one hour, I shall forget how hard it was to birth you and cut my losses. I still have my daddy's pistol, you know."

"Don't you want to know what happened?"

"I know what happened. Go. I don't want to see you until you've got a clean face."

I looked down the fence line. There were no women standing there—yet. But soon, in that miraculous way Coalwood had, the adventures of Jake the jokester, John the union boss, and Sonny the moron going down in the mine would be all over town, and probably with it the secret of long-wall mining on 11 East. I wondered if that was what Jake had in mind all along. Coalwood's back was up against the wall, and Coalwood better know about it, company secrets or no. I was certain I was going to be the butt of the story, little Sonny Hickam dragged down into the mine by Jake the steel company man only to be chased out by his daddy. That's the way the gossipers would turn it around. I'd been around long enough to know that.

As I trudged to the basement steps for my penitent shower,

Poteet came over with something in her mouth. She spat it out on my boots. It was a dead mole. I didn't know whether it was a gift or a sign of her disrespect at my appearance. I caught sight of the Christmas tree Dad and I had dragged in. It hadn't moved an inch except maybe sagging a bit in its corner. Mom was piling seeds on the picnic table nearby to feed the birds. There must have been at least a hundred of them—chickadees, tufted titmice, house sparrows, cardinals, and nuthatches—all eating like there was no tomorrow. Everything in the mountains must be starving, I thought. The Christmas tree looked lonely, but it wasn't abandoned. Birds were using it as a staging area for their assault on the picnic table. I still felt sorry for it.

I went down into the basement and began the process of scrubbing the coal off me, concentrating on my face. Coal miners went around looking like Cleopatra if they didn't work really hard at getting the dust out of the moist crevices around their eyes. I used Lava soap and ended up getting it in my eyes. It burned like heck, the start of a long series of punishments, I suspected.

When I came upstairs, I looked for Mom to let her inspect my cleanliness, but I didn't see her. Maybe she had gone down the row to see Mrs. Sharitz or Mrs. Keneda. I went upstairs to my room to reflect on the day's events. Daisy Mae raised her fuzzy head when I came into the room. She had been sleeping on the bed. She yawned and then curled up and went right back to sleep. I thought about joining her. It had been a long day, beginning with a rocket launch and ending with a trip to the bottom of the Coalwood mine. But there was too much buzzing around in my mind to sleep, so I sat down with a piece of notebook paper and a pencil and began to do some rocket work, the calculations I needed to produce a drawing of a smooth-throated rocket nozzle. Calculating angles was hard enough, but curves were even harder. Not only were the mathematics tricky, but drawing the result was going to be tough, too. For one thing, I would need some way of making a smooth arc to describe the throat to Mr. Caton. Engineers used a variety of instruments for this, but I didn't have them. I made a first run on the calculations but gave up trying to make a drawing.

I was bone tired and, besides that, I was frustrated by not having the right tools.

Then I remembered that I was also supposed to plan the Christmas Pageant. I hauled out my list of problems and added to it two things: *Curved throat* and *Christmas Pageant*. I still thought there was something missing. What was it? I crossed off *Billy,* at least. That gave me some satisfaction even though I hadn't personally done anything to solve his problem.

I was getting my second wind. I decided to draw up a list of things that would have to be done for the pageant even though I didn't see ever pulling the thing off. I started writing everything I could think of, trying to remember what had been done during previous pageants. I also thought about what we might do to make it a little different. When I looked at the result, I shook my head. It was impossible in the short time left. Then I heard Mom call me down to supper. I threw my pencil down. Launching rockets and working in the coal mine, especially on the same day, can give a growing boy quite an appetite.

When I entered the kitchen, there was no Dad, but there was Mom—and Jim. My enthusiasm surprised even me. "Jim!" I erupted joyfully.

"What?" He was stuffing his mouth full of potato cake. Two huge bags of laundry with his name on it were piled next to the basement door.

"You're home!" I had a huge, silly grin on my face. I was really glad to see him. I didn't know why but I just was. Jim, good old Jim!

He raised his eyebrows. "Are you okay?"

Mom looked at me over the rim of her coffee cup. "You want to hug your brother, Sonny?" she asked. "I'm sure he won't mind." Her remark brought me back to some semblance of reality. I cringed and Jim did, too. Mom waved me to my chair. "Did you know Sonny's decided to work in the coal mines, Jim? He started today."

Fortunately, Jim had gone back to eating and wasn't paying any attention to her sarcastic remarks. I kept my head down and didn't reply, either. I knew better than to help Mom stir her own pot, especially when I was the stew meat.

After supper, I went back upstairs. I sat down and continued working my calculations, even though I wasn't in the mood for it. I was about to just give up and go to bed when Mom pushed open my door. "You've had a pretty long day, haven't you?" she asked.

"Yes, ma'am," I answered, letting a little pitifulness creep into my voice. It was a tactic I didn't even have to think about. Vast experience with Elsie Hickam told me that a little pitifulness might lead to sympathy and then—home free.

No such luck this time. "It's about to get longer," she said, without a trace of sympathy in her voice. "I need a chauffeur to Welch and you're it. Jimmie's going to do his own laundry and he's got a ton of it."

My brother doing his own laundry was perhaps the most difficult of all the day's events for me to comprehend. "Why do I have to drive you to Welch?" I asked.

I waited for her to tell me "Because I said so." Instead, she smiled and said, "Because you, Sonny boy, just got drafted into the Starvation Army."

I almost didn't see it until it was too late. I slammed on the Buick's brakes and skidded toward the buck standing in the middle of the road just past New Camp. We slid up next to it, its eyes bright coals in the headlights. Mom braced herself with a hand on the dash, but at the last instant the deer bounded out of the way. We watched its white tail flipping into the darkness. Mom sat back, holding her heart. "I didn't see it, either," she said. Then she said, "It was so skinny I could count its ribs."

My heart was pounding. Shakily, I started the Buick again and eased up a short straight stretch before beginning the long series of turns that would take us to the top of Welch Mountain. I still didn't exactly know where we were going and why.

Mom was still upset over the deer. "The poor animals," she said. "They're starving, even the birds. It's terrible the way a little less rain in the summer can cause so much trouble for the critters in the winter."

I remembered something I'd learned in biology class. "Coach Mams taught us that everything on the planet is connected—the air, water, weather, animals, and people. If one gets out of whack, all the rest do, too."

When she didn't respond immediately, I knew she wasn't so sure of Coach Mams's concept. She said, instead, "Well, I can't keep enough bird food out. I've never seen the like. Especially since your dad dragged in that old tree. They sit in it and demand food all day long."

I didn't particularly want to stay on the topic of hungry animals because it wouldn't take long, I figured, before it led to Chipper. I cast around for a change in subject and lit on what I thought would be a safer one. "Jim and I could decorate the tree," I offered. "Even if you're going to Myrtle Beach."

Mom crossed her arms. "I'm not going to Myrtle Beach. How could I go down there after you dragged me up Six Hollow and showed me all that mess?"

"Really?" I couldn't help but grin. Mom was going to be home for Christmas! I never imagined that such a thing would be a reason for joy. I mean, that's where she was supposed to be, wasn't she? But this year it was a wondrous revelation. But what did Six Hollow have to do with it? There was a mystery.

She appraised my grin. "Well, I'm glad you're pleased . . ."

"Yes, ma'am!" I chortled.

She continued in a bitter voice. ". . . that I can't do something that might have allowed your father and me some future happiness."

I dropped my grin, wiped it clear off my face. It appeared I was on dangerous ground with just about any subject I chose. I drove on. Welch Mountain was just one curve after another, back and forth, back and forth. As we crested the top of the mountain and started the dizzy spiral downward, I decided to go ahead and get the worst subject out of the way. I figured I might as well. I couldn't see how I could make it worse than it was. "I promise I won't ever go down in the coal mine again, Mom," I said.

To my surprise, she laughed. "Oh, Sonny, I knew you were going before you went. Jake asked me first. You really think he'd risk me coming after him?" She barked out another short laugh. "I know his game." She was quiet for a moment and then said, "I thought it would be good for your dad to see you down there. You on your own, not because he made you go but because you wanted to see what he was doing. Sorry if it didn't work out. Just like last year with you and your dad and Poppy. I keep trying to figure out how to get you two close and it keeps backfiring on me."

Driving to Welch in the cold darkness had already reminded me of Poppy. "Dad was right to be mad," I said. "I acted like a coward. I just couldn't stay in that room."

"Sonny, I wouldn't have stayed in that room with those two Hickams for a million dollars. You did better than I would have done, better than just about anybody. Nobody's blaming you."

"Dad is," I said bitterly.

"No, he's not. He got mad at you because he just lost his dad and needed to take it out on somebody. He knows that and I bet he's ashamed of it. Only thing about your dad is he forgets to tell you what he feels, especially when he's been wrong. So I'm telling you now. Take Poppy off your list. Your dad's not mad at you and wherever Poppy is, he isn't, either. That much I know."

Her words filled my heart and I could feel a warm sense of redemption flooding my mind. Dad had forgiven me. I didn't need to hear it from him. Mom was good enough. Then something else she had said struck me. My inner warmth vanished. "My list?" I said aloud. "You looked at my list?"

"Sure," she answered. "It was in your desk drawer. Why wouldn't I look at it?"

I was outraged but knew better than to show it. "Oh, I don't know," I said. "Maybe because it was at the bottom of the drawer under a bunch of other stuff that belongs to me."

Despite my careful response, she caught a wisp of my true feelings. "Sonny, as long as you live in my house, anything you bring into it is fair game. But, before you ask, no, the reverse isn't true. Adults have things that kids aren't allowed to see."

"Is there some sense to that?" I asked, emboldened by my anger.

"No. It's just the way things are. Let me tell you something. Someday you may have kids of your own. You'll want to know what they're up to and you'll do just about anything to find out. When they get mad about it, you tell them ol' Granny Elsie Hickam taught this to you: Parents can do any dang thing they want if it's to make sure their kids get brought up right. That's the way God set things up and no amount of crying and whining can change it."

I chose not to argue anymore with her about it. I knew I wouldn't get very far, anyway. I resolved to hide my list, though, as soon as we got home. I also reviewed all the other things in my desk and concluded there wasn't anything in there I cared if Mom saw, anyway, even the dozen or so never-finished love letters to Dorothy Plunk. Finally, I just shrugged. For all I knew, as out-landish as it seemed to me at the time, she might be right. If I had wanted privacy, I should have been born an orphan. Considering what else I got out of the deal, I'd take my folks, thank you very much, nosey mother and all.

We finally reached the last turn on the back side of Welch Mountain, coming out at the Welch High School football field. To make enough level ground to build it, they had bulldozed out a place in the side of the mountain. The next obstacle was Davy Mountain, but, thankfully, we only had to skirt it. We climbed it a little ways and then there was a straight run before we reached the car dealerships in a place everybody called Coney Island. As we passed the parking lots of shiny, chrome-laden cars, I thought of Ginger's boyfriend. I was faintly jealous, but I also thought it must be quite a challenge to sell all those cars to men who were never quite sure if they'd have a job the next day or not. I turned left and drove along the road built above the Tug River. We would soon be in downtown Welch. "Mom, where exactly are we going?" I asked.

"Do you know how to find Welch High School?"

"I think so."

"That's where we're going."

WELCH High School was a rambling brick building built up on the side of a mountain that overlooked the bustling county seat that gave it its name. To me, it was a school for rich kids, all of whom went off to college to become doctors, lawyers, bankers, car dealers, and politicians. I parked in front of the school alongside a couple of big trucks that had cloth covers over their backs. Their doors had SALVATION ARMY painted on them. "Do you know where the gymnasium is?" Mom asked.

I wasn't exactly certain. I had only been to Welch High once before, back in the eighth grade when I had taken the Golden Horseshoe test for West Virginia history. I'd come within a whisker of winning the countywide examination. There was no greater honor for a West Virginia student than winning a Golden Horseshoe.

Mom held my arm as we climbed the steep stone steps to the entrance. It didn't take long to find the gym. I heard the echo of voices and just followed my ears. When we entered it, I saw stacks of boxes, bundles of cloth bags, and what were obviously color-fully wrapped Christmas presents in a pile. Teenage boys and girls were working among the boxes and bags. They seemed to be sorting them into squares marked by masking tape on the floor. Each one had a name—Kimball, Keystone, Iaeger, Elkhorn, North Fork, all the names of the little coal towns in the county. Mom spotted a woman dressed in a navy-blue dress and walked across the gym to her. "I'm Elsie Hickam," she said.

The woman was wearing a Salvation Army uniform, the insignia glittering on her lapel. She looked up from a clipboard. "Oh, Mrs. Hickam! How's your dear husband? I'm Sergeant Martin."

"A bit busy these days, Sergeant." Mom rummaged in her handbag and produced a check. "Here's the money." I peered past her and saw the amount. *Five hundred dollars!* That was a lot of money, and it was a personal check out of Mom's account at the Welch First National Bank. I recognized it because Mom's checks were green. The checks from Mom and Dad's joint account were white.

"A very generous donation, Mrs. Hickam," Sergeant Martin said. "Do you have the list of families and what they need?"

Mom took a sheet of paper from her handbag and unfolded it. "Here you go. When do you think you'll make the deliveries?"

"We'll be making our rounds on Christmas Eve," she said. "Will you be guiding us?"

Mom nodded. "You know where I live. Stop, toot the horn, and I'll come out."

I was astonished. The Salvation Army was coming to Coalwood? That had never happened before. What else had never happened before was my mom using her money for much of anything. She had been saving it for a long time.

Sergeant Martin talked some more to Mom about what the Salvation Army did across the county, and I wandered off, intrigued by the kids who were helping to put the boxes in their squares. I thought maybe they were Welch High students, although I couldn't imagine it since they weren't dressed in tuxedos or formal gowns or anything. They were all dressed pretty much the same as if they were Big Creek students. One of the girls saw me watching. "You want to help?" she asked. She stuck out her hand. "My name's Don Juan Collins." She pronounced Juan with a hard "J."

When I looked at her, she said, "Don't ask. I don't know why my parents named me that but they did. Where are you from?"

When I told her, she warmed to me. "My dad used to work in the Coalwood mine. Is your daddy Homer Hickam? He talks about him all the time."

I confessed my father was none other. A boy came up beside her. "I'm Bill Phipps," he said, sticking out his hand.

"We call him Preacher," Don Juan said. "His daddy's a minister over at Davy."

Other boys and girls came up, introducing themselves. Benny Chaos from Davy said his father was a miner. The Davy mine was just scraping by, he said. A girl with a cheerful grin shook my hand—Fredda Horne was her name. She said her mother worked at the Sears and Roebuck store. Brenda Conn was a majorette. She was tall, with long, honey-colored hair and snapping brown eyes. I instantly wondered if she had a date on the night of the Christmas Formal but I didn't get a chance to ask her. Sergeant Martin came by and suggested we all get to work. I followed Don Juan and helped her move boxes. "We're volunteers," she said when I asked her why she was there. "It's a way to help a lot of our classmates."

"I thought all you Welch kids were rich," I said.

She laughed. "You ever been up Twin Branch? You won't find poorer kids in the whole state."

I looked at the Welch students with new respect. They knew how to have fun, too. Brenda came over and asked if Big Creek students could dance. It was a challenge I took up. "I reckon we can," I said.

Preacher ran to the principal's office and turned on a radio over the loudspeaker in the gymnasium. WLS in Chicago was playing rock and roll. After we finished our work, I showed Brenda that a Dugout-trained boy had a move or two. We danced until Mom came to get me to drive her home.

MOM was quiet as I steered us back and forth, back and forth, and back and forth again through the steep curves of Welch Mountain. I didn't question her or make any comment at all about her donation. I had a feeling it was too painful a subject. I decided to compliment her about something else. "I saw Dreama's new tooth the other day. It's just a temporary but it looks good. You did a good thing there, Mom." I didn't elaborate further. I knew that she knew everything else that had happened on the day Santa Claus Clowers had come to the Big Store.

"I wish now I hadn't done it," she replied.

Her response surprised me. "Why?"

"Because it's wrong to try to make right what can't be made right, that's why," she said firmly, and then fell silent.

I decided to tell her something I was pretty sure she hadn't heard, about what Dreama wanted to be. "She can't be a Coalwood girl," Mom snapped. "It wouldn't matter if she lived there a million years."

"Because she's with Cuke?" I asked.

"She's not with Cuke," Mom replied. "She's moved into the Club House. Dr. Hale asked me if she could stay there until he got her the new crown. I played like I was your dad again, said that would be fine, but as soon as her tooth gets fixed, she has to go."

I absorbed the news. "I'm glad she's not with Cuke anymore."

"Sonny," she said, sighing, "with a girl like that, it's going to be one Cuke after another. Or worse. Look at what she's done. She's managed to get a free place to stay. She's gotten free work from both Dr. Lassiter and Dr. Hale. She's got Dr. Hale even giving her money for food. Next thing you know, she'll be asking for the government to send her money. That's not the way we do things in Coalwood. It's okay for people to help out people, like the Starvation Army does, but you don't want to get it started where people expect everything to be free without working for it. No, Coalwood will be better off without her."

I wanted to gnaw some more on what Mom had said about Dreama, but I instinctively knew she had said all she was going to say. I asked her again about the Christmas tree. "Jim and I will put it up, decorate it and everything," I said. I figured she would like that.

She didn't, though. "I don't think I could stand to look at it," she said sadly. "It would make me think of Chipper." Her voice nearly cracked. "He so loved to play in the Christmas tree."

I cringed. I had managed to get her on the very subject I had tried to avoid all evening. I just decided to shut up. "So how did you like the Starvation Army?" Mom asked as I slowed the Buick at the sign marking the start of Coalwood.

"The Salvation Army, you mean?"

"That's what I said. It's your dad's favorite charity. I guess it's mine now, too," she added grumpily.

"I liked the Welch High kids I met tonight," I said.

"Did you think you wouldn't?"

"I always thought they were a snooty bunch."

Mom laughed. "When I went to Gary High, we always thought kids from Big Creek were the snooty ones. When we played them in girls' basketball, we beat the tar out of them. I was the top scorer of the game. I thought I was really the cat's meow because I had shown those rich Big Creek girls what a poor Gary girl could do."

I drove on, thinking how every time I thought I knew all there was to know about my mother, she surprised me in one way or another. She was one interesting lady. Mother or not, I figured I was just lucky to know her.

THE CHRISTMAS FORMAL

THE NEXT MORNING, I woke up and thought: *It's Christmas Formal day and I am a senior and I don't have a date.* Then I thought: *Things could be worse. I could have a date with a girl I didn't want to take.* I could look on the bright side of things if I put my mind to it.

I heard sounds outside, men on the day shift walking to the mine. There was no strike, not yet. After breakfast, I reviewed the nozzle calculations I'd made the day before. I was fresher and could concentrate on them. I had them done in short order, and then I worked on the engineering drawing. I wasn't satisfied with the result, but it would have to do. I didn't have time to make it any better. I hoped Mr. Caton could make sense of it. I borrowed the Buick for a quick run down to the machine shop. Mr. Caton looked over my drawing. "The curves don't look right," he said.

"I had to freehand draw them," I said by way of apology.

He nodded. "Well, I'll give it my best shot, but interior curves like this are going to take some time to get right. If the strike happens, I'll have to stop."

"I understand, sir," I assured him.

"Got something for you," he said, and reached under his workbench. It was a nozzle. "I made another one like the last one and then smoothed it out some. You might want to test it to see if smoothing helps before I add in the putty."

"Yessir," I said. "I'll do it today." And I did, even though the other boys moaned and groaned about it. They had things to do to get ready for the Christmas Formal, they said. They needed to wash cars, go to Welch to get corsages for their girls, and shine their shoes. I took no pity on them. They'd pushed me to get things done and I'd done it. Now, I guessed I could push a little, too. If they didn't want to go to Cape Coalwood with me, I'd go by myself. At that threat, they gave in. They were too afraid I might have fun without them.

I used Mr. Caton's smoothed nozzle in a preloaded casement I hurriedly named *Auk XXIV*. As it would turn out, I came to regret the day's launch, teaching me again that nothing much good ever came out of something not carefully planned. First the cork holding the igniter fell out; then some miners led by Pooky Suggs, a local ne'er-do-well, yelled catcalls at us. Finally, we got the launch off. There was less erosion in the smooth nozzle, but I knew the real test wouldn't come until we tried the one with the putty liner. All in all, I thought the launch was mostly a waste of effort. I was sorry I'd put the boys through it. When I reflected on it, I knew I'd done it mostly because I was jealous they were going to the Christmas Formal and I wasn't.

"We're just going to go and do it," said Sonny Hickam, leader of the Rocket Boys, this past weekend as your intrepid reporter once more made the journey to Cape Coalwood to watch the latest creation of the Big Creek Missile Agency. True to his word, the boy scientist pressed the button and Auk XXIII-A blasted off with a whoosh of fire and smoke. A cry of joy erupted from the mouths of the assembled multitude as the silvery missile flew heavenward. Oh, Rocket Boys, thy fleet creations are like spears thrown by the Gods! Exult, exult! Exult at the dazzling brilliance of these, our Rocket Boys of Coalwood. . . . And a Merry Christmas to all from the staff of this newspaper and the happiest of new years as we begin the certain to be grand decade of the sixties.—The McDowell County Banner, *Christmas 1959 issue*

I finished reading Basil's latest and then shook my head. Roy Lee laughed. "Every time I read something Basil wrote, I feel like I've been sprinkled with pixie dust."

"Peter Pan," I said. "Great book."

"I liked the Walt Disney version better," Roy Lee replied amiably. "Except I still can't figure out how anybody could stick a shadow on with soap. Since when is soap any kind of glue?"

We were on our way to the Christmas Formal. Roy Lee had come to the house and insisted I go. "You're a senior and I say you should be there, even if nobody wanted to go with you."

I felt his last statement was a misreading of history, but I kept quiet. I dressed up in what I had, a brown sport coat, white shirt, tan pants, and loafers. Roy Lee looked over my plan for the Christmas Pageant while I dressed. "Man, oh, man, why don't you just build the Taj Mahal?"

"If we're going to do it, we're going to do it right," I said. "Not that we're going to do it. I didn't see any of the boys—including you, I might add—up here asking how they could help."

Roy Lee shook his head. "We can get started on the blame thing tomorrow. Now stop stalling and get ready."

We first went to Cucumber to pick up Roy Lee's date, a friendly and buxom cheerleader named Holly Faye Reed. It was the first time they'd gone out together. He went inside her tiny little house—her father was a coal miner, of course—and returned quickly, with Holly Faye holding up her dress to keep the hem out of the mud. She was wearing a low-cut lime-green formal gown with lots of ruffles. On her wrist was the pink carnation corsage Roy Lee had given her. Roy Lee held the door open for her. "Hi, Sonny," she said in a surprised voice as she climbed in.

After Roy Lee settled in behind the steering wheel, she pondered him. "He needed a ride," he said, feeling her gaze.

She turned. "Who's your date?" she asked me.

"I don't have one."

She pondered Roy Lee again.

"I asked him to come along," he said.

"Why don't you have a date?" she asked me.

"I couldn't get one."

She pondered Roy Lee once more, a little harder this time.

"I didn't want him staying home all alone, all right?" He tried to find first gear. He found instead several others at the same time. The gearbox sounded like somebody was inside beating on it with a hammer.

"Do you go on all of Roy Lee's dates?" she asked me.

"Pretty much," I answered, just for the heck of it.

She pondered Roy Lee as hard as she could. He had turned on the radio. The Monotones were singing "The Book of Love." "I wonder, wonder, who, do-do-do, who wrote the book of love?" Roy Lee sang along with them, about as off key as you could get, and pretending not to notice that he was getting hard-pondered.

"I don't think that's what they're really saying," I said from the backseat.

Holly Faye stopped pondering Roy Lee long enough to frown at me. "What do you think they're saying?"

"Well, listen. It's 'I wonder, wonder, who, do-do-do, *who let the moo cow out?*'"

"Oh, that's silly," Holly Faye said, but listened intently. "You know what? You're right. They *are* saying 'who let the moo cow out'!"

"You're both nuts," Roy Lee griped. "My God, can't a boy enjoy a song anymore without people making fun of it?"

Holly Faye and I ignored Roy Lee and sang together. *I wonder, wonder, who, do-do-do, who let the moo cow out?* She nearly collapsed with laughter.

"You're really funny, Sonny," Holly Faye said. She was on her knees, half hanging over the front seat to face me. In that position, the tops of her breasts were completely exposed, not that I noticed.

I grinned at her. "I think you're the best cheerleader on the squad," I said. "You're the loudest one."

"Gee, you really think so?" She was chewing gum, and I could smell its fruity sweetness coming from her ruby red lips. "Well, I think you're the cutest, toughest little drummer in the band."

While Holly Faye and I continued to admire each other, Roy

Lee's foot kept getting heavier and heavier on the accelerator. We were tearing through the curves. "Hey!" Holly Faye yelped when he slid around one. She nearly fell in his lap.

"Oh, baby," Roy Lee said. "Talk to me, baby. I'm having trouble staying awake on this dark road."

Holly Faye giggled and put her head on his shoulder. Roy Lee's eyes flashed in the rearview mirror. I gave him my best innocent look. He grinned. Good ol' Roy Lee. The Big Creek lovemaster was in his glory.

The Big Creek gym was ablaze with crepe paper but the lights were turned down as far as the chaperones would allow. Swaying couples danced before me. I sat alone and watched from the auditorium. The Big Creek gym was unique. It was actually a big stage with auditorium seating. Curtains allowed it to be sectioned off into a smaller stage for play productions. For basketball games or dances, it could all be opened up. It was kind of fun, sitting and watching and listening to the music, provided by a colored band out of Bradshaw. They were good and getting better as the night proceeded. Every so often, they'd take a break, disappear, and then come back, looser to the bone. I suspected you wouldn't have wanted to strike a match near their breath, though.

After a while, I started feeling a bit sorry for myself. Everybody seemed to be having a lot of fun. I wondered how Ginger was doing over at the Welch dance. That thought didn't cheer me up. I was thinking about sneaking out and thumbing home when a vision of loveliness appeared at the edge of the stage. "Sonny?" It was Melba June Monroe.

"Right here," I said.

"What are you doing down there?"

"Roy Lee forced me to come."

Melba June made her way down the steps and edged between the seats, which wasn't easy in her full-skirted, pastel-blue, mostly ruffles and lace party dress. I also noticed it was tight at all the right places above her waist. She sat down beside me, and my legs were suddenly covered with ruffles as her dress lapped over the chair into my lap. She sighed. "My date sure is boring," she said.

"I'm sorry," I replied.

"I read about you in the paper today."

"Basil is a great writer. He'll use three adjectives when one will do. I admire that."

"I liked what he wrote about you."

"I'm glad."

"Sonny?"

"Uh huh?"

"Do you think Roy Lee would give me a lift home? I don't want to go with Holder."

"Why are you asking me?"

"Because I guess I'd have to share the backseat with you," she replied demurely. "And I wouldn't want to crowd you." She fluttered her long eyelashes.

"You wouldn't crowd me," I promised, although I hoped she would.

She moved closer to me, my lap piling up with even more ruffles and lace. Her voice got throaty. "I just love your rockets."

If Basil had been there at that moment, I would have hugged him, no matter what Roy Lee would have thought of it. Instead, I stretched and let my hand kind of creep along the top of Melba June's seat until it brushed against her bare shoulder. She leaned back, so I got a full touch of skin. I suddenly pitied the angels in heaven. I was going to get to sit with Melba June Monroe in the backseat of a car in the dark. I thought: *Merry Christmas!*

THE SECOND SON

COALWOOD HAD BEEN anticipating it for months. Carol Todd and Jimmy (Slug) DeHaven's wedding was to be the social event of the year. Carol was one of the prettiest and nicest girls in Coalwood. She had taken a job with the coal company as a stenographer, but she was a lot more than that. She had the responsibility to keep track of all the mine's records, to write letters for Dad and the other managers when they were too busy to do it themselves (which was nearly all the time), and generally keep all the paperwork flowing for the company the way it was supposed to. Slug DeHaven was something of a homegrown junior engineer. He had survived Dad's boot camp and then taken a position on Olga Coal's engineering staff. Everybody in town agreed that it was important to give Carol and Slug a good send-off in life. Dad promised to leave 11 East long enough to go to the wedding. At the direct request of Carol's mother, Mr. Dubonnet promised to hold off one more day before he took his miners out on strike. It was declared a day of peace, if not rest. Mom was going to spend the whole day at the church helping to decorate.

The wedding was to be officiated by a new pastor. There had been some last-minute turmoil when Reverend and Mrs. Schrieber had packed their bags and left town. They had left behind a letter in the parsonage. It wasn't a nice letter. I heard later there were words in it like "old-fashioned" and "mean-spirited citizenry." Hurried phone calls to Methodist headquarters in Charleston resulted in the assignment to Coalwood of one of their most experienced and respected preachers, the Reverend George Clay, who had taken temporary lodging in the Club House.

I slept in until around ten o'clock that morning. I was tired but feeling pretty good about myself. Melba June had helped a lot in that direction. By the time Roy Lee dropped Holly Faye off at her house and then drove Melba June to Bartley, I'd pretty much been kissed until my lips were sore. When we had come up for a breath, Melba June had asked me if I would take her to the junior-senior prom in the spring. I couldn't think of a better idea. The Big Creek lovemaster was proud, mostly of himself. "Worked out just like I planned," he snickered when he let me off at my house.

While I was having breakfast in the kitchen, Sherman and Quentin came by. Quentin had double-dated with Sherman and had spent the night at his house. He was going to hang around for the wedding, too, then hitch back to Bartley on Christmas Eve. He was pleased when I told him I'd turned over the nozzle drawing to the machine shop. He seemed otherwise in a contemplative mood. Maybe Mary Kay Yates had something to do with it, I thought. "How'd your date go, Q?" I asked.

Sherman chuckled. "All the way over to the dance, Quentin explained to Mary Kay the principles of magnetism and interacting currents. On the way back, she explained it to him."

Quentin blushed. "It is remarkable, is it not, how darkness, warmth, and going around curves in the backseat of a car can stimulate the libido?"

Sherman smirked. I had no room to poke fun at Quentin. I'd sort of discovered the same thing myself with Melba June.

"You got the Christmas Pageant plan done?" Sherman asked.

I handed it over. He whistled. "You think you're Cecil B. DeMille or somebody?"

"If we're going to do it, we should do it right."

Sherman fussed over my plan for a bit, making some suggestions. I wrote them down. Nothing was going to get done today, anyway. Everybody was gearing up for Carol and Slug's wedding. "Tomorrow," Sherman said. "We'll get going then."

"The union will probably be on strike tomorrow," I pointed out. "And there's no way we could possibly do all this in a day even if the company agreed to help. It just can't be done."

Sherman frowned at me. "A lot of people used to say that about us and our rockets, too."

I refused to be anything but logical about the pageant. "We just don't have time to do everything, Sherman."

"Then we'll do what we can in the time we have," he answered reasonably. "Don't give up before you start!"

I knew Sherman was right, but I was too proud to confess it. I tried another tactic to bring him in on my side of things. I put it in the form of a statement wrapped in the pure cloak of righteousness. "This is what I believe," I said nobly. I jutted my chin forward. "If you can't do a thing perfectly, it's not worth doing at all."

Sherman stared balefully at me, then shook his head. "I can't argue with that," he said grimly.

I thought I would be happy if I made Sherman agree with me, but I wasn't. It was just another one of those instances when I got exactly what I wanted, and then knew it wasn't what I wanted at all. I watched unhappily as he got up, put on his coat, and limped out of the kitchen.

Quentin pensively regarded me. "You know, Sonny boy," he said, "there's an evolutionary principle for what happens when an animal reaches perfection."

I leaned my head on my hand. "And what would that be, Q?" I asked tiredly.

Quentin got up, pulled on his jacket, and jammed a toboggan on his head. "It perishes," he said, and then followed Sherman. The slap of the screen door on the porch was like a slap in my face.

I spent most of the day in the basement loading a casement with zincoshine, preparing it for the new curved nozzle when and if

Mr. Caton could build it. While I was there, Dad came in from the mine to get ready for the wedding. For a man who'd hardly slept for weeks, he seemed spry enough, although there was perpetual worry on his face and he was coughing a lot, his condition probably aggravated by all the extra coal and rock dust he was having to breathe on 11 East. Jim came down in the basement to greet Dad with a request for the Buick. Dad turned him down flat. "If you take the Buick, how will your mother and I get to the wedding?" Dad asked. When Jim didn't answer, Dad said, "You can go with us and Sonny."

I piped up, "I'm going with Roy Lee!" For a teenager, there was nothing more humiliating than to go anywhere in the backseat of your parents' car.

"But I have a date for the wedding," Jim explained to Dad. "She can't get over here unless I go get her."

Dad stripped and climbed in the shower and started the water running. "The answer's no, Jim. Sorry. Why don't you just take a Coalwood girl?" He pulled the shower curtain closed.

Jim stared unhappily at the shower. "Did you tell Dad you're quitting college yet?" I asked, careful to keep my voice below the noise of the running water.

His eyes shifted to me. "I'd forgotten what a little creep you really are," he said.

"And I'd forgotten what a big jerk you really are," I said back.

"Idiot."

"Moron."

"Sister."

"Bonehead."

We turned away. We had said too much, our insults the closest we could come to showing affection. I hoped I wasn't getting soft on my big brother.

When I came upstairs, I found Mom on the Captain's porch looking outside. She'd just gotten back from her decorating at the church. She was watching Jim standing on the shoulder opposite the gas station. He was dressed up, a long overcoat over a suit and tie. He had his thumb out. I couldn't believe my eyes. "Jim's thumbing?" It was an unheralded event. I hitched all the time, but Jim always said it was like begging.

"He looks cold," Mom said. "I wish he had on his gloves. I wonder who his date is?"

I knew because I'd seen them together at the Christmas Formal. "Her name is Patsy Hoops. She's a junior."

"Where does she live?"

"Yukon. Do you think Jim and Patsy are going to thumb back to Coalwood?"

Mom gave me a dirty look, fully earned. "That isn't funny."

I agreed. But I did wonder how Jim was going to get back to Coalwood with his date. He had to have a plan.

"Go upstairs and look on Jimmie's dresser," Mom ordered me. "I laid out some new gloves for him. He must've forgotten them."

"Did you get me some new gloves, too?" I asked.

"The last pair of gloves I got you, you took them down to Cape Coalwood and ruined them." Mom huffed out a laugh. "I don't think so."

I climbed upstairs to Jim's room and sure enough, his new gloves were lying out in plain view, a nice pair of brown leather ones. I didn't think Jim had forgotten them. I thought he just wanted to look cold. I had to take my hat off to my brother. It was a pretty smart move. In only a matter of few minutes, I bet to myself, Mom would turn to Dad (who was hiding behind the *Welch Daily News*) and say "Homer, we could catch a ride down to the church with somebody. Let Jimmie have the car."

When I got back downstairs with the gloves, Mom was just coming off the porch into the living room. "Homer," she said, "why don't we go down in your company truck? Then Jimmie can have the Buick."

I was off a little on my prediction, but not by much. But then I saw it didn't matter, anyway. Jim was climbing into a car. He had given one last plaintive look in the direction of the house, but honor demanded that he get inside the ride that had stopped for him. I pointed and Mom looked. "Oh, good," she said, but she didn't sound very enthusiastic.

Then, nearly as soon as Jim's ride disappeared around the curve just past the mine, it started to snow. "Look!" I said.

"Oh, my good Lord," Mom said.

The snow got heavier as it got darker, and pretty soon it started to stick and build up on the fence. Mom kept going back and forth to the Captain's porch to look out toward the tipple to see if cars were still on the road. "We should have let him have the Buick, Homer," she said. It had been her mantra for the last hour.

"He'd still have to drive through the snow," Dad said, pointing out the obvious. He had switched to a *Reader's Digest,* too small to hide behind.

"The Buick's heavy," Mom said. "It's got traction."

Dad put up a stout defense. "Um," he said.

By six o'clock the snow had really started to pile up. Mom couldn't put off getting dressed any longer, so she went upstairs to her room. She reappeared in a pale green wool suit with a pretty yellow rose corsage pinned to it. The official wedding colors were green and yellow. Dad had put on his rarely worn church clothes, a charcoal-gray suit with a black tie.

Mom gave one last worried look up the road toward the mine. I hadn't noticed any cars coming from that direction for over an hour. The snow on the road sparkled under the tipple lights' harsh glare. "We should go after him in your truck," she told Dad.

"Where would we look?"

Mom had no answer. "We should have let him have the car," she said again.

"Let's go, Elsie," Dad said. "Jim can take care of himself."

"Let's call the state police," Mom said suddenly.

"And tell them what?"

Mom couldn't answer his question, but she gazed longingly at the home phone, which had been installed during the summer. The home phone was rarely used, but theoretically it was a connection to the outside world, perhaps even to the state police, which had an outpost in Welch. I often looked at the home phone and wondered what Wernher von Braun's number was. Somewhere on the other end of the thin wire that went out of the back of that telephone sat the greatest rocket scientist there ever was. I never got the courage to pick it up to see if he was really there.

Mom and Dad finally left, the Buick slowly turning the corner and heading down toward Coalwood Main. Roy Lee wasn't due to pick me up for another hour. He didn't see any reason to be early. We couldn't get at the cake until after the ceremony was over anyway.

I went upstairs to dress. I decided to wear the same clothes I'd worn to the Christmas Formal even though the collar on my shirt was smudged with lipstick and the sport coat smelled of a certain girl's perfume. To change my ensemble a little, I put on a peacock-blue tie. When I was in the bathroom looking in the mirror to tie it, I heard an odd but very loud noise—abrupt and metallic—coming from the direction of the tipple. The house hadn't shaken, so I didn't think it was a mountain bump. I went into my room and looked at the gas station. In its lights, I could see the snow still coming down. Then I looked up at the tipple and I saw a bright light pointing up from the creek that ran alongside the mine. The company had built a stone wall to channel the creek at that spot. I puzzled over the light for a moment and then noticed skid marks through the snow on the road. That's when I realized a car had slid off the road and into the creek. I could see no movement, no one on the road, nothing but the headlight flaring up out of the creek.

I flung open my closet, grabbed my pea-coat, and ran outside through the front gate. Before I got more than a couple of steps, my feet slipped out from under me and I fell flat on my back. Loafers weren't much good on fresh snow. I picked myself up and began to shuffle, trying to maintain traction. As I neared where the car had gone off the road, I saw a woman appear out of the shadows. I shuffled up to her, my loafers full of ice and snow. "Hey, you all right?" I called.

The tipple light caught her face. It was Patsy Hoops. I looked down into the creek. The car was upside down. "Where's Jim?" I demanded.

Patsy just looked at me. Oddly, she wasn't wet. "Where's Jim?" I demanded again, and then I saw that the passenger side of the car was open but the driver's door was shut. The dark water of the creek rumbled menacingly around the half-submerged car. Patsy must have climbed up on the bottom of the car to get to the road. That meant Jim was still down there!

I stepped up on the low rock wall to see what I could see. I teetered there for a second, and then my loafers slipped on the ice and I went howling into the creek. I tried to clutch rocks to slow my backward voyage downstream, but they were too slippery. Then my back thumped up against a boulder and I desperately clung to it.

I heard shouts. There were men on the road, running past, heading for the car. They didn't see me. "Help!" I called hoarsely, but they kept going. "Help," I gasped, the shock of the freezing water all but robbing me of my voice.

I heard someone on the creek bank. Then I felt the collar of my coat tighten around my neck. Somebody pulled me out. Whoever it was had to be strong. I was thoroughly waterlogged. I crawled to my knees to see him going back up the bank and over the low wall. I struggled to follow. I'd lost my loafers, and my coat felt like it weighed ten tons. There were people at the spot where the car had gone off the road. Where was Jim? Maybe he was still in the car, drowned! I pushed my way through them. I recognized Tug and Hug. It was the hoot-owl rock-dusting crew. "Jim," I gasped at them. They looked at me with wide eyes. "Jim." I pointed at the car, my teeth chattering so hard it took about five seconds to utter the single syllable.

"What?" Jim said, and when my eyes coalesced on one of the men, I saw it was actually my brother. Not even his tie was askew.

I, however, was a total wreck, loaferless, pea-coat thick and stiff with ice, my pants soaked and torn and freezing to my legs, and my blue tie frozen at an angle away from my chest. "Did—did—did . . ." That's all I could get out between my chattering teeth.

Jim eyed me and shook his head. "Yes, I pulled you out. What were you doing in the creek anyway, you moron? I went over to the mine to call Tag and then the church to let Mom and

Dad know I'd had a wreck and when I came back, you'd gone swimming."

"How—How—How—" I pointed at the car, so he'd get my meaning.

"The car didn't fall in until we got out," Jim said. "It was balanced on the wall. We were lucky."

"Ya'll sure were," Hug said. "Whose car is that?"

"It's my daddy's," Patsy said.

Jim put a protective arm around her. "I borrowed it. Dumb thing to do, I guess."

Patsy cuddled against him. "You saved my life," she cooed. "You were so brave! Then you saved Sonny's life, too. You were even braver."

"You drove all the way across Coalwood Mountain in this snow?" Hug marveled. "You must be some good driver."

"Hell, ol' Jim's good at just about anything he does," Tug said. "You ever seen him play football?"

I just stood there, equal parts freezing and mortified, listening to Jim receive praise even though he'd just wrecked his girlfriend's father's car. Oh, sure, he'd dragged me out of the creek, but I would have gotten out on my own, I was certain of it. My next thought was what the fence line would make of all this. I instinctively knew. It would be glossed over that Jim had wrecked the car, but what would be remembered, and discussed forever, was that I had fallen in the creek! Why hadn't Patsy told me Jim was okay, had gone to call Tag? I gave her a dirty look, but she was enjoying the attention of Jim, not to mention Tug and Hug. I considered flinging myself back into the creek, but I wasn't sure anybody would notice or care.

The Buick eased to a stop beside us. Dad was first out. "You okay, son?" he asked Jim.

"Yes, sir," he said. "I guess I messed up."

"It's not your fault. This curve is banked all wrong. It can get you even when it's not slick."

Mom hugged Jim. "Oh, thank the good Lord you're all right."

"Hi, Mom," I said.

She shot a frown in my direction. "What happened to *you*?"

"I fell in." There was no use reporting that I had tried to be a hero when no heroics were required.

She took inventory. "Where's your loafers?" I tried to shrug, but my coat was too heavy to get my shoulders up. "Go home, get dry, put something else on, and get to the church," she said. "Hurry up. They're holding the wedding until we get back."

I stood for a moment longer, perhaps thinking maybe she or Dad would offer me a ride in the Buick, but when no such offer came, I shuffled back home in my frozen socks. The Buick passed me just as I reached the front gate, Jim and Patsy snuggled in the backseat.

In my room, I stood on the furnace register until some blood got moving in my feet again. Roy Lee tooted the horn outside and, when I didn't appear, he came inside and up the stairs. "Why aren't you ready?" he demanded. I gave him a condensed version of my little adventure. He laughed out loud. "You're just not hero material, Sonny."

"I guess you're right, Roy Lee," I said grumpily. I pulled on a pair of jeans and a flannel shirt and a pair of tennis shoes. It was all I had left to wear.

"Is this the way you're going to dress at Cape Canaveral?" Roy Lee asked. "Maybe I was wrong about those rocket women being after you."

"Shut up, Roy Lee," I grumbled. Then I thought of something I needed to know. "Roy Lee, would you tell me the truth about something, honest, flat-out, no holds barred if I ask you a question?"

"Sure, if you'll get moving."

I went down the stairs with him and out into the backyard. Poteet zipped by and then leapt high in the air, catching a snowflake on her laughing tongue. Dandy trundled after her and then flung himself down in the snow, rolling over. At least the dogs were having fun.

We settled into Roy Lee's car and slowly drove down Main Street. The road was covered with snow and ice. So were the houses. Christmas greens and colorful lights on every window lit our way. "Do you remember that poem about snow we used to say in grade school?" Roy Lee asked.

Roy Lee always knew how to cheer me up. We recited it together:

O the snow, the beautiful snow
Filling the sky and the earth below.
Over the house-tops, over the street,
Over the heads of the people you meet,
Dancing, flirting, skimming along,
Beautiful snow, it can do nothing wrong.

When we approached Cuke's dreary house, I told Roy Lee, just in case he hadn't heard, that Dreama had left Cuke.

He knew all about it but had an update. "I heard she went back with him," he said. "Mom said she saw her going into Cuke's house yesterday."

There was only one light showing through the dirt-caked windows as we passed Cuke's place. He was a notorious miser, never burning more than one light in his house at a time. I wondered if Dreama was in there, sitting near that one light, and what she was doing, and what she was thinking. I could not, for the life of me, imagine what thoughts might be running through her head.

"So what honest, flat-out, no-holds-barred thing did you want to know?" Roy Lee asked.

I laid it on him. "Did you ever notice that Mom and Dad like Jim better than me?"

Roy Lee kept his eyes on the road, carefully steering. "Yes, I have, now that you mention it," he said. "I always thought my folks liked my older brother more than me, too, and you know what? I think they really did. It used to bother me until I finally looked at it this way. When a couple of young folks have their first baby . . . I mean—think about it—a boy and a girl who're just doing it in bed every night and having a good time all of a sudden find out that they're a man and a woman with a baby. It's bound to make them different and that baby's got to mean everything to them. It's them—man, woman, and baby—against the whole damn world! Then the second kid comes along but it's not the same. It just can't be. You know what I think, Sonny? I think you can't beat history. You're the second son. That means you're number two and that's all there is to it. Your mom and dad love you just fine, probably more than you deserve, but just not the same or as much as Jim. Does that answer your question?"

A COALWOOD WEDDING

I THOUGHT ABOUT what Roy Lee said all the way to the Coalwood Community Church, my heart in the icy cold vise of truth where hearts tend to suffer. I concluded Roy Lee was right. It was just history, that's all it was. I had wondered for a long time why my mother and dad seemed to dote on Jim more than me, but, deep down in my heart, I'd never believed it was really true. But now I completely understood the entire matter. Mom and Dad loved me—more than enough—but just not the same as Jim. It was history, see? Second son and second forever in everything for all time no matter what. I realized I could go out and ride one of my rockets right up to the moon—*the moon!*—and I'd still just be the second son in their eyes. I knew now that Little Richard hadn't got it entirely right. It was History, not God, at the controls of the great Potter's Wheel and it ground without cease, thought, or remorse.

Then I thought: Wait a minute! Could this be the thing that came out of nowhere every once in a while and made me sad? Had my list, if I'd put it all together, added up to that? Was it because, deep down in my heart, I knew that no matter what I did in my life, Jim was always going to be the favorite son? I applied Quentin's logic test to it. It seemed to fit, and I felt a sense of grim satisfaction, as if I'd finally found the piece that went in a particularly aggravating place in a jigsaw puzzle. But if that was so, why then did I do what I did next? Without a thought, I looked up and prayed: *Dear God, what is it that's really bothering me?*

Instantly, I knew what I'd done. A groan escaped my lips. Roy Lee looked over at me. "What?" he asked.

I couldn't tell him. I didn't even know how to tell myself. I just crossed my fingers. *Just kidding, God,* I prayed. But I knew I was in trouble. I had asked God to give me something I really didn't want. The truth was I'd been hiding from the answer to what was bothering me all along because I suspected it was worse than anything I could imagine. Now, I'd opened myself up to it. It was coming. I could feel it. And there was no place to hide.

IT turned out to be a beautiful wedding, although I struggled to stay focused on it. I spotted Miss Riley with Jake in one of the pews up front. That pleased me. Now I knew what her message had meant. I wondered how she was going to get home in all the snow, though. It occurred to me that getting home—if home was somewhere else other than Coalwood—might be a problem for a lot of people at the wedding. But there were worse things than to find yourself stuck in Coalwood, I reflected. Mrs. Davenport could always find extra rooms at the Club House, if need be, and just about anybody in Coalwood would open up their homes to someone who needed a place to sleep. As long as the stay was a short one, Coalwood would open its arms to anybody. That made me think of Dreama. Our town was changing but it still had its rules on who was welcome and who wasn't.

Tommy Todd, Carol's first cousin, sang "If I Could Tell You," "Always," and "The Lord's Prayer" to Jeannette Odle's organ accompaniment. Jeannette was one of Mrs. Dantzler's prized students. Jane Todd Yost, Tommy's sister, was the matron of honor. All the bridesmaids, 1956 Big Creek classmates of the bride, wore green velveteen gowns and yellow chrysanthemum corsages. Carol wore a magnificent white taffeta highlighted by sequins. I'd never seen such a dress and couldn't help but gawk at it. Freddie Allison, a Coalwood boy who'd gone off to study engineering at West Virginia Tech, was the best man, and he, like the groom, wore a navy-blue suit. It was all pretty much glorious. As the wedding progressed, I sensed there was something in the air, something that seemed to transcend all of Coalwood's troubles. It was as if all those troubles had been suspended, just for the moment. By the time Carol came down the aisle on the arm of her father to the triumphant strains of the "Wedding March," nearly every woman in the church was crying. The men sat stiffly upright without looking left or right, as if fearful that the emotional tide that had swept over the women would engulf them, too. But, truth be told, there was no stopping it. Red bandannas came out of hip pockets by the score. When Carol and Slug said their vows, there was outright bawling in the pews, more than a little of it from tough, grizzled miners. Then there was a long sigh from the tearful assembly when the freshly married couple swept up the aisle. If angels had appeared out of thin air at that moment and started flying around the church, I don't think the congregation would have been the least bit surprised, or been capable of choking out much more emotion.

Afterward, at the reception in the church basement, Ginger found me. She was decked out in a powder-blue suit and matching heels. Her blouse had little pearls as buttons and she wore a pearl necklace. I could not imagine how any girl could look prettier. "How was the Welch Formal?" I asked her.

She took my arm. "I didn't have that much fun," she confessed. "Stuart's an okay boy but he doesn't seem to have much spunk. He's going to get a degree in accounting and then come home and run his father's car dealership. He's not like you, with big dreams."

"At least he has a dream of some kind," I said.

She shrugged. "What did you do formal night?"

I felt good for the first time since I'd fallen in the creek. Ginger had that effect on me. She was a first-class pal. "I went!" I said enthusiastically. "Roy Lee made me go. And I had a good time, too. As a matter of fact, after the dance, I—"

"Sonny," she interrupted, "I've been thinking about . . . well, thinking about us. You know what? We really would be a cute couple. My mother says so, too."

Uh oh, I thought. "I guess we would be, Ginger, but—"

"I know I'm just a sophomore," she said. "But if you wanted to take me to the junior-senior prom, I'd be pleased to go."

I gulped. "I can't," I confessed, feeling miserable. "I'm going to take Melba June Monroe. We got together at the formal."

"Oh." Ginger released my arm. Her eyes were a little misty.

"I'm sorry," I said, and I was.

"We're never going to get together, are we? No matter how much we like each other, either you're going to be with somebody else, or I am."

I thought she was going a little overboard there, but I couldn't deny it had so far worked out that way. "I would have been proud to take you to the junior-senior prom," I said.

"And I would have been proud to go as your date," she answered. The way she said it sounded formal. I could sense the distance she was putting between us. To make it official, I suppose, she turned and walked away without another word.

While I was standing there, trying to figure out what had just happened, Emily Sue Buckberry came up to me. "Do they make girls any nicer than Ginger Dantzler?" she asked.

"Emily Sue," I said, "you know a lot more about these things than I do. Is it written down somewhere that every girl I care anything about either hurts me or I hurt them?"

"It's in the book of love," Emily Sue said, patting my cheek. "You know, 'I wonder, wonder, who, do-do-do, who wrote the book of love?'"

I didn't make any crack about moo cows. This was serious. "I'd sure like to find out who wrote that blamed thing," I said, "and see if I could get a few revisions."

"So would most of the human race, Sonny," Emily Sue replied, and then she gave me a quick hug. "You'll find the right girl. Might take you a couple of tries, though. You know what they say about love. ''Tis better to have loved and lost . . .'"

"Tennyson," I said morosely, recalling Miss Bryson's English lit class.

"The very one," she agreed, and went off into the excited swirl of Coalwood society.

I got some cake and punch and wandered around until I saw Dad talking to Mr. Guy Cox and a few of the other company engineers, including junior engineers Rollie and Frank. Rollie, for some reason, looked a little dejected. Frank was his usual boisterous self. They were all having an animated conversation, so I edged in closer, curious cat that I was. "We're ready to blow the header," I heard Dad say.

"What if there's another header behind it?" Frank worried.

"Then we've got a big problem," Dad said.

"What's this about Sonny falling in the creek?" Mr. Cox asked. I guess he was tired of talking about 11 East and didn't see me standing there.

Dad laughed. I guess he didn't see me, either. "That boy. He was soaked. Lost his shoes right off his feet, too. Lucky for him that Jim's so strong. A normal man would've had trouble pulling Sonny out, he was so heavy with water and ice." He shook his head, chuckling. "That boy."

Everybody joined Dad to laugh heartily. There was no mention of Jim wrecking the car. Frank asked, "You gonna let Sonny go off to Cape Canaveral, Mr. Hickam?"

Dad pondered the question. Then he said, "He's going to have to make better grades if he hopes to go down there."

It felt like my brain had been hit by a nuclear missile. The blood flushed into my face, coursed into a torrent up into my skull, and then swept away every semblance of rational thought. I had put my report card with all A's beside Dad's mail on the dining-room table where he couldn't miss it. It was still there. He hadn't even bothered to open it and take a look. My mouth, pretty much disconnected from my brain, started working and I made no attempt to stop it. "I will so go to Cape Canaveral," I said, stepping up to Dad. "You haven't even looked at my report card, have you?"

When he didn't reply, just stared at me with a frozen expression, I became angrier. "I got all A's! What do you think of that? I'm not a quitter," I spewed, "like your precious Jimmie! Did you know Jimmie's quitting college? Well, he is!"

Dad seemed paralyzed. "Don't you ever make fun of me again," I snarled into his face. "Don't you ever say *anything* about me again!"

"Sonny, I'm sure your dad didn't mean—" Mr. Cox began.

I cut him off. "Shut up. Just shut up!" Tears welled up, a single one trickling down my cheek. To my shame, I couldn't stop it. I don't remember leaving, but I must have because I found myself outside the church, wading into the darkness. It was snowing so hard I couldn't see more than a foot in front of me, but I didn't care and just plowed into it. I hadn't gotten my coat, and I didn't care about that, either. I was halfway home before I stopped and looked around and realized where I was. I stamped the snow, wrapped my arms around myself, and shivered. My heart, which had been pounding in my ears, subsided, and everything came into focus around me, reality returning.

I knew now what had *really* been bothering me all those months. I had built my rockets, learned calculus and differential equations, made good grades, gained the respect, even admiration of my fellow students, my teachers, and even people from all over McDowell County. But my father, my wonderful, glorious father, still thought I was stupid! He believed I wasn't smart enough to make my dreams come true and had said so in front of God and everybody! Nothing I had done all these months as a Rocket Boy mattered a hill of beans. I'd known that all along, and it had made me sad even when I didn't know why. *That was it, the whole thing!* "Why didn't you just tell me that?" I demanded of heaven, looking skyward. Heaven didn't answer, just dumped more snow in my face. I remembered I hadn't asked, not until tonight.

"I give up," I said. "I just give up." After I stumbled a bit farther up the road, I found another way of saying it. I yelled it out, my voice muffled by the building snow. "I quit!"

It felt good, right, and even holy to say it. In another two days, it would be Christmas, the most joyous day of the year. I felt like laughing into the face of the Christmas Spirit, as if such a thing existed. No wonder I hadn't wanted anything to do with the Christmas Pageant from the start. The truth was I hated Christmas because I hated the place I had always known at Christmas—ugly, blighted, mean, and dirty Coalwood, the whole place and everybody in it.

I could hardly wait to make my announcement to one and all.

Guess what, everybody? Merry Christmas and I quit! Laugh at me now, why don't you?

I heard a skittering sound, and then a dark form moved ominously toward me from the deep shadows of the forest. The snow interfered with my vision. It was even sticking to my eyelashes. I wiped at them and peered in the direction of the shape that kept coming toward me. A sudden gust of wind blew the snow swirling away, and I saw it was the buck.

It stopped, stamped its hooves, and stared at me. It seemed to be making an accusation of some sort. "What?" I asked it. Its bones were so sharply etched that I half expected them to poke through its skin. "I don't know what you want," I told it. "I quit."

The buck blocked my path, as if it still hoped that I would do something, or say something. When I just stood there, it turned and walked slowly away, going up the trail into the woods that led past Cuke Snoddy's house. There was still a single light in the front window, but just as the buck disappeared into the shadows, the light abruptly went out. I pondered the sudden darkness. Had someone in the house seen me or the buck? Was that why they had turned the light out? But then I thought—What do I care? I had better things to worry about. I shook my head and turned toward home. I had a worthless list to tear up. It was so funny I felt like laughing out loud. That list had always needed just one word on it. I'd finally figured out what it was: *Dad.*

Dad.

Merry Christmas, Dad. I quit.

28

ONCE LIKE THE BEAUTIFUL SNOW

I WOKE THE next morning, the day before Christmas Eve, in serenity. I had a clear conscience, a clear mind, and a clear conviction. I was a quitter. I savored my quitting and thought of all the quitters I knew or had ever heard about. Going back to the beginning of history, there was that pharaoh who started building his pyramid and then just chopped it off at the top. Was he any deader than the pharaohs who'd built their pyramids all the way up to the stars? I didn't think so. Another fine example of a renowned quitter was Christopher Columbus, who had been heading for China but called it quits just because he ran into America. The assembled Congress of the entire United States thought so much of Columbus, they'd created a holiday in his name. And, oh, yes, there was old Napoleon, who had thrown in the towel at Waterloo and scurried back to Paris with his tail tucked between his legs like Dandy during a thunderstorm. France had built that big quitter a fine tomb and went on about how great he was to this day. There were almost too many famous and great quitters to count. And what about those so-called heroes who didn't quit? What had they gained? Davy Crockett at the Alamo, Scott at the South Pole, and Joan of Arc came to mind. Every last one of those no-quitters had been beaten down and destroyed. The more I thought about it, the more I realized that quitters were the real winners. I wallowed in my newfound wisdom.

Outside my window was nothing but white, and it was still snowing. I saw some miners walking past our house, swinging their lunch buckets, heading for the mine. I saw my dad coming out from the yard to join them. How silly they were, I thought. Couldn't they see it was time to quit 11 East? I pitied them, especially my dad. He thought that all he had to do was work himself to death and all would be well in Coalwood and everywhere else. Poor, poor man. I even felt benevolent toward him for thinking me stupid. Sometimes, people like my father who didn't know how the real world worked thought there was something wrong with quitting and quitters. I knew so much better. I smirked at the sight of him.

Dad looked down Main Street. The other men had stopped, and they were looking, too. Then they went on, heading for the tipple. Dad took a few steps after them, then stopped to look down Main Street again. He called out to the men, but I couldn't hear what he said. One of them in a white helmet—I recognized Mr. Blankenship—said something, and Dad shook his head. He walked back toward the house. I decided to get up. I could hardly wait to tell everybody I'd quit. Maybe I'd get to tell it to Dad first. He'd like that. He'd already given up on me, anyway. Might as well make it official.

I heard the sound of his company truck starting up in the back alley and caught sight of him in it, easing on around the curve, heading down toward Coalwood Main. I idly wondered where he was going. I'd decided to quit being curious, among all the other things I was going to quit doing.

Mom was in the kitchen. She'd just come in from feeding the birds. There was snow melting in her hair. "I quit," I said in greeting.

"So do I," she said, obviously not understanding the vast import of my declaration. "Those birds are going to eat me out of house and home." She had her coffeepot going full bore, its mellow fragrance filling the room. She poured herself a cup. "Want some?" she asked laconically.

"I don't drink coffee," I said. "You won't let me."

She eyed me, then poured me a cup. She went back to the table and slid the cup across the table and nodded toward it. "Have a seat," she said.

I sat and picked up the cup and sniffed it. The aroma was wonderful. Then I took a sip and screwed my face up from its bitterness. "Yuk."

"Something new for you to learn," she said. "What sometimes smells sweet tastes bitter in the trying."

I wasn't going to be tricked away from the message I'd risen to deliver. "I quit," I said once again.

She blew into her coffee. "What are you quitting?"

I hadn't completely made up my mind exactly what the details of my quitting were, so I improvised. "Everything."

She narrowed her eyes. "Sonny, you're into so many things, it would be easier to go ahead and do them than to stop."

"I still quit," I said firmly.

"Let me guess," she said tiredly. "Things haven't worked out for you quite the way you hoped, is that it? Well, I guess they haven't worked out for me, either, but you don't see me quitting."

I felt reckless. "You were going to go to Myrtle Beach."

"Yes, to do a job. So what?"

I could see I wasn't going to convince her. I fell back on my original message. "I quit," I said.

She nodded. "Tell me what you're quitting."

"Building those blamed rockets," I said. "Worrying about my grades. Hoping you and Dad will like me as much as you do Jim. Trying to get Dad to believe I'm not generally stupid. That's just for starters."

"Okay," she said. "Fine by me. But what are you going to do with all your spare time now that you've quit this other stuff? I'm not going to have you lying around the house doing nothing. Come to think of it, I've got about a million things for you to do.

I'll make you a list. You can start by going down in the basement and shoveling coal in the furnace."

I got up and poured the coffee down the drain in the kitchen sink. "Why don't you give this kind of trouble to Jim?" I demanded. "He quit, too, you know."

"He did?"

"You know very well he quit college," I reminded her, as if she needed it.

"I heard you told your dad that last night. Wherever did you get such an idea?"

She was playing with me now, like Lucifer with a mouse, and I wasn't going to let her get away with it. "Mom, you know where I got it. From Jimmie!"

She waved my words away. "Oh, yes, well, I guess your brother did say something like that when he was home for Thanksgiving, but that lasted about as long as Pat stayed in the army. Jim's not going to quit. He's not the type. I guess you are but he's not."

I could see I was going to have to depend on Napoleon, Columbus, and a pharaoh whose name I couldn't think of for my good bad examples. Mom stopped me before I could do it. She pointed at the basement door. "Get on down there and shovel coal. While you're at it, now that you're not going to make rockets anymore, clean up my laundry, won't you? And throw away that moonshine!"

I headed for the basement, not certain how quitting had managed to put me so quickly to work. "On second thought, Sonny," Mom called after me, "don't throw away John Eye's stuff. The way this snow's piling up, I might need it to while away the hours."

I went down into the basement, rolled up my sleeves, and got to work shoveling coal. Lucifer, Dandy, and Poteet were all huddled next to the furnace. I had to step over them to get to the coal pile. I heard the back gate open and footsteps coming down the basement steps. Dad came inside, glanced at me, and kept going. He looked nervous. More than that, he looked scared. He marched up the stairs to the kitchen. Although I had decided to give up being curious, I recalled that I needed to tell Dad that I had quit. That was the excuse I needed. I threw down the shovel and followed him. "Oh, Homer, no!" Mom was saying as I came through the kitchen door.

"I sent Tag down to sort it out," Dad said. "There will be a crowd soon enough."

Mom was sitting with her legs splayed in her chair as if they had suddenly given out. She put a hand over her eyes and turned away. "I just can't believe it."

I couldn't control my curiosity. I guess I was addicted to it. "What is it?" I demanded.

Dad kept his eyes on Mom. "It's none of your business," he said.

"Oh, it is so, Homer," Mom said. She dabbed at her eyes with her apron. "Sonny, your dad just found Dreama Jenkins murdered."

Murdered! I had no words to respond. *Murdered* was something that happened on the television or in movies or in books, not in Coalwood! *Murdered!*

I found my voice. "Who did it?"

"Cuke," Dad said. "Who else? When he didn't show up for work, I went down to his house to get him. I found her but no Cuke."

"How? Why?" Curious-Cat-Satisfaction-Brought-It-Back was definitely alive and well.

"Hunting knife," Dad said grimly. He shuddered. "It was still in her."

"I saw a light in Cuke's window last night!" I erupted. Mom and Dad stared at me. "There was this buck and he went up by Cuke's house. And then the light went out just as I looked and—" I stopped. Had that been when Cuke murdered her? I had no way of knowing, but I would have put money on it.

Mom rose from the table. "Take me down there, Homer."

Dad shook his head. "No, Elsie. You've got no business there."

"Take me. She was a Gary girl. I owe her that much, to make sure she's handled right."

"It's not pretty, Elsie."

"Take me."

Dad gave in and took her. As she left, bundled up, she pointed at her bird feeder, already nearly empty of seeds. "After you finish stoking the furnace, Mr. Quitter, take care of my birds."

I did as I was told and then put on my coat, a toboggan, and some galoshes. Jim came downstairs, and I told him what had happened. He threw on a coat, too, and we headed down Main Street just as fast as we could walk. "I hear you're not quitting," I said.

"I was leaving, not quitting," he corrected me. "Anyway, I told Dad and he said Hickams never quit. It isn't in us to quit."

"Even when it's a good idea?" I asked.

"Especially then, apparently," Jim said grimly. "Guess I'm going to stick it out. I signed a contract and I have to honor it. That's that."

When Jim and I got to Cuke's house, a crowd had formed. I found Roy Lee, Sherman, Quentin, and O'Dell standing together. Billy wasn't there, and I didn't expect him to be. It would take a little time before they heard about this up in Six Hollow. Jim went over and stood with Billy Hardin and some other boys in his class who were home from college or the military for Christmas. "Your mother and dad went inside," Roy Lee said when I walked up. "Tag and Doc's in there, too, and also Jake."

"Why Jake?" I asked.

Roy Lee shrugged. He didn't know.

Everyone stood in knots, chewing the event over. The snow was still falling steadily, sometimes so hard you couldn't even make out Cuke's house at all. Cleo Mallett and her followers were in one group. "It don't surprise me none," she said while her ladies nodded in agreement. "You let in trash, you get this kind of thing. Well, good riddance, I say. She was nothing but a harlot."

Mrs. Mary Alice Cox heard her and came over from the knot of Coalwood school teachers and husbands. "Cleo," she said sweetly, "an ignorant mind can be tolerated as long as it is silent. Kindly keep your trap shut or, by God, I'll shut it for you."

"Don't you dare—" Mrs. Mallett yelped, but when it sank in that she was talking to a Coalwood teacher, she clamped her jaw shut and kept it that way. She knew very well who ultimately defined Coalwood society, and it wasn't the Coalwood Organization of Women.

I spotted Frank and Rollie. Rollie was sitting on a snowbank, his head between his knees. I could see he had thrown up on the clean, white snow. I figured he must have been out drinking all night. Frank stood beside him, his hand on Rollie's shoulder.

For Curious Cat, Mr. Dubonnet and his union men looked to be having the most interesting discussion. I walked over near where they were standing. "This is the end of 11 East," Leo Mallett was saying. He seemed subdued, perhaps mortified by his wife. "Without Cuke," he continued, "they can't get through that rock header."

"It wouldn't have mattered," Mr. Dubonnet said. He patted his coat pocket. "We're going out on strike as of today and staying out. Orders from headquarters."

"I wonder what was on the other side of that header," another man said. It was Mr. Bradley, the motorman who'd taken us to 11 East.

Mr. Dubonnet shrugged. "Another one, probably. It was all a fairy tale from the beginning."

I walked over to Frank and Rollie. "What's wrong with Rollie?" I asked.

Frank gave me a forlorn look. "Unrequited love," he said. "Well, it might have got requited. Rollie's a gentleman. He never told me for sure."

Rollie kept his head down and said nothing. "What are you talking about?" I asked.

Frank nodded toward Cuke's house. "Rollie and Dreama . . . they were seeing each other."

"Are you serious?" I demanded.

Rollie raised his head. His face was pale, his eyes red. Snot ran out of his nose. "I loved her," he said. "She was the sweetest little woman I ever knew. Now, she's gone." He lowered his head again. "All gone," he sobbed.

Frank looked at me and shrugged. Rollie put his hands to his face and moaned. The Book of Love had struck again, I thought. Then I found myself thinking of the rest of the poem Roy Lee and I had quoted so merrily the night before. It wasn't a children's poem about the beautiful snow, not really. There was more to it than that.

Once I was loved for my innocent grace—
Flattered and sought for the charms of my face . . .
Once I was pure as snow, but I fell,
Fell like the snow flakes from heaven to hell . . .
Merciful God, I've fallen so low!
And yet I was once like the beautiful snow. . . .

"I'm sorry, Rollie," I said, and wandered off, finding myself alongside a knot of coal company engineers. Love and Dreama weren't what they were talking about. They had the same thing on their minds as the union men. "Cuke was going to blow the header today," Mr. Cassell said.

"Man may be a murderer but he's the best powder man in the state," Mr. Keefler added.

A memory stirred somewhere in the dim recesses of my mind. I knew another good powder man, now that I thought about it. When the BCMA had first built its rockets, we'd used black powder with little success until that man had advised us how best to handle it.

"I know a good powder man," I said.

The engineers looked at me and then went back to their conversation. "The steel company is going to shut it all down, anyway," Mr. Keefler said. Mr. Keefler was an engineer who wore a white beard, one of the few bearded men in Coalwood. He had been with the company since Mr. Carter's days. "If we don't blow it today, 11 East is dead."

"I know a good powder man," I said.

"I never seen so much rock in all my born days," Mr. Keefler went on. "But I think we were close to busting through. Just a little bit of powder in the right place might have done it."

"I know a good powder man," I said.

"Or brought the whole thing down on our heads," Mr. Cassell said.

I was just about to advise them that I knew a good powder man when I heard someone cry out, "Here they come!" It was Roy Lee. I went back over to stand with the Rocket Boys to watch what I knew was going to be something people in Coalwood would be talking about for a very long time.

The door to Cuke's house opened and the mine rescue team, identified by the green crosses on their helmets, shuffled outside with a stretcher covered with a gray blanket. Mom walked, almost regally, beside it. A Gary girl was seeing another one home. A coal company truck, chains on its tires, waited at the bottom of the path to receive the body.

"Where will they take her?" Quentin asked.

"All dead people are supposed to go to Welch," Roy Lee advised. "Coalwood's got no place for bodies."

Sherman said, "I doubt if anybody is going to Welch today, not with all this ice and snow."

Roy Lee shrugged. "Maybe they'll take her to Doc's office, leave the window open or something. It's cold enough to freeze her, I guess."

Dr. Hale came up alongside Dr. Lassiter, taking him by the arm. He led him off to the side of the road. I thought to sneak over there, hear what they were saying, but then I saw Reverend Richard join the two. He looked like he'd just dropped in from Siberia. He had on a long black coat with a white fur collar and what appeared to be a white rabbit sitting on his head. It was actually his hat, a big fluffy thing. Little would spot me if I got too close, I decided, so I stayed back. He leaned in toward the two doctors and said a few words. Dr. Lassiter scratched his head and then nodded. Dr. Hale shook Little's hand and then walked over to the truck and got in the cab. Dr. Lassiter followed, climbing in beside him. Little walked over to the truck, observed Dreama's body, then bowed his head. His lips moved, saying a prayer, no doubt. I thought if I ever got killed, I sure wanted the Reverend

Little Richard to say the words over me. It was my opinion that nobody was more likely to get you into heaven than that man.

The truck slowly pulled out, its chains clanking. It was heading not for Welch but Coalwood Main. Dad stood with Mom and watched. Jake came out on the porch followed by Tag, who closed Cuke's door. They walked together down the path, separating at the bottom of it. Somebody asked Tag what he was going to do. "Going home, get some breakfast," he said.

"Ain't you gonna go hunt Cuke?" came a demand. It was from Pooky Suggs, standing in a knot of men carrying paper bags. There were bottles in those bags, of that I was certain.

Tag looked up at the snow-covered mountain behind Cuke's house and then at the mountain on the other side of the road and the creek. "You want to go up there, be my guest, Pooky," he said. "He's hiding up there, I'm sure of it. He's probably watching us now. But he'll either come down, give himself up, or he'll freeze, one or the other. That's the only choice he has. Give up"—he raised his voice—"or we'll find your body in the spring! Hear that, Cuke?"

No answer came back from the mountains, just the silence of the snow. Tag shook his head and started walking home. I saw Jake standing with the engineers. I went over to him. "He was the only powder man I trusted for this job," Jake was saying as I walked up. "Guess we'll stop. All we can do."

"I know a good powder man," I said.

Jake looked at me. "Who? Quentin? I don't think so, Sonny, but thanks, anyway."

"You know who, Jake. Remember when he helped us with our black powder?"

Jake frowned at me, but then I could almost see the light go on in his brain. He looked up at the knot of union men, now dispersing. "Hold on!" he called out. "Hold on!"

29

LIFE IS WHAT YOU MAKE IT

MR. DUBONNET'S BOOTS were aimed toward his house, but he turned his head at Jake's cry: "Hold on, John!"

Mr. Dubonnet leaned in toward him as Jake put his arm over his shoulder. Then he straightened and shook Jake's arm off. Mr. Mallett and the other union men came slogging back through the snow to see what was happening.

Reverend Richard came over and greeted me. "Hey, Sonny boy," he said.

"Hello, Reverend. Isn't it awful?"

Little contemplated Cuke's house. Mom and Dad were standing in front of it, talking things over with the school teachers and their husbands. I noticed Little was wearing a handmuff and envied him for it. It looked warm, and my hands were cold in my threadbare gloves. "I did not know the woman, although I had tipped my hat to her in the Big Store."

"All she wanted to be was a Coalwood girl. That's strange, isn't it?"

"She will get her wish," Little said.

"What do you mean?"

"She is in God's arms," he said, "but her body will repose in the cemetery on Mudhole Mountain. Dr. Hale asked if I was willing to let this girl be placed there. He said she had no family, said this was where she wanted to be. I agreed and it will be done."

Over the years, I had heard the story that such a cemetery existed. When Coalwood had been founded, so the story went, Mr. Carter had agreed to let colored people bury their dead on Mudhole Mountain because there was no cemetery for them closer than a hundred miles away. But, since then, colored cemeteries had opened in Welch, Kimball, and Bluefield. To my knowledge, no one, black or white, had been buried in Coalwood for years. "Do you think she knows, Reverend?" I asked. Then I raised the stakes. "Or do we know anything after we're dead? Tell me the truth."

Little looked me over. "Do you want a sermon?"

I squared my shoulders. I was a Rocket Boy. A rocket wasn't worth flying if you didn't know how it worked. Living was the same way and dying was just part of life, I figured. "I just want the truth," I said staunchly.

"The straight dope?"

"Straight as an arrow."

"You sure?"

"I'm sure."

"All right. Here it is. Yes, she knows because you know. Do you understand?"

I was honest with him. "No, sir."

"We're all one, Sonny. It don't matter if you're colored or white, American or Russian. God decided in his wisdom to put us in vessels that die, but He also gave us a spirit that can't die. That spirit keeps us connected. Our bodies may turn to dust, but as long as one of us is still alive, all our spirits go on."

I grappled with Little's explanation. It must be, I decided, like the equations for complex variables I had studied in my calculus book. I couldn't understand how they worked but I believed, with all my heart, they were true. Some things you just have to accept. "What about Cuke, Reverend?" I wondered. "What happens to people like him when they die?"

He didn't hesitate. "Cuke Snoddy will burn in hell, of that I am certain." He mused on his answer a bit and then added, "Or maybe the Lord will be merciful. It isn't for me to say."

Even a Rocket Boy could only absorb so much truth. I'd need to ponder all Little had said, but I doubted if I'd ever really understand it. I'd read where Wernher von Braun had been asked about religion and he'd said, in effect, that sometimes you just had to stop worrying about it and just believe. Maybe God had created complex variables, or even death itself to convince us of that, I thought.

Little changed the subject. "I heard you and Mr. Homer had it out last night."

There was no use asking him how he knew. "Yes, sir, it's so. And now I know what the thing is that's really been bothering me all these weeks."

"That your daddy thinks no better of you now than when you started shooting off your rockets?"

"Yes, sir," I said bitterly. "He thinks I'm not smart enough to ever go down to Cape Canaveral."

"That's what I thought it was from the get-go."

"Then why didn't you tell me?" I demanded.

He ignored my tone. "So what are you going to do about it?"

"I've quit," I answered. "Just given up. My rockets and everything else I can think of."

Little said, "You can't quit building your rockets, Sonny Hickam. You could no more quit than the sun can quit coming up in the morning or the moon at night. Besides, what would the people of Coalwood be without their Rocket Boys? You are part of who we are."

When I didn't answer, he went on. "But on this matter of your daddy, you need to see him as he really is." He pointed his muff at Dad, who was talking to Jake. Mr. Dubonnet was standing some paces off, his hands jammed in his pockets, his head down, kicking at the snow. "Your daddy *is* Coalwood. Without him, Coalwood would die."

"I had hoped—" I began.

"You should have prayed," Little interrupted.

"Yes, sir. But I just wanted Dad to—"

"Wanting a man to do something is just wishful thinking," Little snapped. "No one can change a man's heart, save himself or God. But I want you to think on all the things your daddy gives you, Sonny. Think about where you live, the warmth of your house, your room to study, all the books you have to read. All those things come from your daddy. That's the way he shows you his love."

"I want him to think I'm smart."

"There's still plenty of time for you to prove it."

"And I want him to care, Reverend. Not just give me a roof over my head but really care about me."

"Then keep going and he may. Stop and he never will."

He had me beaten down. "Why is life so hard, Reverend?" I asked.

Little frowned at me. "Why, life is what you make it, Sonny boy. It don't matter who you are. Sure, God molds you a little on his wheel but, in the end, it's all up to you. You got to take what you got and do the best you can with it."

"Yes, sir," I said, grappling with the enormity of it all.

"Now I want you to look over there," Little said, nodding toward my parents, Jake, and Mr. Dubonnet.

Obediently, I looked. Mom had taken a step toward Mr. Dubonnet, and the union boss had taken off his hat. He looked at her with a crooked smile.

"Is there a sadder memory than a lost love?" Little asked, holding his handmuff up to his heart.

The wind blew down the hollow behind Cuke's house, and Mom's voice wafted over to us, crystal clear. "John, I want all this fighting between you and Homer to stop," she said.

Dad pushed past Jake and tugged on Mom's arm. "Elsie, what are you doing?" he demanded.

"I'm tired of it, Homer," Mom said, pulling her arm away. "I swan, since the day I met you and John at Gary High School, you've been fighting over one thing if not another. Won't you stop for just one day?"

"You're a good woman, Elsie," Mr. Dubonnet said. "Too good for the likes of him." He nodded toward Dad.

Mom shook her finger at Mr. Dubonnet. "John, if all you're going to do is talk stupid, you can just shut up."

"Go home, Dubonnet," Dad growled. "You're not needed."

Mr. Dubonnet had flushed crimson at Mom's words. He put his hat back on and tilted his chin. "What do you say to that, Jake?"

After a quick glance at Dad, Jake said, "John, I need you to blow that header."

Dad said, "He hasn't done any powder work in ten years. He'll have the whole section down on our heads."

"He either does it or it doesn't get done," Jake replied.

Mom said something to Dad, so softly I couldn't hear. His face clouded, then he lowered his eyes while she went past him, walking up Main Street toward the house.

Jake said, "See you at the mine, John."

Dad's and Mr. Dubonnet's eyes locked for a moment and then, after they had burned holes in each other, broke contact and they stomped away in opposite directions. Jake stepped up to me. "Thanks," he said. "Looks like we got us a powder man."

The snow kept coming down as everybody walked away from Cuke's house. "Hey, Sonny," Quentin called. "Look what Mr. Caton gave us for Christmas."

Quentin was bareheaded and bare-handed and only had a thin coat. He was wearing his usual leather brogans, one of them untied. He had to keep stamping his feet to keep warm, but somehow he was glowing as if he were under a warm, tropical sun. I looked at the thing in his raw, chapped hand. It was a glorious, gleaming, perfectly machined, curve-throated, ceramic-lined De Laval Coalwood machine-shop-crafted rocket nozzle.

Quentin's hand became blurred, then he disappeared entirely in a swirl of snowflakes. I looked around at shadowy forms slowly disappearing into the blizzard until finally I was alone within a brilliant white concavity. I could feel its pressure, as if there were giant hands on me. From somewhere behind the translucent veil, I heard a slow laugh. *Heh-heh-heh.* It sounded a lot like the Reverend Little Richard.

I found Mom in her kitchen. She had a paint roller in her hand and was staring at her beach mural. "What are you going to do, Mom?" I asked her.

"Rid the world of this monstrosity," she said, and dipped the roller in a tray of white paint.

"Why?"

"Because some dreams don't deserve to come true," she answered. "It's time I accepted that."

"Quentin's here," I told her.

Mom turned to see Quentin, and her eyes brightened. How she loved that boy.

"I believe I can assist you in the proper form of the gulls' wings in your painting, Mrs. Hickam," Quentin said. He gave me a sour glance. "Sonny, as usual, failed to give me the context of his question concerning the gull's wing. That's why I gave him a short answer and for that, on his behalf, I apologize. The shape of a bird's wing is, of course, dependent upon the requirements of speed and maneuverability for which the gull, that is to say the birds of the genus *Larus* in this case, have developed a unique airfoil. Of course, to gain a proper appreciation of the wing, it will be necessary for us to discuss the extinct *Archaeopteryx*, which, while probably flightless, nonetheless demonstrated the physical characteristics necessary for the evolution of the modern birds as we know them today."

Mom stared at Quentin, then pushed a chair out from the kitchen table with her foot. "Well, sit right down, Quentin. God knows it looks like a good day to discuss the *Archaeopteryx.*" She put the paint roller down. "Would you like some breakfast? Some eggs and bacon? How about some waffles with hot maple syrup?"

"Why, yes, ma'am, that would suit me just fine," Quentin said, taking the chair. Mom went to her kitchen cabinets and started rattling pots and pans. "Well, Mrs. Hickam, you see," Quentin went on, "this creature was as much reptile as it was bird. As a matter of fact, it had teeth, although it also had feathers and a head of low mass . . ."

"Do tell," Mom said, cracking eggs as fast as she could go.

"I'm going down in the basement," I said, relieved that just the sight of Quentin had revived Mom's spirits. I was not at all certain, however, that I could withstand a lecture on birds and reptiles from him. Mr. Caton's nozzle was safely in my coat pocket. "I'm going to whip up a batch of zincoshine. I've got a casement nearly loaded."

"Don't use up all the 'shine," Mom said. "I may have need of it yet."

"Yes, ma'am."

"But, wait, why are you loading a rocket?" she asked. "I thought you'd quit building those things."

"Quit?" Quentin's eyebrows went up.

"Just a passing fancy," I said.

I was called up for breakfast shortly afterward, and then, with Mom at her mural and Quentin supervising the shape of the wings of the gulls, I walked through the snow down to Coalwood Main while the fresh zincoshine cured in the casement. There was somebody I needed to see down there. Along the way, I met a line of men going toward the mine. They had their heads down against the snow. Tug and Hug were among them. "Extra crews for 11 East," Tug told me at my question as to where they were going.

"We got a lot of rock to move," Hug added.

I found Mr. Cox at his desk in the engineer's office beside the Big Store. He was one of my favorite adults in Coalwood, and I had told him to shut up while yelling at my dad. A star athlete as a youth and still one of the best tennis players in West Virginia, Mr. Cox had always been warm and friendly to me. I had no right to smart-mouth him and it bothered me. "I'm sorry I yelled at you," I said. "I had no right to do that."

Mr. Cox reared back in his chair and crossed his arms across his khaki work shirt. "Heck, Sonny, I wouldn't have blamed you if you'd kicked me in the shins." A big grin spread across his face. "You had something to say and, by golly, you said it!"

I couldn't let him make it easy for me. "I'm still sorry and I apologize," I said. "I acted like a moron."

Mr. Cox nodded. "You did, you did. Apology accepted!" He drummed his fingers on his chair's armrest. "Say, you want me to teach you how to play tennis this spring?"

I knew he was trying to make me feel better, so I told him I'd like that just fine and then walked to the Dantzler house. Mrs. Dantzler, dressed like she was about to attend a party in New York or something, answered the door. Ginger, hearing my voice, came up behind her and gave me a wan smile. She was wearing a fuzzy pink robe and fuzzy pink house shoes. My boots were too snowy for me to come in, so I talked to them from the porch. In case they didn't know, I told them about Dreama, and about 11 East. Of course, they had heard all about everything. Mrs. Dantzler's eyes flashed. "It is a terrible thing that happened to that girl, but it convinces me all the more that we must have our pageant. If Coalwood ever needed to pull together, it's right now, seems to me. The pageant would do that."

I looked around. The snow was still falling. It was hard just to walk through it. I thought Mrs. Dantzler was right, but I didn't see how it was possible and said so. "So you figure if you say it's impossible, then it's all right not to try?" she demanded. "I want you to go home and think about that, Sonny Hickam. I've already seen you quit one thing on me, young man. I don't care to see another."

Despite Mrs. Dantzler's challenge, I still couldn't see what I could do. The snow showed no sign of slowing down, and anyway, until the situation on 11 East got resolved one way or another, how could there be a Christmas Pageant? Besides the Dantzlers, who else would help to put it on? The Rocket Boys? The Coalwood teachers? I thought they were like most of the people in Coalwood, huddled around their Warm Morning stoves and waiting word on 11 East.

I trudged home in the continuing blizzard. Drifting snow had nearly covered the fences. I used a narrow path beaten down in the center of the road, moving to one side to allow miners heading home to pass by. They were coated in brown and white rock dust. "Dubonnet blew the header," Mr. Kirk told me. "But all we got was more rock. We loaded it until another crew came down. All three shifts are taking turns until we get it done, one way or another."

"What's going to happen now?"

He shrugged. "They're arguing about it. Dubonnet says the coal's not back there, just more rock. Your dad wants to give it another go. Jake's not sure what to do."

I went home and kept loading the casement. Mom was on the Captain's porch, keeping an eye on the mine while pretending not to. Quentin had fallen asleep on the couch. Jim came down into the basement. "Let's put up the Christmas tree," he said.

I told him Mom had said she didn't want it. "Let's do it anyway," he said.

Who was I to argue with my big brother? Anyway, it seemed like as good a thing to do as any. We poked around the basement until we found the big steel base Mr. Bolt had built for us a couple of years ago to hold Mom's usual big trees, and then took it upstairs and put it in place in its traditional living-room spot.

Mom cast an intolerant eye on our work. "Stop it," she said.

"It's nearly Christmas, Mom," Jim replied.

Mom shook her head. "I'm sorry, Jimmie. I don't feel much like Christmas. With Dreama and all this . . ." She waved back toward the tipple and fell silent.

Jim sighed, then sadly abandoned the effort and went up to his room to read and listen to music. Then, the inevitable happened in a West Virginia blizzard. The electricity went off. I thought of the mine ventilating fans. If they were off, 11 East was going to fill up with methane. An hour later, even though the trees outside were sagging under the weight of the snow, the power came back on. "God bless Appalachian Power and Light," Mom said.

Miners kept going back and forth, coated brown and white.

The rock header was covering them all with dust and failure. I couldn't stand it any longer. "I'm going to go up to the mine," I told Mom.

She nodded and kept reading. I suggested to Quentin that he might like to go as well. He agreed, and we walked up the path that led to the tipple. A bank of snow as high as our heads had built up on one side of it. We stood at the man-hoist and watched for a while. The men coming out of the shaft, even though covered with rock dust, seemed happy and confident. It didn't matter if they were union or management. They were working together against a common enemy. I felt pride for the miners of Coalwood, no matter how their war in 11 East turned out.

Quentin got cold watching, so we retreated into Dad's office. I sat behind his big desk while Quentin perused the mine maps tacked to the wall. "A complex affair," he said. He sniffed, then pulled out a big red bandanna from his hip pocket and gave his nose a good blow. "There are aspects to coal mining that require a greater intellectual capacity than I might have supposed."

Mr. Chris Todd came inside. He supervised the lamphouse. "Saw you boys. Thought you might like some of this." He provided mugs of hot chocolate.

"Any news?" I asked him.

"They're getting ready to blow a double charge," he answered.

"Going for it, by damn!" Quentin said, smacking his fist into his hand. He was as caught up in it as anybody.

I worried. The fans had been down for nearly an hour before the electricity had come back. Had the methane built up in the meantime? Mr. Todd sipped at a mug with us. "That was quite a thing at the wedding the other night, Sonny," he said.

"Yes, sir. I apologize."

"No need." He pondered me. "What Homer said was not right. We all told him so after you left."

That surprised me. I didn't realize anybody in Coalwood ever corrected my father. "What did he say?"

"He agreed, said he wished it was Christmas."

I didn't understand why he wanted it to be Christmas and said so. Mr. Todd took off his helmet and ran his thin fingers through his bright red hair. "A boy shouldn't think something about his father when the truth's a whole different thing," he said.

He opened up a cabinet and took out two brightly wrapped boxes, one about the size of a book, the other one narrow and about a foot long. He put them down on Dad's desk and then pushed them across to me. "These are your Christmas presents from your dad. I'm not going to tell you to do it, but you might just want to give yourself an early Christmas."

I frowned at the presents while Quentin came over to look. Mr. Todd walked out, going back to the lamphouse. "What do you think, Q?" I asked.

Quentin grinned. "I'd open them if they were mine!"

The folds of the wrapping paper on the presents were clumsily made and too much tape had been used. Dad must have wrapped them himself, I thought. My fingers trembled when I touched the paper. I tore at the narrow present first, just a bit, then a bit more. Then Curious Cat took over and ripped the paper away.

Inside I found a white box made of thin cardboard. I opened it and saw a long brown leather case that had a buckled flap on one end. I took it out and unbuckled it. I unsheathed a flat bar made of plastic and wood, covered with tiny numbers. A sliding scale moved in grooves along its edges, and there was also a tongue of plastic-covered wood down its center. It was also covered with numbers, etched into the plastic. I scratched my head. "What is it?"

"It's a Keuffel and Esser log-log desitrig, you twit," Quentin said in reverent tones. "A slide rule, Sonny! Haven't you seen Wernher von Braun on television? This is the instrument he is always fiddling with! It will allow you to instantly take powers, use logarithms, determine the trigonometric functions! It is a most prodigious instrument."

I held the slide rule and moved its wooden tongue back and forth, feeling it slide smoothly in its grooves as if on greased ball bearings. I didn't know how to work it, but I knew I would learn.

I handed the slide rule to Quentin and pulled the paper away from the second box. Inside was a another thin-papered white box. It held a case made out of black leatherette. The letters K&E were engraved on it in gilt. It had a snap front. I unsnapped it and the box unfolded. Inside, on a scarlet cushion, was a display of gleaming metal instruments. I recognized one of them: a drawing compass. But such a compass! It had a thumbscrew for fine settings and a levered pencil holder. I looked up at Quentin for an explanation.

"Professional drawing instruments, Sonny!"

I handled each device. There were several types of pens, a straight edge marked in metric as well as the English scale, the compass, an engineer's curve. I didn't have to say it to myself or to anybody else. These things represented what my father truly thought of my work. It wasn't likely that Homer Hickam would give professional engineering tools to anybody, even a second son, who didn't measure up to his standards.

I stayed with my presents for the rest of the day. Quentin played with the slide rule for a while and then went back to my house, where he'd decided to take up residence until the blizzard abated. I knew Mom would be glad to see him.

The snow kept falling and the men kept going in and out of the mine. I was hoping to see one of them with at least a little coal dirt on him, but still they paraded in brown and white. I kept going outside the office and standing at the lift, wishing that I could put on a helmet and a lamp and join my dad at his work down in the mine.

The man-hoist bell rang and the lift came up. Mr. McGlothlin, one of the foremen, was on it. I fell in beside him as he went into the bathhouse. "Another header," he said, so tired he had trouble raising his boot up the step to the doorway of the bathhouse. "They're drilling a hole in it now."

Miners passed us, going in for a shower. One of them was singing "In the Sweet Bye and Bye." "It's over, boys," he said tiredly. He got no argument from the rest.

It was nearly midnight when I was startled awake. Dad's office shook, the books on his shelf falling over. A framed photograph of Captain Laird fell from its nail, crashing onto the floor, the glass shattering. There was a general raising of voices outside. Men were huddled at the shaft. The snow was still falling. I stepped off the porch and fell into a drift nearly over my head. I swam out of it and made my way to the man-hoist. "We don't know what it was," Mr. Todd said, his eyes filled with worry. "A mountain bump, maybe." I looked back toward my house. The light on the Captain's porch was on. I was certain Mom was there, watching.

The minutes ticked by and then an hour. The snow muffled everything, even the voices of the miners standing around waiting. A group of them had arrived out of the mine after the ground had shook. They'd been on the main line coming back, they said, and felt it, whatever it was, but kept coming. Another group of miners, this one led by Mr. Mahoney, an engineer just come on duty, had gone down to see what had happened. Mr. Todd kept trying to call 11 East on the black phone. There was no answer. I was shivering, the snow building up on my shoulders and my bare head. Mr. Todd ordered me back inside Dad's office to get warm.

Just as I sat down, the lights flickered once, then went off. I sat in the darkness, waiting, holding my breath. It was all I could do. Outside, I heard generators start up with a whine. At least the man-hoist would have power. But with the fans down . . .

I sat for a long time, breathing in the smell of Dad's office, his old mine maps, his desk, his grimy typewriter. Then I again fell asleep. When I woke, the lights were back on. Somehow, Appalachian Power and Light had come through again. I started to get up to see what was happening at the man-hoist, but just then the office door was flung open and there stood my dad, his eyes gleaming like white marbles on a face black as pitch. He looked at the slide rule and the drawing instruments he had given me, but before he could say anything, Mr. Dubonnet pushed past him, followed by Jake. They both had huge grins, their teeth like pearls lined up on ebony cloth. "We got that bastard!" Jake crowed. "We got him good!"

3 0

THE COALWOOD WAY

IN A PLACE other than Coalwood, perhaps my father and I would have put our arms around each other and had a nice hug. Instead, what happened was that he cast an unhappy eye on the presents I had opened, mumbled something about what could happen to a boy who was too curious for his own good, lurched to his desk, and, after I got out of it, sat down in his chair—hard. He lowered his head on his arms and fell instantly asleep.

Other men tromped inside the office, all covered with coal dust. Dieter and Gerhard were two of them. "It's a nine-foot-high seam," Dieter said happily. "Perfect for long-wall. We will have our machinery operating at peak efficiency within a month."

Mr. Dubonnet did not allow the victory to remain unsullied for long. "This won't solve much, no matter what he thinks," he said, nodding toward Dad. "It only gives us another set of problems."

"What do you mean, John?" Jake demanded. "We'll soon be doubling our production!"

"Yes," Mr. Dubonnet said grimly, "but without any increase in the number of miners. Production will be up but employment will be down. It is always the result of mechanization."

"You're wrong. We'll be hiring, not cutting off," Jake said. "You'll see."

The next round of town uncertainties was beginning. It was

the Coalwood way I knew so well, and I didn't see any reason to listen to it. "Help me with Dad," I asked Jake, but it was Mr. Dubonnet who responded.

"Get up, Homer. Time to go home." Mr. Dubonnet put his hands under Dad's arms and lifted him to his feet.

Dad stood, wavering. Mr. Dubonnet put Dad's arm around my neck. I walked him through the office, the miners who had crowded inside smiling at us. "Way to go, Homer," one of them said. Somebody else said, "The Captain would be proud, Homer." There was a murmur of agreement for the sentiment.

As soon as we were outside the office door and onto the porch, I heard Mr. Dubonnet and Jake start to argue again, and then I heard other voices join the debate about what the victory over 11 East had really meant. I didn't care. I just wanted to get Dad home. I helped him along the grooved path that led down from the tipple to the road. I felt like it was a path of glory. All that my father had said he was going to do, he had done. Other men would sort it out, maybe even decide he shouldn't have done it, but he had gone after his dream and grabbed it with both hands. What could be more glorious than that?

Dad tottered along, his head bobbing up and down like it was on a string. Then his knees buckled. I had to stop and brace myself to hold him up. He came awake and looked at me as if I were a stranger, which, in so many ways, I suppose I was. "What are you doing?" he slurred.

"I'm taking you home, Dad."

He blinked at me, and a hint of recognition came onto his face. "Take me home, Sonny," he said. "I'm pretty tired."

"Yes, sir." Together, father and second son, we shuffled along the path of glory toward the light in the Captain's house on the corner.

A PAGE FROM JEREMIAH

I WOKE ON the couch. It was morning. I remembered bringing Dad home and Mom gathering him in. "Good Lord, Homer," she said, and then walked him upstairs. Quentin was asleep in my bed, Daisy Mae curled up between his legs. I retreated to the couch.

I'd had a nightmare. I had dreamed I was asleep and all around me was turmoil, things breaking, curses, and then a huge crash. I looked around and, in the light of the early dawn filtering through the living-room windows, I saw that the Christmas tree was inside, more or less erect in its stand. It was tilting at an odd angle, but it was there. Then I noticed Jim was sitting across from me on Dad's footstool. Billy Rose was also there, in a chair beside the tree. I thought I was still dreaming. I closed my eyes. When I opened them, both boys were still there. "What?" I demanded.

"Look," Jim said, and showed me his finger.

I found my glasses. Jim's fingertip was bloody. It looked as if he'd been bitten by a snake. "What happened?"

"I just wanted a Christmas tree," he said. "So I figured I would go ahead and put it up on my own. I got out this morning and saw Billy walking down the road."

Billy said, "I was coming to your house, anyway. I thought maybe I could shovel snow or do some kind of chore for your mother."

"I asked Billy to help me with the tree and we got it inside."

"There was a bird in it," Billy said.

"We spent a good part of the last hour chasing it. I finally chased it out the back door."

That explained the noises in my dream. "Did the bird bite you?"

Jim shook his head. "No, after it went outside, I came back in here and Billy said he heard another bird rustling in the tree. I reached inside to scare it out."

"Was it a bird?"

"No."

"A snake?"

"No. Worse."

Both my eyes and brain were still bleary. "What?"

He pointed to the coffee table where the mangled Hickam family Bible rested. It was open, and on it sat something fuzzy and gray. A page had been torn from the Bible and the thing seemed to be eating it. I blinked again and then I knew what the thing was. "Chipper!"

At his name, the little squirrel squawked and jumped to the top of the couch, ran along it, and leaped for the curtains where it swung, its half-tail jerking spasmodically. "I think he's been living in that tree for a while," Jim mused.

"That would explain why Mom's birdseed got eaten up so fast," I said.

"Chipper!" It was Mom, come down from upstairs to see about the commotion. She was dressed in her housecoat. Chipper stopped fussing and threw himself down on the floor and zipped up Mom's robe and then on top of her head, digging a nest in her hair. "My little boy," she said, delighted.

I had my eyes focused enough to look at the Bible. Chipper had eaten an entire page from Jeremiah. "Jim and Billy found Chipper," I said, giving credit (or blame) where credit (or blame) was due.

"He bit me," Jim said unhappily. Billy just grinned a proud grin.

"Thank you, Jimmie. And thank you, too, Billy. I just can't thank you enough."

Chipper came down out of Mom's hair and into her arms, where she held him like a baby, his little paws curling happily. "My little boy, my little boy," she crooned to him. "I know you've been far, far away but you just had to come home to me, didn't you? You never gave up, did you?"

Jim and I looked at each other and shrugged. The Hickam family, for better or worse, was back together again. The Prodigal Squirrel returneth.

Mom looked up from Chipper, then at Jim and me. "What day is it?" she asked.

"Why, Christmas Eve," Jim said.

She crossed to the Captain's porch and put a critical eye on the outside world. The snow had stopped, but it had piled up over the fence. The road was covered with it, too. "The Starvation Army won't come," she said grimly. "They won't be able to get over the mountain." She took a deep breath. Chipper jumped up on her shoulder, his little rat face taking on a look of studied concentration. Mom's face did, too, although she didn't look like a rat. She just looked tired, but as I watched, there was a transformation. It seemed to me that she began to glow, as if an inner fire that had been damped down had burst again into flame.

"Jimmie," she said, "I want you to go find Jake Mosby. Most likely, he's either still at the mine or down at the Club House. Wherever you find him, roust him out and tell him he needs to get the road cleared to Welch. Tell him he owes me and if he wants to argue with me about it, he can do it later but otherwise we don't have time for his usual foolishness. Tell him the Starvation Army is coming to Coalwood and he needs to clear a path for them, no matter what it takes."

"Yes, ma'am," Jim said.

"Put chains on the Buick so you can get around."

"Yes, ma'am."

"When you finish with Jake, get back here. I've got to get over to Welch. You're the best driver in Coalwood. If anybody can get me there, it's you."

"Yes, ma'am. I'll get Jake and then I'll drive you to Welch." Jim spoke with fierce determination. He grabbed his coat and headed outside.

"I want to help, too, Mrs. Hickam," Billy said. "I'll shovel you a path to Welch if that's what it takes."

"Thank you, dear," she said. "I believe you."

I felt left out. "What can I do?" I asked.

"I can't use a quitter," she said.

"I don't think I'm a quitter anymore," I replied softly.

"I'm not surprised. You boys don't know a thing about quitting. I guess you haven't seen enough of it to learn."

Mom looked out at the tipple. A towering plume of steam rose from the shaft and climbed through the man-hoist, curling and spreading until it disappeared into the layer of thick white clouds that covered the valley. She shook her head and crossed her arms as if she were cold. "Some things need quitting, though. Not many, but some. You just got to know the difference."

She faced Billy and me, and her lips were pressed together in that way she had when she'd made up her mind about something. "But that's for another time." She pondered the undecorated Christmas tree. "You two want to know what you can do? I'll tell you. Do the impossible. It seems like a good day for it."

I puzzled over her words, and then I knew what Mom wanted me to do. It was impossible, of course, but I couldn't wait to do it.

THE KINGS OF COALWOOD

IT TOOK FOURTEEN feverish hours of work by at least a hundred people to complete the necessary preparations. By then, it was already nine o'clock at night. While my assembled army moved up and down Main Street, we shared the road with a growling convoy of company trucks. A company bulldozer had first opened up Main Street, then the road going past the tipple, and then Six Hollow. The trucks were filled with grit dug out of the Six slack dump. The bulldozer turned toward Welch Mountain, the trucks following, men on the back shoveling the coal tailing off onto the road. It made a nasty mess but it provided traction. Jim and Mom drove behind the trucks, the Buick gradually turning gray from the wet slack. The procession slowly disappeared up the road past Substation Row toward New Camp and the mountain.

According to my plan, everybody had something to do. Quentin and Billy took on the lighting and pyrotechnics. They went to work in my basement laboratory. Sherman and Roy Lee were put in charge of the players. Sherman helped Roy Lee put chains on his car and they started their visits, explaining to each person what role they'd been assigned. Everyone enthusiastically joined up except my dad, who was still asleep and would stay in bed all day. When Dad was finally roused and told what we had done and the part he was to play, he resisted it. "I'm no actor," he said, but then he gave in when I told him what Mom was doing. Mom was doing her duty and he was going to have to do his, too.

O'Dell was put in charge of general scrounging. Red drove the garbage truck to take him around. O'Dell was after as many extension cords and as much electrical cabling as he could find. I also asked him to see about taking care of the snow on the Club House lawn and maybe somewhere for the audience to sit. Mr. McDuff and Mr. Lindley took on the carpentry work and didn't bother asking for the necessary company paperwork. The same was true for the machine shop. Mr. Bolt said he'd get right on my designs and called in a half dozen of his best men. Soon, the machine shop was afire with activity, sparks flying from welders and the buzz of saws and lathes.

All day long, we gained momentum as more and more people became aware of what we were doing. Ginger took charge of the music after puzzling over my plan. "Do we dare do this to traditional Christmas music?" she asked.

"Yes," I said. I felt as if I was in a state of grace. She said she'd get right on it.

When construction of the sets began on the Club House lawn, there were more people trying to help than there was room. Mr. McDuff finally had to send some of them home. With the help of half the people of Frog Level to push when they got stuck, O'Dell and his brothers and Red transported the spoiling hay bales from Trigger and Champion's barn to act as seats for the audience. Little kids shoveled snow all day to make room. A hay bale, it turned out, was as comfortable a seat as there was.

There was no set time for the pageant to begin. It would start when it was ready and not a moment before or a moment later. People seemed to understand we were putting together something more than a Christmas pageant. It was a celebration of Coalwood.

As the shadows lengthened, Billy and Quentin arrived from the lab with their hardware. They reported wonderful news: Two big Salvation Army trucks had arrived, a filthy Buick leading the way. The convoy had turned up toward Six Hollow. Snakeroot, Mudhole, and Frog Level wouldn't be forgotten, either. No child was going to lack for food or Christmas presents in Coalwood this year.

The audience started to arrive in twos and fours and then entire families. They walked in from all the sections of Coalwood and settled in on the hay bales. Some of the men had come straight from the mine after a cleanup shift on 11 East. They still wore their helmets and coal-smeared clothes. Their wives sat close to them, and their children clung to their legs, heedless of the dirt. The snow had stopped, but then it started up again. The blackened roads started to pale, then became a pristine white once more. Every so often, there would be the noise of a small avalanche coming off the post office or church roofs. Nobody worried. There was a cheerfulness in the air, a deep and pleased contentment that overcame the damp cold of the snow.

I saw Roy Lee riding the bulldozer on the road toward Frog Level. "Where's he going?" I asked Quentin.

"Part of my plan," he said, his hands a blur as he spliced electrical wire.

"What plan would that be?"

"I'll do my work, you do yours," he snapped.

Except for the glow from a single lamp, the Club House was kept dark so as to not distract from the pageant sets on the lawn. There were two sets, a manger and a tower. The manger had an open front and a canted roof. The tower was set on the other side of the lawn and was about fifteen feet high. The snow was packed down around the sets so there was room for the players to move.

As the last-minute preparations swirled around the Club House, and the people gathered on the hay bales or stood in the street, there was still the occasional hammer put to nail. I saw Billy Mahoney, just in a few days before from college, come from behind a set, his coat dotted with sawdust. All the boys and girls who had left Coalwood but were home for a visit from college or the military or jobs in far-off places had enthusiastically turned out to help. I looked around, picking them out. Billy Hardin and Eddie Auxier could be seen moving a sawhorse off, to hide it behind a bush. Claudia Allison, dressed in jeans, emerged with a bucket of nails and disappeared into the shadows. The Todd boys, Johnny and Bill, hammered the final boards into place on the tower and reported to Mr. McDuff, who reported to me.

Quentin and Billy were in the final stages of wiring two electrical breadboards. The breadboards were two squares of plywood with electrical leads and switches. They were marked with a number corresponding to the places in my script where lighting or pyrotechnics was needed. Their plan and equipment were simple and crude, which gave me some hope that they might actually work.

Mom arrived with Jim. I was too busy to talk to them. They took their seats on a hay bale up front. She looked exhausted. Jim looked proud.

I felt a soft shoulder nudge mine and looked and saw that Dorothy Plunk was standing beside me. The other girls of Linda DeHaven's snowed-in slumber party were taking their places on the porch. They were going to sing a medley of doo-wop Christmas songs while the audience gathered. Lynn Ridenour, Janice Taylor, Eleanor Marie Dantzler, and Guylinda Cox, all college students, joined them. Dorothy said, "I hear you've got a girlfriend. I'm jealous."

I found myself staring into eyes that were like deep blue lakes. Our faces were just inches apart and she moved in closer. "You know where to find me if you ever need me," she said. She kissed me on my cheek, a quick peck, and then went up on the porch with the doo-wop girls. I saw Emily Sue give me a look from the porch with a knowing smile. *I wonder, wonder, who, do-do-do, who wrote the book of love?*

I heard a distant thunder down toward Frog Level. I was puzzled. A thunderstorm during a blizzard?

Quentin said, "Anytime you want to stop romancing and help out would be much appreciated by Billy and me."

Mrs. Dantzler sat down at the Club House piano, which had been moved out on the porch. The doo-wop girls began to sing softly as she played, then louder as their confidence built. They went through "Jingle Bell Rock," "Blue Christmas," and "Rudolph,

the Red-Nosed Reindeer" while Quentin and Billy worked fever-
ishly on their equipment. I did what I could, stringing extension
cords and testing lights. Tug and Hug came by and pitched in, too.

Finally, when Quentin and Billy said their preparations were
complete, I went up on the Club House porch and huddled with
Ginger. "Are you ready?"

"I was born ready."

"Then I guess it's time."

"This is going to be fun," she said.

"It has been so far."

I looked out over the audience that grew by the minute. The
street was crowded with people from the Big Store all the way
down to the Community Church. I wished that Reverend Richard
could see it. I had stopped by during the day and invited him and
his church to the pageant, but he said they were having Christmas
Eve services and a dedication of his new windows. The windows
were still covered with canvas, so I couldn't see what was so special
about them. "We'll come up directly just as soon as we're done,"
he said mysteriously. I showed him my script, and he puzzled over
it for a while. As he did, my confidence cracked a bit.

"Is it wrong, Reverend?" I asked worriedly.

He handed the script back and then took off his glasses, slowly
folding them with his long, delicate fingers. He inserted the glasses
into his coat pocket and patted the pocket. It was as if he needed a
moment to choose the right words. "For this story, every place is
Bethlehem," he said softly, "and every time is now. It is not wrong.
Some will say it is brazen. But it is not wrong." Little's face was
creased by a sudden smile. "God will laugh, of that I am certain."

I had looked past him then, up toward the crest of Mudhole
Mountain. He caught my gaze. "Miss Dreama's home now, Sonny.
Mr. Dantzler donated her a box of pine and men of my congregation dug her grave. She has a good place to rest, and a fine view of
mountains and sky."

As the girls finished their songs on the porch, I thought about
Dreama and imagined the snow, the beautiful snow, covering her
"good place to rest." There was rich soil on Mudhole Mountain.

When the snow melted, and spring warmed the hills, her grave would be covered by mountain phlox and fire-pink dancing in the light, blown by gentle southerly breezes. I thought she'd like that.

The Community Church choir, dressed in their maroon robes, gathered on the Club House porch steps. Ginger blew softly into a pitch pipe and the choir warmed their throats. Mrs. Dantzler began to play and then the choir began to sing. They started with "O Little Town of Bethlehem" and the crowd quieted to hear the familiar words. Except they were not entirely familiar.

> *O little town of Coalwood,*
> *In the Appalachian hills so steep;*
> *Your men go down every day*
> *To mine your coal so deep.*
>
> *Yet in your depths there shineth*
> *A light the best there be,*
> *You're tough and hard at times, it's true,*
> *But you're the place for me.*

At the end of my revision of the ancient, reverent classic, there was a low murmuring in the audience, then a few chuckles, then a pleased hum. I took a deep, relieved breath. They liked it. I would have been happy with a simple lack of outrage.

Mr. McDuff had built a low wooden stage for the speakers at the bottom of the porch steps. Billy threw the switch that turned on a small spotlight, scrounged by O'Dell from the mine. It lit the stage, and Sherman greeted one and all and gave a prayer, a short, easy one asking for the guidance of the good Lord and a hope for peace everywhere. Billy threw the second switch, and a dim light came on within the manger set. It was filled with straw. Champion's head poked through a window. He was placidly eating from a bucket. It was filled with carrots, scrounged from the vegetable section of the Big Store. Sherman's voice rolled across the assembly:

And it came to pass in those days, that there went out a decree from Governor Underwood up in Charleston that everybody should go and visit their home town for a reunion. And all went, every one into the town where they were born.

As the choir quietly began to hum, I threw another switch and a small spotlight came on at the top of the manger. Slug DeHaven, wearing a miner's helmet and work clothes, stepped into the spot. He held Trigger's bridle. Trigger was wearing a wreath of Christmas greens around his neck and bells on his harness. He stamped his feet, somehow knowing that he had a good part. His bells jingled prettily. Sherman kept reading.

And a man named Joe who had to go upstate to work because of the economy came unto the city of Mr. Carter, which is called Coalwood in McDowell County, because Joe had been born there, his father a miner as was his father's father.

Slug led Trigger into the light. Sitting sideways on the saddle was Carol, his new bride. She and Slug had been trapped in Coalwood by the snow, their Myrtle Beach honeymoon put off on account of winter. Carol was dressed in a plain cloth coat and a kerchief around her head. Both hands gripped the saddlehorn. It had taken a lot of convincing to get Carol up on Trigger, but now that she was aboard, she didn't plan on coming off by mistake. Trigger whinnied at Champion, and Champion withdrew his nose from his bucket long enough to prick up his ears and snort.

Joe brought Mary with him because he loved her. She was pregnant and probably should have stayed at home. But Joe wanted her to see Coalwood, the town where he'd been born and raised. He was proud of it. It was filled with hard-working, God-fearing people and he knew he and Mary would be safe there.

Slug led Trigger and Carol over to the Club House steps. Mrs. Davenport, her hands crossed in front of her, waited for them. Slug mimed speaking to her, and she shook her head as if to say "no."

But there was no room for them at the Club House, there being a bunch of junior engineers down from Ohio to learn how to mine coal, and Germans come to teach Coalwood miners how to mine the long-wall way. But wait, the Club House manager said . . .

Mrs. Davenport raised her finger theatrically and pointed toward the manger set.

There is a mule barn in Coalwood. It is old and no one has used it for many a year. It was here old man Carter kept his mules, which he loved exceedingly, and from where they were sent away to be rendered when he sold the company. There you will find shelter. I even have the key.

Mrs. Davenport held up a key and Slug took it and led Trigger over to the manger. He helped Carol, still maintaining a grip on the saddlehorn, to the ground. O'Dell slipped out from behind a bush and took Trigger's reins and moved him discreetly away. His bells jingled into the darkness. Champion whinnied after him. Slug and Carol took up seats on hay bales positioned in the manger. Billy turned the lights down.

And lo, it was Mary's time so she brought forth her firstborn son, and wrapped him in a Salvation Army blanket, and laid him in the straw.

The light came back on, revealing a cradle between Slug and Carol, and in it was a real baby boy, loaned out by a mother from up Snakeroot Hollow. You could just see her coat as she disappeared around the corner of the manger. Every once in a while, she'd peek out from behind to make certain her baby was all right.

Carol rocked the cradle, looking at the baby, her face aglow with the love only a young woman can show for a child. The baby, dressed in blue, slept. It was a good baby. Sherman and Roy Lee had picked the right one for the part. I just hoped they hadn't given it any of John Eye's magic stuff to keep it quiet. I wouldn't have put it past Roy Lee.

Billy brought another light up, this one on the tower. Eight men, dressed in their mining clothes, stood in front of it, fiddling with their batteries and lamps as if preparing to go down into the mine.

It was time for Quentin's first pyrotechnics. A puff of smoke erupted from the top of the platform. It was a small bucket of rocket candy. I gleefully smacked Quentin on his back. "It worked!" I whispered furiously into his ear.

"Of course, old boy," he shrugged.

From the smoke appeared Linda DeHaven on the platform. She was wearing a white robe and big paper wings. She waved away the smoke and then raised her arms in a blessing while the choir sang the special words to "The First Noel."

On this Noel the angel did say
Was to certain poor miners
With scrip for their pay
With scrip for their pay, it was a hoot-owl shift
Huddled at the tipple awaiting the lift.

Noel, Noel, Noel, Noel
Born is the babe whose story we tell . . .

Sherman continued:

And there was up the road at the Number One Portal the hoot-owl shift putting on their lamps and batteries and getting ready to go inside.

And lo, the angel of the Lord came upon them at the man-hoist, and the glory of the Lord shone round about them; and being coal miners they were duly impressed but not afraid.

And the angel said unto them, Behold, I bring you good tidings of great joy for unto you is born this day a Savior, which is Christ the Lord.

And this shall be a sign unto you: Ye shall find the babe wrapped in a Salvation Army blanket, lying in Mr. Carter's old mule barn.

The choir then burst into "Hark! The Herald Angels Sing," the words modified according to the idea that Sherman had put into my mind when we watched the little fawn die on Sis's Mountain, that neither place nor time is without meaning to God, only the story He wishes to tell.

Hark! the herald angels sing,
Glory to the newborn King!
Peace in the coalfields, and mercy mild,
Company and union reconciled.
Joyful, all ye miners, rise,
Join the triumph of the skies;
With the angels yell out good,
Christ is born here in Coalwood.
Hark! the herald angels sing,
Glory to the newborn King!

When all the voices died away, Sherman proceeded:

And it came to pass, the miners said one to another, Let us now go down past Tipple Row on Main Street and past the school and the Big Store and the Club House and the Community Church and Snakeroot Hollow and the machine shops; let us go even unto Middletown before Mudhole and Frog Level and stop at the old mule barn, and see this thing which is come to pass, which the Lord hath made known unto us.

And they came with haste, swinging their lunch buckets, and found Mary and Joe and the baby just as the angel said they would.

The miners walked across the Club House lawn to the manger and took off their helmets and knelt to the side of the sleeping baby in the cradle. The choir sang:

Joy to the world! The Lord has come:
Let's now receive our King.
Let ev'ry family, show Him our love,
And Coalwood's people sing,
And Coalwood's people sing,
And Coalwood's, let Coalwood's people sing.

Joy to the town! Our Savior reigns:
Let all their songs employ,
While mountains, mines, and hollows,
And slack dumps and coal trains,
Repeat the sounding joy,
Repeat the sounding joy.
Repeat, repeat the sounding joy.

When the choir finished, Sherman began to read again.

Now, behold, there were three Kings in Coalwood,
Saying, we have seen his star, and a rocket, too, and are come to worship him.

What was coming next was tricky. At the crest of the wide pavement between the Club House and the Community Church sat a small rocket, topped by the cargo canister Mr. Bolt had given me just after Veterans Day. Quentin and Billy had loaded the rocket with rocket candy, a propellant that burned hot and long and produced a pretty pink exhaust. Tug and Hug monitored the rocket, keeping curious folk from approaching too close.

Quentin threw the switch. I held my breath, crossed my fingers, and closed my eyes. Actually, I squinted. But I opened them wide when I heard the rocket take off. It flew perfectly. *Good old rocket candy!* The audience let out a long, slow "ooooooh" as the rocket climbed, the pink flame from its tail shooting up into the darkness. At around a thousand feet, a mix of flash powder in the cargo canister went off, producing a big white and red burst of streaming fireflies. Presently, we heard something crash into the trees behind the church. I let out a long sigh of relief. The audience broke into sustained applause.

Billy threw a switch that went to colored lights strung around a Christmas star (an aluminum construction courtesy of the machine shop) on top of the manger. It looked glorious. Quentin got up and took a little bow. I made him stop it. I had been against the idea of the rocket, launched so close to a seated audience. "You worry too much, old boy," Quentin said in disdain.

And lo, they followed his special star till it stopped over the mule barn.

There was the sound of tire chains slapping the snow-covered road, and an Olga Coal Company Jeep pulled up at the Club House entrance.

Then the Kings of Coalwood rejoiced with exceeding great joy.
  And so they gave Him gifts.
  First came the Company King who brought the baby a gift of West Virginia coal, the black diamond from which steel is made. For without coal, steel fails, and without steel, the country fails.

My dad, wearing his old cowhide jacket and white foreman's helmet, climbed awkwardly from behind the wheel of the Jeep and walked up the steps to the Club House sidewalk. In his outstretched hands was a white pillow, and on it was a large chunk of very black coal, sparkling even in the muted light. He stopped at the cradle in the manger, bowed, and went down on one knee, placing the pillow at the cradle's foot.

Second came the Union King who brought a gift of West Virginia labor, without which there would be no coal, or steel, or country, either.

Mr. Dubonnet got out of the Jeep, dressed in his miner's clothes and his black helmet. He carried a coal shovel. He knelt beside Dad, jostling him a little, which earned a dirty look, and put the shovel down beside the pillow.

And third came the Teacher King who brought the baby the greatest of West Virginia gifts, education, by which He might learn to read and write and understand our history and traditions and see an end to all ignorance.

Jake went over and helped Miss Riley out of the Jeep. Although I'd originally selected Mr. Likens, the Coalwood school principal, to play the part, he and his teachers had decided to give the honor to Miss Riley, instead. Technically, of course, she was a queen, but sometimes a writer has to trust his audience to understand that words are as much art as definition.

Miss Riley, wearing a tweed coat and borrowed galoshes that were too big for her, leaned against Jake and then straightened and came forward on her own. She carried school books. She put them at the end of the cradle beside the coal and the shovel and then knelt with Dad and Mr. Dubonnet.

Then they worshipped Him as did all the people of Coalwood who had come together as never before.

Roy Lee suddenly appeared from the shadow of the Club House. He worked his way over to me and Quentin and Billy. He had the casement I had loaded during the past two days. "Look!"

he whispered. The casement was discolored, as if it had gotten very hot.

"I had Roy Lee static-test our new nozzle," Quentin told me. He was also whispering. "I couldn't wait to see if we'd solved the problem."

I was furious. "Couldn't you have asked me?"

"The ignorant hesitate," Quentin sniffed. "The intelligent demonstrate."

I stared at him. "What?" His Quentinese had finally beaten me.

"I stuck the casement nosefirst in the slack," Roy Lee said, ignoring our little tiff, "and lit the fuse. Man, it was loud!"

I recalled the odd thunder I'd heard coming in the direction of Frog Level.

"Did it work?" Bill whispered eagerly.

Roy Lee used a flashlight to show us the results. "Look!"

We all peered inside the casement at the nozzle. "Not a trace of erosion," Quentin said aloud. "Is this not the most rigorous result there could possibly be? It's a miracle!"

It was, but I hushed them, anyway. Quentin, Roy Lee, and Billy fell silent.

Ginger, having donned a choir robe, climbed to the top of the Club House steps and turned. Her smile was radiant. Her mother gave her a nearly inaudible cue on the pitch pipe, and then she began to sing in the purest, lightest voice anyone had ever heard. Each note was perfect. It was as if they had substance, made of the finest and purest crystal, floating from Ginger to cross the sky.

Silent night
Holy night
Coalwood's calm
Coalwood's bright

It had started to snow again and it seemed as if a white, translucent veil had been drawn across the Club House lawn. I heard a murmur of voices and then I saw that people on the front row of hay bales were standing up. Miss Riley was on her feet, too, and then Slug, Carol, Dad, and Mr. Dubonnet got up, too. Champion was making little neighing noises. The baby's mother came and got her child out of the cradle, holding him close. They were all looking at a dark form that I couldn't quite make out that had come around the manger. Then, as the snow lifted, I saw what it was. "A deer!" Quentin said.

It was the buck. It came into the manger and started grazing on the hay. Champion nickered a greeting. Then, another deer, this one a doe, crept up to the first row of hay bales. The people that had been sitting on them stood up to make room. "Look, Mommy," one little girl cried. "It's Santa Claus's reindeer!"

The doe stuck her big black nose into the hay and snatched a clutch of it, chewing and swallowing in nervous gulps. Then another doe came out of the darkness and then, from around the Club House, came three more does and a fawn. Ginger sang on.

Round yon virgin
Mother and child
Holy infant
So tender and mild

Shock was giving way to small chuckles. Soon, everyone was raptly watching as the deer made their way through the bales. "Merry Christmas," I heard Sherman say. "I think we're seeing a real miracle."

Sleep in heavenly peace,
Sleep in heavenly peace.

As Ginger finished, another voice picked up on her final, perfect note. It was a woman's voice, deeper, throatier. Then a chorus of voices. In front of the Community Church stood a vast choir, dressed in gold. I thought at first it truly was an angelic host. Then a woman stepped out and sang "Silent Night" to the syncopated claps of the others, all swaying to a beat I had never imagined could be applied to the ancient song. I spotted a man standing apart from them, dressed in a suit of what appeared golden armor. It was actually gold lamé and wearing it was none other than the Reverend Julius "Little" Richard. The Mudhole Church of Distinct Christianity choir kept singing, and soon everybody was singing with them and clapping along. I looked and Ginger was doing a little dance on the Club House porch, singing and clapping enthusiastically in time with the Mudhole chorus.

When the choir was finished, Little stood in front of them. "My friends, you were so kind to invite me and my flock to this gathering but we had a gathering of our own planned, I swan, and so we are a mite late. I invite you now to walk back with us, praising God all the way, to see all that there is to see."

And so we did, all the people, leaving the famished deer to eat their fill. The Mudhole church choir in gold mixed in with the Coalwood church choir in maroon. They began to sing "Joy to the World." Everybody joined in. I looked over my shoulder, and the deer were still happily eating the hay. To them, there was joy indeed.

As we passed the old mule barn, the site of our fictional manger, I could see Little's church. Built into the front of the church were two perfectly round windows. With the light from inside the church shining through them, they looked like the sun and the moon. "What does it mean, Reverend?"

"What does it mean? Why, child, those windows are meant to be the potter's wheels. Remember the verse from Jeremiah?"

Little walked on to be with the joined choirs gathered beneath the glowing circles. They began to sing "Go, Tell It on the Mountain." I kept looking at Little's windows.

Behold, as the clay is in the potter's hand, so are ye in mine.

Every Christmas carol anybody could think of was sung, and we held hands or locked elbows and swayed in time with the music. Then, finally, I could feel the perfect thing was complete. Everybody else seemed to know it, too, and people started walking home in warm groups of the spiritually satiated. I walked behind my mother and father. They were holding hands, like school kids in love.

When we reached the Big Store, I could see a small cluster of people gathered at its side. As we got closer, I saw that they were looking at a man standing on the loading dock. He had his head bowed and was shivering, his arms wrapped around himself. When he unwrapped them, I saw he was carrying a shotgun. It was Cuke Snoddy and, in the way of Coalwood, the light of the grand evening had given way to something of darkness.

Cuke was weeping, wiping at his nose and sniffling. He was swinging the shotgun around.

Tag stood on the concrete apron the trucks used to unload at the dock. He had his hands on his hips. His pistol was in its holster. "Cuke, you can't be with decent people now," he said. "Come down from there and let's get you started on your way."

Cuke said, "I didn't mean to kill her. I just wanted to scare her a little. Then I got so mad at her, I didn't know what I was doing. Don't you see?"

"It isn't for me to see," Tag said quietly. "Come down, Cuke."

"I won't ever hurt nobody again," Cuke sniveled. "Why can't I just go home? Be like I always was?"

"Because you've crossed the line of decency, Cuke. A man who crosses the line of decency must leave us forever. It's our way, you know that."

Cuke stamped his feet in the snow on the dock. "What will become of me?"

"You will be locked up forever and we will think of you as dead," Tag said without a trace of pity in his voice.

"I couldn't stand that," Cuke moaned. "Might as well end it now," he said.

"Stop it, Cuke," Tag said. "You're scaring the ladies."

"Tell them not to look, then," Cuke said.

"Cuke, there's been enough killing in Coalwood to last us a long, long time," Tag said tiredly. He went slowly up the wooden steps to the dock as if his shoes weighed a ton apiece. Cuke backed away. Tag put out his hand. "Give me the shotgun and I'll get you some food. You can sleep tonight in a warm place, too. You don't even have to think. You can just sleep."

Tag put his hand on the shotgun, then tightened his fist around it. Cuke let it go. Tag handed the gun down to someone in the crowd and then took Cuke by his arm and led him to the street. He looked over at Mr. Dubonnet. "I'll lock him in the union hall, John, unless you got any objections."

Mr. Dubonnet said, "He's still a member of the union until we get around to kicking him out."

"Will you help me, Mr. Dubonnet?" Cuke asked.

"No, Cuke. I will not," Mr. Dubonnet replied grimly.

Mom and Dad and Jim and everybody else began to walk up Main Street while Tag led Cuke to the union hall. Cuke slipped once, went down on one knee, and Tag tenderly lifted him up. Then they went inside and the door was closed and a light came on.

I found myself alone except for the deer still grazing on the Club House lawn. I watched them for a long while. "It was a wonderful Christmas Pageant, wasn't it?" Ginger asked, walking up the street from her house. "I saw you standing out here all alone," she added.

"I'm pretty sure this one will go down in history," I said.

She took my arm. "Are you all right?"

"Perfect. You?"

"Yes."

"I'm going up on the Club House roof," I said. "Do you want to go with me?"

"You can go on the Club House roof?"

I laughed. "Come on. I'll show you."

I took her hand and helped her as she took the final step off the rickety wooden ladder onto the roof. Most of the snow had been cleared by people who had watched the pageant from there. "There's where our telescope is set up," I said, pointing at the telescope's heavy base underneath its canvas shroud. "We keep the telescope downstairs and only bring it up when we need it."

"You look at the stars up here?"

"I do when it's clear. And sometimes, I just look at Coalwood."

I led her to the edge of the roof. Beneath us, in the lights from the company buildings, the snow glistened as if a giant had scattered a billion diamonds across the ground. The air was fragrant with hay and Christmas greens. In the distance, I could hear the gurgling of the little creek that ran behind the machine shop, and up on the mountains the low note of the winter wind passing through the leafless trees. Coalwood's industrial symphony had paused, just for a moment, to listen to the ancient things that someday would reclaim their places.

"I love coming up here," I said.

"I've never seen Coalwood from this angle," Ginger said. "It really is pretty, isn't it?"

"I can't imagine anywhere prettier."

Then I realized it was past midnight, and it was Christmas, the last one I would ever know as a Coalwood boy. I stood, watching, and listening, and smelling the fragrances, and then I knew that it wasn't so, that I would never leave Coalwood, not at Christmas or any other time. Coalwood was my potter's wheel. It had shaped me into who I was. And no matter where I went or what I did, I would forever be a Coalwood boy whose father . . . I smiled . . . whose father, even though it was against his better judgment, respected his second son enough to give him drawing instruments and a slide rule to build his rockets. And whose mother . . . I broke out in a grin . . . whose mother loved him enough to give him the gift of inspired vexations so that he could rise above his own petty ones.

My parents, and all the people of Coalwood, had given me the only true gifts they could give, that of their wisdom, and of their dreams, and of their love. All fear, sadness, and anger inside me had vanished. I knew who I was and where I came from and who my people were. I was ready to leave because I could never leave.

Ginger leaned against me. "Sleepy?" I asked.

"Yes."

"Do you want to go home?"

"No."

We sat down on the edge of the Club House roof and watched Coalwood together. Ginger put her head on my shoulder. She began to breathe slowly and rhythmically. I thought she was asleep, but then she said, as if from a faraway place, "I still think we would have made a cute couple."

I raised my eyes from Coalwood and peered into the sky. It was covered by a dense layer of clouds, but I kept looking. Somewhere up there, I was certain there were stars as far as we could see.